A Puritan Catechism for Families

A Puritan Catechism for Families

Originally published as:

The Catechising of Families

Richard Baxter

For those that are past the common small catechisms, and would grow to a more rooted faith, and to the fuller understanding of all that is commonly needful to a safe, holy, comfortable and profitable life.

LEXHAM PRESS

Contents

— *The Reasons and Use of this Book*

Man is born without knowledge, but not without a capacity and faculty of knowing; this is his excellency and essence: nature, experience, and God's word, tell us the great necessity of knowledge. As the soul's essential form is the virtue of vital action, understanding, and will, conjunct; so holiness is holy life, light, and love, conjunct. The wisest men are the best, and the best the wisest; but a counterfeit of knowledge is the great deceiver of the world. Millions take the knowledge of bare words, with the grammatical and logical sense, instead of the knowledge of the things themselves, which by these are signified; as if the glass would nourish without the wine, or the dish without the meat, or the clothing or skin were all the man; God, and holiness, and heaven, are better known by many serious unlearned Christians that cannot accurately dispute about them, than by many learned men, who can excellently speak of that which their souls are unacquainted with. The hypocrite's religion is but an art; the true Christian's is a habit, which is a divine nature.

But yet the words are signs, by which we are helped to know the things, and must diligently be learned to that end; and though men cannot reach the heart, God hath appointed parents, and masters, and teachers, to instruct their inferiors by words, and hath written the Scripture to that use, that by them his Spirit may teach or illuminate the mind, and renew the heart: God worketh on man as man; and we must know by signs, till we know by intuition.

It is a thing well known, that the church aboundeth with catechisms, and systems of divinity; and doth there yet need more? Their scope and substance is the same; they differ most, (1) In choice of matter, that there be nothing left out that is needful, nor needless uncertainties and disputes put in. (2) That the method or order of them be true, agreeable to the matter and sacred Scripture. (3) And that they be not blotted with any drops of disgraceful error. These are the requisites to desirable catechisms.

No doubt but they should be sorted into three degrees, suited to the childhood, youth, and maturer age of Christians. (I) The essentials of Christianity are all contained generally in baptism; this must be understood, and therefore expounded; the Creed, Lord's Prayer, and Decalogue, the summaries of things to be believed, desired (in hope) and practised, were from the beginning taken for a good exposition to those that were to be baptised: these three, as expounding baptism, are themselves a good catechism, the understanding of the Lord's Supper being added for communicants. (II) But here also children will be childish, and learn the words while they are mindless of the sense; therefore an explication of these in other words hath ever been thought a great part of the work of a teaching ministry; whence the ancients have left us their expositions of the creed, &c.

But here the difficulty is made insuperable by the learner's indisposition; if such a catechism be short, and much put in few words, the vulgar cannot understand it; if it be long, and in many words, they cannot learn and remember it. (III) For remedy of this, a larger catechism yet is needful; not to be learnt without book, but to be a full exposition of the shorter which they learn; that they may have recourse to this for a more full and particular understanding of a shorter, whose general words they can remember.

Accordingly, having in my Poor Man's Family Book written two catechisms of the former rank, I here add the third, for those that have learned the two first: far am I from thinking that I have done any one of these to perfection; I never yet saw a catechism without some notable imperfection: and no doubt mine are not free from such. But while I avoid what I see amiss in others, I hope God will illuminate some to do yet better, and to avoid what is amiss in mine. The degree which yet pretendeth to greater accurateness in method, I have given in a Latin *Methodus Theologiæ*.

The uses for which I have written this are these. (I) For masters of families, who should endeavour to raise their children and servants to a good degree of knowledge: I have divided it into short chapters, that on the Lord's days, or at nights, when they have leisure, the master may read to them one chapter at a time, that is, the exposition of one article of the creed, one petition of the Lord's Prayer, and one commandment expounded.

(II) For schoolmasters to cause their riper rank of scholars to learn: I am past doubt, that it is a heinous crime in the schoolmasters of England, that they devote but one hour or two in a week to the learning of the catechism, while all the rest of the week is devoted to the learning of Lilly, Ovid, Virgil, Horace, Cicero, Livy, Terence, and such like; besides the loss and sinful omission, it seduceth youth to think that common knowledge (which is only subsidiary and ornamental) is more excellent or necessary than to know God, Christ, the gospel, duty, and salvation; besides which, all knowledge (further than it helpeth or serveth this) is but fooling and doting, and as dangerous diversion and perversion of the mind, as grosser sensual delights. He is not worthy the name of a christian schoolmaster, who maketh it not his chief work to teach his scholars the knowledge of Christ, and life everlasting.

(III) But if they go from the country schools before they are capable of the larger catechisms, (as to their great loss most make too much haste away,) why may not their next tutors make it their chief work to train up their pupils as the disciples of Jesus; and yet not neglect either Aristotle, or any natural light? To our present universities, I am not so vain as to offer such instructions; (though to some small part of them I directed my *Methodus Theologiæ;*) I learned not of them, and I presume not to make myself their teacher: their late guides, their worldly interest, and their genius, have made my writings odious to many, even that which they like they will not read. But I have oft, with lamentation, wondered why godly ministers do no more of the work now appropriated to universities for their own sons? Those men whose church zeal would ruin nonconformists, if they teach many, either boys or men, have no law against parents teaching their own children.

(1) Are you fit for the ministry yourselves? If so, cannot you teach others what you know? If you are defective in some useful knowledge, let them elsewhere learn that afterwards.

(2) Is there any so greatly obliged to take care of them as yourselves? Will you be like those parents who set godfathers at the font, to vow and promise to do the parents' part? And how do such undertakers use to

perform it? Or will you be like the women of this unnatural age, who get children, and (not through disability, but wealth, pride, and coyness) disdain to nurse them, but cast that on hired women, as obliged more by money, than themselves by nature, to all that care.

(3) Cannot you do more at least to ground them well in religion, before you send them from you for other learning? Or are you of the mind, that to cant over the catechism is divinity enough, before they have read Aristotle, or studied the sciences? And that they must be proficients in logic and philosophy, before they make sure of their salvation; and must read Smiglecius, Ariago, Zabarel, Suarez, or be fooled by Cartesius, Gassendus, or Hobs, before they will study the gospel and cross of Jesus Christ?

I am no undervaluer of any academical advantages: when the stream of academies runs pure and holy, they are blessed helps to men's salvation: when their stream is sensual, worldly, corrupt, and malignant, they are seminaries for hell, and the devil's schools, to train up his most powerful soldiers to fight against serious godliness in Christ's own livery and name; and to send youth thither, is worse than to send them to a brothel-house, or a pest-house.

(4) Are there not fewer temptations in your own houses, than they are like to find abroad in the world? You can keep them from the company of sensual, voluptuous lads, and of learned, reverend enemies of serious Christianity, and of worldly men, whose godliness is gain, and would draw them ambitiously to study preferment, and espouse them to the world, which, in baptism, they renounced; if you cannot keep them from such snares, how shall they be kept where such abound?

(5) And one of the greatest motives of all, for your keeping them long enough at home, is, that you will thereby have time to judge whether they are like to become fit for the ministry, or not: oh, how many good men send plagues into the church, by devoting unproved lade to the ministry, hoping that God will hereafter give them grace, and make them fit, who never promised it! When you send them at fifteen or sixteen years of age to the university, from under your own eye, you are unlikely to know what they will prove, unless it be some few that are very early sanctified by grace; and when they have been a few years at the university, be they never so unmeet, they will thrust themselves into the ministry, and, (miserable men,) for a benefice, take the

charge of souls; whereas, if you will keep them with you till twenty years of age, you may see what they are like to prove, and dispose of them accordingly.

If you say, they will lose the advantage of their degrees, it is an objection unfit for a Christian's mouth; will you prefer names, and airy titles, before wisdom, piety, and men's salvation, and the church's good? Must they go out of their way for a peacock's feather, when they are in a race as for life or death?

If you say, they will lose their time at home, the shame then is yours, or they are like to lose it more abroad: teach them to read the Scriptures (at least the gospel) in the original tongues, and to understand and practise things necessary to salvation, which all arts and sciences must subserve, and they do not lose their time; and at ripeness of age they will get more other learning in a year, than before they will do in many; and what they learn will be their own, when boys learn words without the sense.

If you say, they will want the advantage of academical disputes; I answer, if reading fill them with matter, nature and common use will teach them how to utter it: the world hath too many disputers; books may soon teach them the true order of disputing, and a few days' experience may show the rest.

If you say, you have not time to teach them, I answer, you have no greater work to do, and a little time will serve with willing, teachable youth, and no other are to be intended for the ministry; what boys get by hearing their tutors they oft bestow small labour to digest, but take up with bare words, and second notions: but when they are set to get it from their books themselves, harder study better digesteth it; it is they that must bestow much time, the teacher need not bestow very much: country schools may teach them Latin, Greek, and Hebrew, let them stay there till they attain it; you may then teach them the common rudiments of logic, and see them well settled in divinity and serious religion; and then, if academies prove safe and needful, they will go out better fortified against all the temptations which they must expect.

It is certain, that inconveniences are not so bad as mischiefs; and it is certain that all our natures, as corrupt, are dark, carnal, and malignant, and need the sanctifying grace of Christ; and it is certain, that as grace useth all things to its increase, so this serpentine nature will turn studies, learning, and all such things, to serve itself; and that carnal, sensual, malignant nature, cultivated by human learning, is too usually ripened and sublimated into diabolism, and maketh the most potent servants of the devil against Christ: and if this be but gilded with sacred ornaments and titles, and pretences of the church's peace and order, it is garrisoned and fortified, and a stronger hold for sin and Satan than open vice: and it is certain, that as the rage of drunkards is raised in their riotous meetings, and as conjunction, example, and noise put more valour into armies than separated persons have, so combined societies of learned, reverenced malignity do confirm the individuals, and raise them to the height of wickedness: so that universities are either, if holy, a copy of paradise, or, if malignant, the chief militia of the malicious enemy of man, except a malignant hierarchy or clergy, who are malignant academies grown up to maturity.

If any say that there is no great and solid learning to be got elsewhere, let them think where great Augustin, and most of the great lights of the church for four hundred years, attained their knowledge; and whether the Scaligers, Salmasius, Grotius, Selden, and such others, got not more by laborious, secret reading, than by academical tutors and disputes: and whether such famous men as John Reignolds, Blondel, &c., even in the universities, got not their great learning by searching the same books which may be read in another place. If any say, that I speak against that which I want myself, I only desire that it may not be those who cast by my Catholic Theology, *Methodus Theologiæ*, &c., with no other accusation, but because they are too scholastical, accurate, and hard for them.

I here bewail it as my great sin against God, that in the youth of my ministry, pride made me often blush with shame for want of academical degrees; but usually God will not have us bring our own human honour to his service, but fetch honour from him, in faithful serving him: fringes and laces must be last set on when the garment is made, and not be the ground, or *stamen*, of it. There have been men that have desired their sons to learn all the oriental tongues, and the rare antiquities, and critical, applauded sort of learning, not for its own worth, but that they might preach the gospel with the advantage of a greater name and honour: and this course hath so taken up and formed such students into the quality of their studies, when their souls should have been taken up with faith and love, and heavenly desires and hopes, that it hath overthrown the end to which it was intended, and rendered such students unfit for the sacred ministry, and caused them to turn to other things: when others, who (as Usher, Bochart, Blondel, &c.) have first taken in a digested body of saving truth, have after added these critical studies at full maturity, and have become rare blessings to the church.

Let those that think all this digressive, or unmeet for the preface to a catechism, pardon that which the world's miscarriages and necessities bespeak.

If at least masters of families, by such helps, diligently used, will keep up knowledge and religion in their houses, it is not public failings in ministers, nor the want of what is desirable in the assemblies, that will root out religion from the land: but if the faithful prove few, they must be content with their personal comforts and rewards; there is nothing amiss in the heavenly society, and the world which we are entering into. Come, Lord Jesus, come quickly. Amen.

London, Oct. 3, 1682.

PART I

1

The Introduction

Q. 1. What is it which must be taught and learned?

A. All must be taught, and must learn, (1) What to know and believe. (2) What to love, and choose, and hope for. (3) What they must do, or practise.[1]

Q. 2. What is it that we must learn to know and believe?

A. We must learn to know ourselves, and our concerns.[2]

Q. 3. What must we know of ourselves?

A. We must know what we are, and what condition we are in.[3]

Q. 4. What mean you by our concerns, which we must know?

A. We must know, (1) Whence we are, or who made us. (2) And whither we are going, or for what end he hath made us. (3) And which is the way, or what means must be used, to attain that end.[4]

Q. 5. What must we learn to love, and choose, and hope for?

A. We must learn to love best that which is best in itself, and best to us and others, and to choose the means by which it must be attained; which implieth hating and refusing the contraries.[5]

---

[1] Ps 25:4, 5, and 27:11, 109:12, 33, 66.

[2] Job 34:32.

[3] Heb 6:1–3.

[4] Titus 2:3.

[5] Ps 34:11, and 32:8.

Q. 6. What must we learn to practise?

A. We must practise the means to obtain the end of our lives, and that is our obedience to him that made us.[6]

Q. 7. Cannot we learn this of ourselves, without teachers?

A. There is some part of this which nature itself will teach you, as soon as you come to the free use of reason, and look about you in the world. And there is some part of it that nature alone will not teach you, without a higher teaching from above. And even that which nature teacheth you, you have also need of a teacher's help to learn it speedily and truly. For nature doth not teach all things alike easily, speedily, and surely: it quickly teacheth a child to suck; it quickly teacheth us to eat and drink, and to go and talk; and yet here there is need of help; children learn not to speak without teaching. It teacheth men how to do their worldly business; and yet they have need of masters to teach it them, and will serve an apprenticeship to learn some. Some things nature will teach to none but good wits, upon diligent search and study, and honest willingness to know; which dullards, and slothful, and bad men, reach not.[7]

Q. 8. Who be they that must teach, and who must learn?

A. None is able to teach more than they know themselves; and all that are ignorant have need to learn. But nature hath put all children under a necessity of learning; for, though they are born with a capacity to know, yet not with actual knowledge. And nature hath made it the duty of parents to be the teachers of their children first, and then to get the help of other.[8]

Q. 9. May we give over learning when we are past childhood?[9]

A. No; we must go on to learn as long as we live; for we know but in part, and therefore still have need of more. But those that have neglected to learn in their childhood, have most need of all; it being

---

[6] 1 Kgs 8:36; Micah 4:2.

[7] Isa 28:26; 1 Cor 11:14; Job 12:7, 8; Heb 5:12.

[8] 2 Tim 2:2; Job 32:17; Titus 2:1; Deut 6:7, 8, and 11:19, 20.

[9] Prov 1:5; 9:9; 6:21, 22.

sinful and unnatural to be ignorant at full age, and signifieth great neglect.[10]

Q. 10. Who must teach us at age?

A. Parents and masters must teach their households, and public teachers are officers to teach all publicly; and all that have wisdom should take all fit opportunities, in charity, to teach and edify one another; knowledge and goodness have a communicative nature.[11]

Q. 11. How must parents teach their households?

A. Very familiarly and plainly, according to their capacities, beginning with the plain and necessary things; and this is it which we call catechising, which is nothing but the choosing out of the few plain, necessary matters from all the rest, and in due method, or order, teaching them to the ignorant.[12]

Q. 12. What need we catechisms, while we have the Bible?

A. Because the Bible containeth all the whole body of religious truths, which the ripest Christians should know, but are not all of equal necessity to salvation with the greatest points. And it cannot be expected that ignorant persons can cull out these most necessary points from the rest without help. A man is not a man without a head and heart; but he may be a man if he lose a finger, or a hand, but not an entire man; nor a comely man without hair, nails, and nature's ornaments. So a man cannot be a Christian, or a good or happy man, without the great and most necessary points in the Bible; nor an entire Christian without the rest. Life and death lieth not on all alike. And the skilful must gather the most necessary for the ignorant, which is a catechism.[13]

Q. 13. But is not knowledge the gift of God?

A. Yes; but he giveth it by means. Three things must concur. (1) A right presenting to the learner, which is the teacher's work. (2) A fitness in the learner, by capacity, willingness, and diligence. (3) The blessing of God, without which no man can be wise.[14]

---

[10] Ps 119:99; Heb 5:11, 12; Prov 5:13.

[11] Gal 6:6; Deut 6:7; 1 Tim 2:7; 2 Tim 1:11; Eph 4:11; Tit 2:3.

[12] Heb 3:13; Ezra 7:25; Col 3:16; Heb 5:11, 12, and 6:1, 2; 2 Tim 1:13.

[13] Matt 12:30, 31, 33; 19:19; 22:37, 39; Rom 13:9; Matt 28:19; Matt 23:23; Jas 1:27.

[14] Isa 30:29; Matt 28:19, 20; 1 Tim 1:3; 3:2; 6:2, 3.

And therefore three sorts will be ignorant and erroneous. (1) Those that have not the happiness of true teachers, nor truth presented to them. (2) Those that by sottishness, pride, sensuality, malignity, or sloth, are incapable, or unwilling, to learn. (3) Those that, by wilful sinning against God, are deprived of the necessary blessing of his help and illumination.[15]

---

[15] 2 Tim 2:2, 24; Acts 20:20; 2 Tim 3:17; Heb 5:12, 13; 1 John 2:27; 1 Thess 4:9.

2

How to know Ourselves by Nature

Q. 1. What is the first thing that a man must know?

A. The first in being and excellency is God. But the first in time known by man, or the lowest step where our knowledge beginneth, are the sensible things near us, which we see, hear, feel, &c., and especially ourselves.[1]

Q. 2. What know we of the things which we see, and feel, &c.?

A. A man of sound senses and understanding knoweth them to be such as sense apprehendeth, while they are rightly set before him; the eye seeth light and colours, the ear heareth sounds and words, and so of the rest; and the sound understanding judgeth them to be such as the sense perceiveth, unless distance, or false mediums, deceive us.[2]

Q. 3. But how know you that sense is not deceived? You say that is bread and wine in the sacrament, which the Papists say is not.

A. God hath given us no other faculties but sense, by which to judge of sensible things, as light and darkness, heat and cold, sweet and bitter, soft and hard, &c. Therefore if we be here deceived, God is our deceiver, and we are remediless; even faith and reason suppose our senses, and their true perception; and if that first perception be false, faith and reason could be no truer. God expecteth not that we should

---

[1] 1 John 1:2, 3; Acts 1:3; 4:20; 26:16.

[2] John 20:20, 25, 27.

judge by other faculties than such as he hath given us for the perception of those objects.

Q. 4. What doth a mail first perceive of himself?

A. We first feel that we are real beings; and we perceive that we use and have our senses, that we see, hear, feel, smell, taste; and then we perceive that we understand and think of the things so seen, felt, &c. And that we gather one thing from another, and that we love good, and hate evil, and choose, refuse, and do accordingly.

Q. 5. What do you next know of yourselves?

A. When we perceive that we see, feel, &c., and think, love, hate, &c., we know that we have a power of soul to do all this, for no one doth that which he is not made able to do.

Q. 6. And what do you next know of yourself?

A. When I know what I do, and that I can do it, I know next that I am a substance, endued with this power; for nothing hath no power, nor act, it can do nothing.

Q. 7. What know you next of yourself?

A. I know that this substance, which thinketh, understandeth, and willeth, is an unseen substance; for neither I, nor any mortal man, seeth it; and that is it which is called a spirit.

Q. 8. What next perceive you of yourself?

A. I perceive that in this one substance there is a threefold power, marvellously but one, and yet three, as named from the objects and effects; that is, (1) A power of mere growing motion, common to plants. (2) A power of sense common to beasts. (3) And a power of understanding and reason, about things above sense, proper to a man; three powers in one spiritual substance.

Q. 9. What else do you find in yourself?

A. I find that my spiritual substance, as intellectual, hath also a threefold power in one; that is, (1) Intellectual life, by which I move and act my faculties, and execute my purposes. (2) Understanding. (3) And will, and that these are marvellously diverse, and yet one.

Q. 10. What else find you by yourself?

A. I find that this unseen spirit is here united to a human body, and is in love with it, and careth for it, and is much limited by it, in its perceivings, willings, and workings; and so that a man is an incorporate, understanding spirit, or a human soul and body.

Q. 11. What else perceive you by yourself?

A. I perceive that my higher powers are given me to rule the lower, my reason to rule my senses and appetite, my soul to rule and use my body, as man is made to rule the beasts.

Q. 12. What know you of yourself, as related to others?

A. I see that I am a member of the world of mankind, and that others are better than I, and multitudes better than one; and that the welfare of mankind depends much on their duty to one another; and therefore that I should love all according to their worth, and faithfully endeavour the good of all.

Q. 13. What else know you of yourself?

A. I know that I made not myself, and maintain not myself in life and safety, and therefore that another made me and maintaineth me; and I know that I must die by the separation of my soul and body.

Q. 14. And can we tell what then becomes of the soul?

A. I am now to tell you but how much of it our nature tells as, the rest I shall tell you afterward; we may know, (1) That the soul, being a substance in the body, will be a substance out of it, unless God should destroy it, which we have no cause to think he will. (2) That life, understanding, and will, being its my nature, it will be the same after death, and not a thing of some other kind. (3) That the soul, being naturally active, and the world full of objects, it will not be a sleepy or inactive thing. (4) That its nature here being to mind its interest in another life, by hopes or fears of what will follow, God made not its nature such in vain, and therefore that good or evil in the life that is next will be the lot of all.

3

Of the Natural Knowledge of God and Heaven

Q. 1. You have told me how we know the things which we see and feel, without us and within us; but how can we know any things which we neither see nor feel, but are quite above us?

A. By certain effects and signs which notify them: how little else did man differ from a beast, if he knew no more than he seeth and feeleth? Besides what we know from others that have seen; you see not now that the sun will rise tomorrow, or that man must die; you see not Italy, Spain, France; you see no man's soul: and yet we certainly know that such things are sad will be.

Q. 2. How know you that there is any thing above us, but what we see?

A. (1) We see such things done here on earth, which nothing doth, or can do, which is seen. What thing, that is seen, can give all men and beasts their life, and sense, and safety? And so marvellously form the bodies of all, and govern all the matters of the world? (2) We see that the spaces above us, where sun, moon, and stars are, are so vast, that all this earth is not so much to them, as one inch is to all this land. And we see that the regions above us excel in the glory of purity and splendour: and when this dark spot of earth hath so many millions of men, can we doubt whether those vast and glorious parts are better inhabited? (3) And we find that the grossest things are the basest, and the most invisible the most powerful and noble; as our souls are above our bodies: and therefore the most vast and glorious worlds above us must have the most invisible, powerful, noble inhabitants.[1]

Q. 3. But how know you what those spirits above us are?

A. (1) We partly know what they are, by what they do with us on earth. (2) We know much what they are, by the knowledge of ourselves. If our souls are invisible spirits, essentiated by the power of life, understanding, and will, the spirits above us can be no less, but either such or more excellent. And he that made us must needs be more excellent than his work.

Q. 4. How know you who made us?

A. He that made all things must needs be our Maker, that is God.

Q. 5. What mean you by God? and what is he?

A. I mean the eternal, infinite, glorious Spirit, and Life, most perfect in active power, understanding and will, of whom, and by whom, and to whom, are all things; being the Creator, Governor, and End of all. This is that God whom all things do declare.

Q. 6. How know you that there is such a God?

A. By his works (and I shall afterwards tell you more fully by his word). Man did not make himself; beasts, birds, fishes, trees, and plants, make not themselves: the earth, and water, and air, made not themselves: and if the souls of men have a maker, the spirits next above them must have a maker: and so on, till you come to a first cause, that was made by none. There must be a first cause, and there can be but one.

Q. 7. Why may not there be many gods, or spirits, that were made by none, but are eternally of themselves?

A. Because it is a contradiction; the same would be both perfect and imperfect: perfect, because he is of himself eternally, without a cause, and so dependent upon none: and yet imperfect, because he hath but a part of that being that is said to be perfect: for many are more than one, and all make up the absolute, perfect Being, and one of them is but a part of all: and to be a part, is to be imperfect. However many subordinate created spirits may unfitly be called gods, there can be but one uncreated God, in the first and proper sense.

Q. 8. How know you that God is eternal, without beginning?

---

[1] Rom 1:19, 20, 21.

A. Because else there was a time when there was nothing, if there were a time when there was no God. And then there never would have been any thing: for nothing can make nothing.

Q. 9. But how can man conceive of an eternal, uncaused Being?

A. That such a God there is, is the most certain, easy truth, and that he hath all the perfection before described: but neither man nor angel can know him comprehensively.

Q. 10. What mean you by his infiniteness?

A. That his being and perfection have no limits or measure, but incomprehensibly comprehend all places and beings.

Q. 11. What is this God to us?

A. He is our Maker, and therefore our absolute Owner, our Supreme Ruler, and our chief Benefactor, and ultimate End.

Q. 12. And how stand we related to him? What duty do we owe him? And what may we expect from him?

A. We are his creatures, and all that we are, and have, is of him; we are his subjects, made with life, reason, and free-will to be ruled by him: he is the infinite good, and love itself. Therefore we owe him perfect resignation, perfect obedience, and perfect complacency and love: all that we are, and all that we have, and all that we can do, is due to him in the way of our obedience; to pay which, is our own rectitude and felicity, as it is our duty: but all this you may much better learn from his word, than nature alone can teach it you. Though man's nature, and the frame of nature about us, so fully proveth what I have said, as leaveth all the ungodly without excuse.

4

Of God's Kingdom, and the Government of Man, and Providence

Q. 1. I perceive that nothing more concerneth us, than to know God, and our relation and duty to him, and what hope we have from him: therefore, I pray you, open it to me more fully, and first tell me where God is?

A. God being infinite, is not confined in any place, but all place and things are in God; and he is absent from none, but as near to every thing as it is to itself.

Q. 2. Why then do you say that he is in heaven, if he be as much on earth, and every where?

A. God is not more or less in one place, than another, in his being, but he is apparent, and known to us by his working, and so we say, he is in heaven, as he there worketh and shineth forth to the most blessed creatures in heavenly glory. As we say the sun is where it shineth: or, to use a more apt comparison, the soul of man is indivisibly in the whole body, but it doth not work in all parts alike; it understandeth not in the foot, but in the head; it seeth not, heareth not, tasteth not, and smelleth not, in the fingers or lower parts, but in the eye, the ear, and other senses in the head; and therefore when we talk to a man, it is his soul that we talk to, and not his flesh, and yet we look him in the face; not as if the soul were no where but in the face or head, but because it only worketh and appeareth there by those senses, and that understanding which we converse with: even so, we look up to heaven, when we speak to God;

not as if he were no where else, but because heaven is the place of his glorious appearing and operation, and as the head and face of the world, where all true glory and felicity is, and from whence it descendeth to this earth, as the beams of the sun do from his glorious centre.

Q. 3. You begin to make me think that God is the soul of the world, and that we must conceive of him in the world, as we do of the soul of man in his body.

A. You cannot better conceive of God, so you will but take in the points of difference, which are very great; for no creature known to us doth resemble God without vast difference.

The differences are such as these. (1) The soul is part of the man, but God is not a part of the world, or of being: for to be a part is to be less than the whole, and so to be imperfect. (2) We cannot say that the soul is any where out of the body, but the world is finite, and God is infinite, and therefore God is not confined to the world. (3) The soul ruleth not a body, that hath a distinct understanding and free-will of its own to receive its laws, and therefore ruleth it not by proper law, but by despotical motion: but God ruleth men that have understanding and free-will of their own, to know and receive his laws, and therefore he ruleth them partly by a law. (4) The soul doth not use another soul under it to rule the body, but God maketh use of superior spirits to move and rule things, and persons below them, so that there is a great difference between God's ruling the world, and the soul's ruling the body.

But yet there is great likeness also. (1) God is as near every part of the world, as the soul is near the body. (2) God is as truly and fully the cause of all the actions and changes of the world (except sin, which free-will, left to itself, committeth) as the soul is the cause of the actions and changes of the body. (3) The body is no more lifeless without the soul than the world would be without God. Yea, God giveth all its being to the world, and without him it would be nothing; and in this he further differeth from the soul, which giveth not material being to the body.

So that you may well conceive Of God as the soul of the world, so you will but put in that he is far more.

Q. 4. Is not it below God to concern himself with these lower things? Doth he not leave them to those that are under him?

A. It is below God to be unconcerned about any part, even the least of his own works. Men are narrow creatures, and can be but in one place at once, and therefore must do that by others which they cannot do themselves, at least without trouble: but God is infinite, and present with all creatures; and as nothing is in being without him, so nothing can move with out him.

Q. 5. By this you make God to do all things immediately, whereas we see he works by means and second causes: he giveth us light and heat by the sun; he upholdeth us by the earth, &c.

A. The word immediate sometimes signifieth a cause that hath no other cause under it; so the sun is the immediate cause of the emanation of its beams of light: and so God is not always an immediate cause; that is, he hath other causes under him; but sometimes immediate signifieth that which is next a thing, having nothing between them. And so God doth all things immediately: for he is, and he acteth, as near us as we to ourselves, and nothing is between him and us: he is as near the person and the effect, when he useth second causes, as when he useth none.

Q. 6. But is it not a debasing God, to make his providence the cause of every motion of a worm, a bird, a fly, and to mind and move such contemptible things; and so to mind the I thoughts of man?

A. It is a debasing God to think that he is like a finite creature, absent, or insufficient for any of his creatures. That there is not the least thing or motion so small as to be done without him, is most certain to him that will consider, (1) That God's very essence is every where: and wherever he is, he is himself, that is, most powerful, wise, and good: and if such a God be as near to every action, as the most immediate actor is, so that in him they all live, and move, and be, how can he be thought to have no hand in it, as to providence or causality? (2) And it is certain that God upholds continually the very being of every thing that moveth, and all the power by which they move: for that which had no being but from him can have none continued but by him: that which could not make itself cannot continue itself: should not God by his causality continue their being, every creature would turn to nothing. For there can be nothing without a cause, but the first cause, which is God. (3) And it is all one to infiniteness, to mind every creature and motion in the world, and to cause and rule the least, as it is to cause and rule but one.

God is as sufficient for all the world, even every fly and worm, as if he had but one to mind. Seeing, then, that he is as present with every creature as it is with itself, and it hath not the least power but what he continually giveth it, and cannot move at all but by him, and he is as sufficient for all as for one, it is unreasonable to think that the least thing is done without him. Is it a dishonour to the sun, that every eye, even of flies, and ants, and toads, and snakes, as well as men, do see by the light of it; or that it shineth at once upon every pile of grass, and atom? This is but the certain effect of God's infiniteness and perfection.

Q. 7. How doth God govern all things?

A. He governeth several things, according to their several natures which he hath made: lifeless things by their natural inclinations, and by moving force; things that have sense by their sensitive inclinations, and by their objects, and by constraint; and reasonable creatures by their principles, and by laws and moral rules: and all things by his infinite power, wisdom, and will, as being every one part of one world, which is his kingdom: especially man.

Q. 8. What is God's kingdom? And why do you call him our King?

A. I call him our King, because, (1) He only hath absolute right, power, and fitness, to be our Supreme Ruler: (2) And he doth actually rule us as our Sovereign. And in this kingdom, (1) God is the only Supreme King and Head. (2) Angels, or glorified spirits, and men, are the subjects: (3) All the brutes and lifeless creatures are the furniture, and goods, and utensils. (4) Devils and rebellious, wicked men, are the enemies, to be opposed and overcome.

Q. 9. How doth God govern man on earth?

A. The power of God our Lord, Owner, and Mover, moveth us, and disposeth of us, as he doth of all things, to the fulfilling of his will. (1) The wisdom of God our King doth give us sound doctrine, and holy and just laws, with rewards and penalties, and he will judge men, and execute accordingly. (2) And the love of our heavenly Father doth furnish us with all necessary blessings, help us, accept us, and prepare us for the heavenly kingdom.

Q. 10. Why is man ruled by laws, rather than beasts and other things?

A. Because man hath reason, and free-will, which maketh them subjects capable of laws, which beasts are not.

Q. 11. What is that free-will which fits us to be subjects?

A. It is a will made by God, able to determine itself, by God's necessary help, to choose good, and refuse evil; understood to be such, without any necessitating predetermination by any other.

5

Of God's Law of Nature, and Natural Officers

Q. 1. By what laws doth God govern the world?

A. How he governeth the spirits above us, whether by any laws besides the immediate revelation of his will, seen in the face of his glory, or how else, is not much known to us, because it doth not concern us. But this lower world of man he governeth by the law of nature, and by a law of supernatural revelation, given by his Spirit or by messengers from heaven.

Q. 2. What is it that you call the law of nature?

A. In a large and improper sense, some call the inclinations, and forcing, or naturally moving, causes of any creatures, by the name of a law: and so they say that beasts and birds are moved by the law of their nature; and that stones sink downward, and the fire goeth upward, by the law of nature. But this is no law in the proper sense which we are speaking of, whatever you call it.

Q. 3. What is it then that you call a law?

A. Any signification of the will of the ruler, purposely given to the subject, that thereby he may know and be bound to his duty, and know his reward or punishment due. Or any signification of the ruler's will for the government of subjects, constituting what shall be due from them, and to them. A rule to live by, and the rule by which we must be judged.

Q. 4. What, then, is God's law of nature, made for man?

A. It is the signification of God's governing will, by the nature of man himself, and of all other creatures known to man, in which God declareth to man his duty, and his reward or punishment.

Q. 5. How can a man know God's will, and our duty by his nature, and by all other works of God about us?

A. In some things, as surely as by words or writings; but in other things more darkly. I am sure that my nature is made to know and love truth and goodness, and to desire and seek my own felicity; my nature tells me that I was not made by myself, and do not live by myself, and therefore that I am not my own, but his that made me. All things show me that there is a God who must needs be greater, wiser, and better, than all his creatures, and therefore ought to be most honoured, feared, loved, and obeyed: I see multitudes of persons of the same nature with me, and therefore obliged to the same duty to God; I see much of God's work in them which is good, and therefore to be loved; and I see that we are all parts of one world, and made to be useful to one another: these, and many such things, the reason of man may discern in himself and other works of God.

Q. 6. But I thought the law of nature had been every man's natural temper and disposition, which inclineth him to action, and you make it to be only a notifying sign of duty.

A. Figuratively, some call every inclination a law, but it is no such thing that we are speaking of, only a man's natural inclination, among other signs, may notify his duty. But I hope you cannot think that a man's vicious inclination is God's law; then you would make original sin, and the work of the devil, to be God's law. One man's sinful distemper of soul, and another man's bodily distemper (the fruit of sin) inclineth him to wrath, to lust, to idleness, to sinful sports, or drinking, or gluttony, and these are so far from being God's law of nature, that they are the contraries, and the law of Satan in our members, rebelling against the law of God. And though the good inclinations of our common nature (to justice, peace, temperance) be by some called the law of nature, it is not as they are inclinations, but as from them we may know our duty.

Q. 7. Hath God any natural officers under him in governing man? I pray you tell me how far man's power is of God?

A. God hath set up divers sorts of human governing powers under him in the world, which all have their place and order assigned them;

some by nature, as entire; some by the law of nature, since the fall, and some by supernatural revelation, which is not to be here spoken to, but afterward.

Q. 8. Because I have heard some say that God made no government, but men do it by consent for their necessity, I pray you show me what government God made by nature, and in what order?

A. (1) Next to God's own governing right, which is the first, God hath made every man a governor of himself. For God made him with some faculties which must be ruled, (as the appetite, senses, and tongue, and other bodily members, yea, and passions too,) and with some which must rule the rest, as the understanding by guidance, and the will by command. And this self-governing power is so necessary and natural, that no man can take it from us, or forbid us the due exercise of it, any more than they can bind us to sin or to self-destruction.

Q. 9. Which is the next human power in order?

A. (2) The governing power of the husband over the wife, whose very nature, as well as original, shows that she was made to be subject, though under the law of love.

Q. 10. But is not this by consent, rather than by nature?

A. It is by consent that a woman is married: but when she hath made herself a wife, nature maketh her a subject, unless madness, or disability, make the man unmeet for his place.

Q. 11. Which is the next sort of natural government?

A. (3) The parents' government of their children: nature maketh it the duty of parents to rule, and of children to obey. And though some have been so unnatural as to deny this, and say that children owe nothing but reverence and gratitude, yet there is no danger of the common prevalency of such a heresy, which the nature of all mankind confuteth, save that licentious youth will take advantage of it, to disobey their parents, to please their lusts.

Q. 12. What is the human government which God's law of nature hath instituted to man, since his fall and corruption?

A. (4) That is to be afterwards explained: but magistracy, or civil government, is certainly of natural institution, though it is uncertain how God would have governed man in such societies by man, if they had not sinned. The law of nature teacheth man the necessity of civil society, and of government therein, and therefore obligeth man thereto.

Q. 13. This seemeth to be but the effect of men's own perceived necessity, and so to be but their arbitrary choice.

A. Their necessity is natural, and the notice of it is natural, and the desire of remedy is natural, and the fitness of magistracy to its use is natural: therefore it is the law of God in nature that bindeth them to choose and use it; and if any country should choose to live without magistracy, they would sin against the law of nature, and their own good.

Q. 14. But I have heard that God hath made no law, what form of civil government shall be used, but left it to every country's choice.

A. God hath, by nature, made it necessary that there be magistracy; that is, some men in power over societies, to enforce the obedience of God's own common laws, and to make their subordinate laws about undeterminate, mutable matters to that end, for the honour of God, and the good of the society.

But, (1) Whether this government shall be exercised by one or many; (2) And who shall be the persons, God's law hath left undetermined to human liberty: the form and persons are chosen, neither by the said persons, nor by the people only, but by the mutual consent and contract of both. (3) And also by this contract, the degree of power, and order of the exercise, may be stated and limited: but for all that, when human consent hath chosen the persons, the essential power of governing in subordination to God's laws, floweth, not from man, but immediately from God's law of nature.

Q. 15. But what if these sorts of government prove cross to one another, and reason commandeth one thing, a husband another, a parent another, and the magistrate another, which must be obeyed?

A. Each have their proper work and end, which none of the other can forbid. Self-government is the reasonable management of our own faculties and actions in obedience to God, for our own salvation, and no king, or other, can take this from us: and if they forbid us any necessary duty to God, or necessary means of our salvation, they do it without authority, and are not to be therein obeyed.

A husband's power to govern his wife is for the necessary ends of their relation, which the king hath no power to forbid. A parent's power to rule his children is for the necessary education of them, for the welfare of soul and body, and the king hath no power to forbid it. Should he forbid parents to feed their children, or teach them God's laws, or to choose for them orthodox, fit tutors, pastors, and church communion where God is lawfully worshipped, and should he command the children to use the contrary, it is all null and powerless.

But it belongeth to the magistrates only (though not to destroy any of the three former governments, which are all before his in nature and time, yet) to govern them all, by directing the exercise of them in lawful things to the common good.

Q. 16. How far doth the law of nature assure us of God's rewards and punishments?

A. As it assureth us that perfect man owed God perfect obedience, trust, and love, so it certifieth us, (1) That this performed, must needs be acceptable to God, and tend to the felicity of the subject, seeing God's love is our felicity. (2) And that sinning against God's law deserveth punishment. (3) And that governing justice must make such a difference between the obedient and the sinner as the ends of government require. (4) And seeing that before man's obedience, or sin, God made man's soul of a nature not tending to its own mortality, we have cause to expect that man's rewards and punishments should be suitable to such immortal souls. For though he can make brutes immortal, and can annihilate man's soul, or any creature, yet we see that he keeps so close to his natural establishments that we have no reason to think that he will cross them here, and annihilate souls to shorten their rewards or punishments.

Q. 17. But doth nature tell us what kind of rewards and punishments men have?

A. The faculties of the soul being made in their nature to know God in our degree, to love him, to please him, and to rest and rejoice herein, and this in the society of wise, and good, and blessed joyful fellow-creatures, whom also our nature is made to love, it followeth that the perfections of this nature, in these inclinations and actions, is that which God did make our nature for, to be obtained by the obeying of his laws.

And sin being the injurious contempt and forsaking of God, and the most hurtful malady of the soul, and of societies, and to others, it followeth that those that have finally forsaken God, be without the happiness of his love and glory, and under the sense of their sin and his displeasure; and that their own sin will be their misery, as diseases are to the body; and that the societies and persons that by sin they injured or infected, will somewhat contribute to their punishment. Happiness to the good, and misery to the bad, the light and law of nature teacheth man to expect, but all that I have taught you is much more surely and fully known by supernatural revelation.

6

Of Supernatural Revelation of God's Will to Man, and of the Holy Scriptures, or Bible

Q. 1. What do you call supernatural revelation?

A. All that revelation of God's mind to man, which is made by him extraordinarily, above what the common works of nature do make known: though, perhaps, God may use it in some natural second causes, in a way unknown to us.[1]

Q. 2. How many ways hath God thus revealed his will to man?

A. Many ways. (1) By some voice and signs of his presence, which we do not well know what creature he used to it, whether angels, or only at present caused that voice and glory. So he spake to Adam and Eve, and the serpent, and to Moses in the mount, and tabernacle, and in the cleft of the rock. (Exod. 34) And to Abraham, Jacob, &c.[2]

(2) By angels certainly appearing, as sent from God; and so he spake to Abraham, Isaac, Jacob, Lot, Moses, and to very many.[3]

(3) By visions and dreams in their sleep, extraordinary.[4]

---

[1] Matt 11:25, 27; Luke 10:22; Deut 29:29; Matt 16:17; 1 Cor 2:10.

[2] Eph 3:5; 1 Pet 1:12; Dan 2:47, 22, 28, 29; Amos 3:7; Gal 1:18, and 2:2.

[3] Eph 3:3.

[4] 1 Cor 14:6, 26.

(4) By the vision of some signs from heaven in their waking: as Saul (Acts 9) saw the light that cast him down.[5]

(5) By visions and voices in an extasy: as Paul saw Paradise, and heard unutterable things; whether in the body, or out of the body, he knew not. And it is like in such a rapture Daniel an John had their revelations.

(6) By Christ's own voice, as he spake to men on earth, and Paul from heaven.

(7) By the sight of Christ and glory, as Stephen saw him.

(8) By immediate inspiration to the minds of prophets.

(9) By these prophets sent as messengers to others.

(10) By certain uncontrolled miracles.

(11) By a convincing course of extraordinary works of God's providence, as when an angel killed the armies of enemies, or when they killed one another in one night or day, &c.

(12) By extraordinary works of God on the souls of men, as when he suddenly overcometh the strongest vicious habits and customs, and maketh multitudes new and holy persons, by such improbable but assigned means, by which he promised to do it.

Q. 3. These are all excellent things, if we were sure that they were not deceived, nor did deceive. But how shall we be sure of that?

A. It is one thing to ask how they themselves were sure that they were not deceived, and another thing to ask how we are, or others may be sure of it. As to the first, they were sure, as men are of other things which they see, hear, feel, and think. I am sure, by sense and intellectual perception, that I see the light, that I hear, feel, think, &c. The revelation cometh to the person in its own convincing evidence, as light doth to the eye.[6]

Q. 4. They know what they see, hear, feel; but how were they sure that it was of God, and not by some deceiving cause?

A. (1) God himself gave them the evidence of this also in the revelation, that it was from him, and no deceit. But it is no more possible for any of us, that never had such a revelation ourselves, to know sensibly and formally what it is, and how they knew it, than it is for a man born

---

[5]   2 Cor 12:1, 7.

[6]   1 John 1:1–3.

blind to know how other men see, or what seeing is. (2) But, moreover, they also were sure that it was of God, by the proofs by which they make us sure of it. And this leads us up to the other question.[7]

Q. 5. And a question of unspeakable moment it is, how we can be sure of such prophetical revelations delivered to us by others; viz. That they were not deceived, nor deceive us.

A. It is of exceeding consequence, indeed, and therefore deserveth to be understandingly considered and handled.

And here you must first consider the difference of revelation. Some were but made or sent by prophets to some particular persons, about a personal, particular business, as to Abraham, that he should have a son, that Sodom should be burnt; to David, that his son should be his punishment, his child die; to Hezekiah, that he should recover, &c. These none were bound to know and believe, but the persons concerned, to whom they were revealed and sent, till they were made public afterwards. But some revelations were made for whole countries, and some for all the world, and that as God's laws, or covenants, which life and death dependeth on; and these must, accordingly, be made known to all.

Q. 6. I perceive, then, that before we further inquire of the certainty, I should first ask you of the matter; what things they be that God hath supernaturally revealed to man, especially for us all?

A. The particular revelations to and about particular men's matter, are many of them recorded to us for our notice; but there may be thousands more in the world that we know not, nor are concerned to know. What revelation God ever made to any persons throughout the world, as what should befal them when they should die, what wars, or plagues, or famine, should come, &c., little do we know; but what is recorded by God we know.

But as for his laws and promises, which we are all concerned to know, I shall now but name, and afterward open what God hath revealed.

(I) He revealed to Adam, besides the law of nature, which was perfecter and clearer to him than it is now to us, a trying prohibition to

---

[7] Heb 2:3, 4.

eat of the fruit of the tree of knowledge, adding the penalty of death to restrain him.[8]

(II) He judged him after his fall to some degree of punishment, but declared his pardoning mercy, and promised victory to, and by the woman's seed, in the war which they now engaged in with Satan, the serpent, and his seed: and he instituted sacrificing to typify the means.[9]

(III) He renewed this covenant with Noah, after the flood.

(IV) He made a special promise to Abraham, to be the God of his seed, as a peculiar people chosen to him out of all the world, and that all nations should be blessed in his seed: and he instituted the sacrament of circumcision to be the seal and symbol.[10]

(V) When his seed were multiplied in Egypt, he brought them out, and in performance of this promise, made them a holy commonwealth, as their Sovereign, and gave them at large a law and sub-governors, which, as political, was proper to that people.[11]

(VI) In the fulness of time God sent his Son to reconcile man to God, to reveal his love and will most fully, and to make and seal the covenant of grace in its last and best edition, and, as King, to rule and judge the redeemed, and sanctify, justify, and glorify, the faithful. These are the public laws and covenants supernaturally revealed.[12]

Q. 7. Is it equally necessary to us to believe every word in the Bible? Or is every word equally certain to us?

A. All truths are truths, which is, to be equally true in themselves: and so, if by certainty you mean nothing but infallible truth, every truth is so certain; and all God's words are true. But if by certain you mean that which is so evident to us, that we may ourselves be fully certain of the truth, so the parts of God's word have different degrees of certainty. We suppose false translations and false printings are none of God's word; nor the words of Satan, or fallible men, recited in the Bible, save only the historical assertion that such words were spoken by them.

---

[8] Gen 2:16, 17, and 3:15.

[9] Gen 4:4, and 9:1, 2–8.

[10] Gen 12:2, 3, and 17:1, 2, 4, 6–11.

[11] Exod 2. &c., 20. &c.

[12] John 1 and 3:16; Gal 4:4–6, and 1:4; Matt 28:10, 20.

But that which is God's word, indeed, is none of it so for void of proof but that we may come to a certainty that it is true: and if we had equal evidence that every word is God's word, we should have equal evidence that all is true: for that God cannot lie is the foundation truth of all our certainty. But God did not reveal every truth in the Bible with equal, evidencing attestation from heaven. Some of them much more concern us than others, and therefore were more fully sealed and attested.[13]

Q. 8. How are we sure of the law that was given to Adam, and that he sinned, as is written, and had after a pardoning law?

A. (1) The law of nature given him is yet God's common law to the world, saving the strictness of it as a condition to life. (2) The fall of man hath too full proof in all the pravity of mankind from the birth. (3) The pardoning act is evident in the execution: God giveth all men mercy, contrary to their deserts, and useth none in the utmost rigour. (4) The notorious enmity between Christ and Satan, and their seeds, through all ages and places of the world, doth prove the sentence, and the law of grace. (5) The universal curse, or punishment, on mankind, showeth somewhat of the cause. (6) The tradition of sacrificing was so universally received over all the world, as confirmeth to us that God delivered it to Adam, as a symbol and a type of the grace then promised. (7) But our fullest proof of all that history, is that which after proved the word that revealed it to us.[14]

Q. 9. How are we certain that the law of Moses was God's law?

A. By a course of wonderful miracles wrought to prepare them to receive it, and to attest it. The ten marvellous plagues of Egypt; the passage through the Red Sea; the opening of the rock to give them water; feeding them with manna; raining twice quails upon them; the sight of the flaming mount, with the terrible concomitants; the sight of the pillar of fire by night, and cloud by day, which conducted them; the sight of the cloud and symbol of God's presence at the door of the tabernacle; the miraculous destruction of the rebellious, even by the opening of the earth; and the performance of God's promises mises to them: all

---

[13] Heb 7:22, and 9:15–18; 9:13; 8:10; 10:10; and 10:16; Matt 4.

[14] Ps 14; Rom 3; Ps 114:9; Acts 14:17; 1 John 3:8; Rom 3:21, 23, and 4:12, 15–17; 2 Kgs 10:19; Acts 14:13, 18; 1 Cor 10:20.

these were full proofs that it was of God. But we have yet fuller proof in Christ's latter testimony, which confirmeth all this to us.

Q. 10. These were full proofs to those that saw them. But are we certain that the records of them in the Scripture are true?

A. (1) Consider that they were written, by Moses, to that very people who are said to see them.[15] And if one should now write to us Englishmen, that God brought us out of another land by ten such public miracles, as the frogs, the flies, the lice, the darkness, the waters turned blood, the death of their cattle, and of all their first-born; that he opened the Sea, and brought us through it on foot; that he opened rocks; fed us with manna; rained quails for a month's food; spake from a flaming mount, and opened the mount to swallow up rebels, &c. When we know all this to be false, would not all men deride and abhor the reporter? Would any of us receive a law, and that of such operous, numerous, costly services, by the motive of such a report as this?

(2) Consider that this law so delivered was on this ground entertained, and unchangeably kept, by them from generation to generation, it being taken for an heinous crime to alter it in one word.[16]

(3) Consider that practised, sacramental symbols, from the first day, were so uninterruptedly kept, as was a fuller proof of the fact than the bare writings. (1) All their males, from the promise to Abraham, were constantly circumcised (save in the wilderness travels) and are to this day. (2) From the very night that the first-born were killed in Egypt, and they driven hastily out, they yearly continued the eating of the passover with unleavened bread, as in a hasting posture. (3) Since the law given in the wilderness, they constantly used the sacrifices, the oblations, the tabernacle, the priesthood and ceremonies, as that law prescribed them. And the national, constant use of these was, an ascertaining tradition of the matters of fact which were their cause. (4) Yea, so tenacious were they of this law, that (as they taught the very syllables of it to their children, and kept in the ark the very tables of stone that had the ten commandments, so) they were enemies to Christianity,

---

[15] Deut 1:31; 3:21, 22; 4:3, 9; 5:24; 10:21; 11:7; and 29:3; Josh 24:7.

[16] Deut 12:22.

because the Christians were against the Gentiles' observation of their law, and for its abrogation.

(4) Consider again, that the matter of fact, and the divine institution, is since made certain to us by Christ's testimony.

Q. 11. But seeing this law doth not bind us now, nor the particular messages of the prophets were sent to us, is it any of our concern now to know or believe them? It belongeth to those that they were made for, and sent to; but what are they to us?

A. There is not the same necessity to know them, and so to be such that they were all of God, as there is to know and believe the gospel: but it is greatly our duty and concern to believe them; (1) Because they were preparatory to the gospel, and bore an antecedent testimony to it (2) Because the gospel itself beareth witness of their truth, which therefore, if we believe it, we must believe. (3) Because by the Holy Ghost's direction all now make up our books of sacred records, which is the certain word of God, though not all of the same necessity and evidence.

And here I must tell you a great and needful truth, which ignorant Christians, fearing to confess, by over-doing, tempt men to infidelity. The Scripture is like a man's body, where some parts are but for the preservation of the rest, and may be maimed, without death: the sense is the soul of the Scripture, and the letters but the body, or vehicle. The doctrine of the Creed, Lord's Prayer, and Decalogue, and Baptism, and Lord's Supper, is the vital part, and Christianity itself. The Old Testament letter (written as we have it about Ezra's time) is that vehicle which is as imperfect as the revelation of those times was: but as after Christ's incarnation and ascension the Spirit was more abundantly given, and the revelation more perfect and sealed, so the doctrine is more full, and the vehicle or body, that is the words, are less imperfect, and more sure to us; so that he that doubts of the truth of some words in the Old Testament, or of some small circumstantials in the New, hath no reason, therefore, to doubt of the Christian religion, of which these writings are but the vehicle, or body, sufficient to ascertain us of the truth of the history and doctrine. Be sure, first, that Christ is the very Son of God, and it inferreth the certainty of all his words, and enforceth our own religion.

Q. 12. I perceive, then, that our main question is, both as to necessity and evidence, how we are sure that the gospel is true, and the records of it the very word of God?

A. It is so: and as it is that must rule and judge the church, so we have to us fuller proof of this than of the Old Testament; because, that the narrowness of the Jews' country, in comparison of the christian world, and the many thousand years' distance, and a language whose phrase and proverbial speeches, and the very sense of the common words of it, must needs make it more unknown to us, than the language that the gospel is recorded in. And it is not the least proof of the truth of the Old Testament, that it is attested and confirmed by the New.

Q. 13. Will you first tell me, how the apostles, and that first age, were sure that the gospel of Christ was the very word of God?

A. Here I must first tell you, that the great mystery of the blessed Trinity, Father, Son, and Holy Ghost, being one God, is made necessary to us to be believed, not only as to the eternal unsearchable, Inexistence, but especially for the knowledge of God's three great sorts of works on man: that is, as our Creator, and the God of nature; as our Redeemer, and the God of governing and reconciling grace, and as our Sanctifier, and the Applier and Perfecter of all to fit us to glory. And so the Son, as Redeemer, is the way to the Father, (to know him and his love, and be reconciled to him,) and the Holy Ghost is the witness of the Son. The proof, therefore, of the gospel of Christ, in one word, is the Holy Ghost; that is, the certain testimony of God's Spirit. And this testimony consisteth of these several parts. (1) The foregoing testimony of the Spirit by all the prophecies of the Old Testament, and the typical prefigurations, which became a fuller proof than before, when they were seen all to be fulfilled in Christ; yet many were fulfilled before. When Abraham had no child, he was promised the multiplication of his seed, and that all nations should be blessed therein. (Gen. 12:2; and 13:16; and 15:5; and 17:2; and 18:11, 12.) The four hundred years of their abode in Egypt and Canaan before were foretold, and punctually fulfilled. (Gen. 15:13, 14; Exod. 12:31, 32.) So was Jacob's prophecy of Judah's sceptre, (Gen. 42:8-10,) and Joseph's dreams: and verily Balaam's last prophecy was marvellous; who, when he had blessed Israel, and foretold their victories, foretold also the sceptre of David and Christ, and the success of the Assyrians; and after that of Chittim against the Hebrews themselves.

(Numb. 24) And who seeing not the fulfilling of the terrible prophecy of Moses against the Jews. (Deut. 31) Josiah by name, and his deeds, were foretold three hundred years before he was born. (1 Kings 13:2; 2 Kings 23:15.) Oft was the captivity of the Jews foretold, and the destruction of Babylon, and the Jews' return, by Cyrus, named long before he was born, and the very time foretold. From the beginning Christ was promised, and the circumstances of his coming foretold: (Gen. 3:15; 26:4; and 49:10; Deut. 18:15; Psalm 2; 27; 89; and 110; Isa. 53, and 11:1; Jer. 33:15; Mic. 5:2:) that he should be born of a virgin, (Isa. 7:14,) in Bethlehem, (Mic. 5:2,) and then the infants killed; (Jer. 31:15;) that he should come into the temple, as the angel of the covenant whom they desired, but they should not endure therein when he came, because he came as a refiner; (Mal. 3:1, 3;) that he should go into Egypt, and return thence; (Isa. 19:1; Hos. 11:1;) that one should go before him to prepare the way; (Mal. 3:1;) that he should do wonders for the people; (Isa. 35:5;) that a familiar should betray him, and that for thirty pieces of silver, (Psalm 41:9; and 55:13, 14; Zech. 11:12, 13,) and a potter's field be bought with them. All his persecution, and abuse, and sufferings, are foretold, (Isa. 1:6; and 53; Psalm 69:21; 22:18; and 118:22; Isa. 6:9,) even to the circumstances of giving him vinegar, casting lots for his garments, suffering as a malefactor; yea, the very time is foretold; (Dan. 9:25, 26;) and that then the second temple should be destroyed.

(2) The second part of the Spirit's testimony, or the certain proof of christian truth is, the inherent constitutive proof of testimony in the inimitable excellency of the person and gospel of Christ, which is the image and superscription of God. The person of Christ was of such excellency of wisdom, goodness, and power, apparent in his doctrine, works, and patience, all sinless, and full of holy love to God and man, as is not consistent with being the deceiver of the world. His gospel, in the very constitution of it, hath the impress of God. He that hath the Spirit of God, will find that in the gospel, which is so suitable to the divine nature, as will make it the easier to him to believe it. Angels preached the sum of it. (Luke 2:14.) It is all but the fore-promised and prefigured redemption of man historically delivered, and the doctrine,[17] laws, and

---

[17] Col 1:15–19; Prov 30:5; Heb 4:12; 1 Peter 1:23; 1 John 2:14; John 8:48; 12:48; 14:25; 15:3; Acts 14:3; and 20:32; Rom 10:8. Eph 5:20; Phil 2:16; 1 Thess 1:5; Jas 1:2; Matt 12:26;,

promises of saving grace most fully promulgated; it is the wonderful revelation of the power, wisdom, and goodness, the truth, justice, and holiness of God, especially his love to man; and of his marvellous design for the recovery, sanctifying, and saving of sinners, and removing all the impediments of their repentance and salvation; it is so wholly fitted to the glorifying of God, and the reparation of depraved nature, and the purifying and perfecting of man's soul to the guidance of men's lives in the ways of true wisdom, godliness, righteousness, soberness, mutual love and peace, that men may live profitably to others, and live and die in the sense of God's love, and in a safe and comfortable state; that we may be sure so good a thing had a good cause; for had it been the device of men, they must have been very bad men that would put God's name to it, and tell so many lies from generation to generation, to deceive the world; and it is not to be imagined, that from Moses's time to the writing of John's Revelations, there should arise a succession of men of such a strange self-contradicting constitution as should be so good as to devise the most holy, and righteous, and self-denying doctrines, for the great good of mankind, and yet all of them so odiously wicked as to belie God, and deceive men, and do all this good in so bad a manner, with so bad a heart.

And if any blasphemer would father it upon evil spirits, what a contradiction would he speak! As if Satan would promote the greatest good, for the honour of God and benefit of man, while he is the greatest hater of God and man; and as if he would devise a doctrine to reproach himself, and destroy his own kingdom, and bless mankind; and so were at once the best and the worst.

Indeed the holy Scriptures do bear the very image and superscription of God in their ends, matter and manner, and prove themselves to be his word: for God hath not given us external proofs that such a book of doctrine is his, which is itself no better than human works, and hath no intrinsic proof of its divine original;[18] but the intrinsic and extrinsic evidences concur. What book, like the sacred Scriptures, hath taught the world the knowledge of God; the creation of the world;

Mark 4:15; Luke 10:18; Acts 26:18; Rom 16:20; Rev 20:2, 3.

[18] 2 Pet 1:20; 2 Tim 3:15, 16; Matt 5:16, 44, 45.

the end, and hope, and felicity of man; what the heavenly glory is, and how procured, and how to be obtained, and by whom; how man became sinful and miserable; and how he is recovered; and what wonders of love God hath shown to sinners, to win their hearts in love to him? What book hath so taught men to live by faith, and the hopes of glory, above all the lusts of sense and flesh, and to refer all things in this world to spiritual, holy and heavenly ends; to love others as ourselves, and to do good to all, even to our enemies; to live in such union, and communion, and peace, as is caused by this vital grace of love, and not like a heap of sand, that every spurn or blast of cross interest will separate? What book so teacheth man to love God above all, and to pray to him, and absolutely obey him with constant pleasure, and to trust him absolutely with soul, body, and estate, and cast all our care upon him; and, in a word, to converse in heaven while we are on earth; and to live as saints, that we may live as angels?[19]

Q. 14. But how few be there that do all this?

A. (1) I shall further answer that anon: none do it in perfection, but all sound Christians do it in sincerity. (2) But at present, it is the perfection of the doctrine of Christ, and of the sacred Scriptures that I am proving; and it is not men's breaking the law that will prove that God made it not.

Q. 15. You have told me of the foregoing testimony of the Spirit of Christ and the gospel, and of the inherent constitutive testimony, or proof; is there any other?

A. Yes, (3). There is the concomitant testimony, by the works of Christ. Nicodemus could say, "We know that thou art a teacher come from God, for no man can do the works that thou doest, except God were with him." (John 3:2.) He cleansed the lepers with his word; he cast out devils; he healed the lame, the deaf, the blind, yea, those that were born blind; he healed palsies, fevers, and all manner of sicknesses, with a touch, or a word; he turned water into wine; he fed twice many thousands by miracle; he walked on the sea, and made Peter do the same;

---

[19] John 3:3, 5; Titus 2:14; 1 Peter 2:9; Rom 8:9; Matt 5:20; Heb 12:14; Matt 18:3; 2 Cor 5:17; Rom 8:14.

the winds and sea obeyed his command: he raised the dead. This course of miracles was the most evident testimony of God.

And he was brought into the world by miracle: born of a virgin; foretold and named Jesus, by an angel; preached to shepherds by angels from heaven; a star conducting the eastern wise men to the place; John, his foregoer, named by an angel, and Zacharias struck dumb for not believing it; prophesied of by Anna and Simeon; owned at his baptism by the visible descent of the Spirit, in the shape of a dove, and by a voice of God from heaven, and the like again at his transfiguration, when Moses and Elias appeared with him, and he did shine in glory; and at his death the earth trembled, the sun was obscured, and the air darkened, and the vail of the temple rent; but the fullest evidence was Christ's own resurrection from the dead, his oft appearing to his disciples after, and conversing with them at times for forty days, and giving them their commission, and promising them the Spirit, and ascending into heaven in their sight. And all this was the fuller testimony, in that he had oft over and over foretold them of it, that he must be put to death, and rise again the third day, before he entered into his glory; and the Jews knew it, and were not able to prevent it, angels terrifying the soldiers on the watch; yea, the disciples understood it not, and, therefore, believed it not, and Peter dissuaded him from such talk of his sufferings, till Christ called him Satan, (doing like Satan that had tempted him, when he fasted forty days,) to show that the disciples were no contrivers of a deceit herein.

Q. 16. Is there yet any further witness of the Holy Ghost?

A. Yes, (4). There was the consequent testimony of the Spirit by the apostles, and other first publishers of the gospel; Christ bid them wait at Jerusalem for this gift, and promised them that when he was ascended he would send that Paraclete, Advocate, or Comforter, that should be better than his visible presence, and should lead them into all truth, and bring all things to their remembrance, and teach them what to say; that is, to enable them to perform the work to which he had commissioned them, which was to go into all the world, and preach the gospel, and disciple the nations, baptising them, and teaching them to observe all things that he had commanded them; which they performed partly by word, and partly by writing, and partly by practice, baptising, gathering churches, establishing offices and officers; and he promised to be with them to the end of the world; that is, with their persons for their time, and with their doctrine, ordinary successors, and the whole church ever after.[20]

On the day of Pentecost, even the Lord's day, when they were assembled, this promise was so far performed to them, that the Holy Ghost suddenly fell on all the assembly, in the likeness of fiery, cloven tongues, after the noise as of a rushing wind, and they were filled with the Spirit, and spake in the tongues of all the countries near them, the praises and wondrous works of God. After which they were endued with the various miraculous gifts of the Spirit; that is, the use of the tongues which they had never learned; the interpretation of them, prophesying, miracles, healing all diseases, insomuch that those that came under the shadow of Peter, and those that had but clothes from the body of Paul, were all healed; the lame and blind cured, devils cast out, the dead raised, some enemies struck blind, some sinners struck dead; and, which was yet greater, by their preaching or praying, or laying on of hands, God gave the same miraculous gift of the Spirit to others; and that not to a few, but ordinarily to the faithful, some having one such gift, and some another.

And as Christ had promised that when he was lifted up he would draw all men to him, so he blessed the labours of the apostles, prophets, and evangelists, accordingly; many thousands being converted at a sermon, and multitudes still added to the church. And when the preachers were forbidden and imprisoned, Christ strengthened them, and angels miraculously delivered them. When Peter was in prison, designed for death, the angel of God loosed his bolts, and opened the doors, and led him forth. When Paul and Silas had been scourged, and were in the stocks in the prison, an earthquake sets them free, and prepareth for the conversion of the jailer and his house. And Christ himself had before appeared to Paul in glory, when he was going on in persecution, and struck him down in blindness, and preached to him with a voice from heaven, and converted him, and sent him as his apostle into the world. By these miracles was the world converted.

---

[20] John 16; Acts 2; Matt 28:20. The whole Book of the Acts of the Apostles is the history of these miracles. Gal 3:1–4; John 7:3, 9; Rom 1:4; 1 Cor 12:4, 7–9, 11, 13.

And as Christ had promised them that they should do greater works than those which he himself did, so indeed their miracles did more to convert the world than the works of Christ in person had done. For, (1) Those which were wrought by one man would leave suspicious men more doubtful of the truth than that which is done by many, at a distance from each other, and in several places. (2) And that which was done but in one small country would be more doubted of than that which is done in much of the world. Sometimes, indeed, thousands, but usually twelve men, were the witnesses of what Christ said and did; but what these witnesses said and did to prove their testimony, thousands in many lands did see and hear.

Q. 17. But why was it that Christ forbade some to declare that he was the Christ?

A. Because the time was not come, till the evidences were given by which it must be proved; it was not a matter to be rashly believed, and taken upon the bare word of himself or any other. That a man living in a mean condition was the Son of God, and Saviour, and Lord, and Teacher, of the world, and the Judge of all men, was not to believed without good proof: and the chief proof was to be from all Christ's own miracles, and his resurrection, and ascension, and the great gift of the Holy Ghost, and the tongues and miracles of the apostles and other disciples; and these were not all done or given then; yet because the Jews received Moses and the prophets, he sometimes showed how they prophesied of him; yea, his very doctrine, whose frame had a self-evidencing light, was not fully revealed till it was done by the Spirit in the apostles.[21]

Q. 18. But though all these miracles were wrought, how could it be certain that they were the attestation of God, when it is said that magicians, false prophets, and anti-christ may do such things?

A. (1) I shall first mind you, that though we were never so uncertain of the nature of a miracle, whether it be wrought by any created cause, yet we are agreed that, by miracles, we mean such works which were wrought quite out of and against the common course of second courses, called nature; and we are sure that as no work can be done without

---

[21] Luke 4:22, and 24:27, 32, 45; John 5:39; Acts 17:2, 11, and 18:28; Rom 1:2, and 16:26; 1 Cor 15:3, 4; 2 Pet 1:19, 20; Heb 2:3, 4; Rom 3:4; John 3:2; 1 John 5:10; Titus 2:2.

God's promotion, or permission, at least, so especially the course of nature cannot be altered and overruled but by God's knowledge, consent, and execution; whatever second cause unknown to us may be in it, certainly God is the first cause.

(2) And it is most certain that the most perfect Governor of the world is not the great deceiver of the world, and is not so wanting in power, wisdom and goodness, as to rule them by a lie; yea, and an unresistable and remediless deceit; this is rather the description of Satan.

(3) And man must know the will of God by some signs or other, or else he cannot do it; and what signs can the wit of man devise, by which they that would fain know the will of God may come to be certain of it, if such a course of miracles may deceive us? Would you believe if some came from the dead as witnesses? or, if an angel, or many angels, came from heaven? All these could give you no more certainty than such miracles may do.[22]

(4) And you must note, that the proof of miracles lieth not on this, that angels, or other spirits, or second causes, can do no such things, but that they cannot do it without God, and that God will not do it to confirm a lie, or any thing which he would not have man believe; for then either man must believe nothing sent from God, though it were by an host of angels, or else he must say, 'I am unavoidably deceived by God himself; for I have no possible means left to know the fallacy.'

(5) Therefore you must note, that whenever God permitteth a magician, or false prophet, to do any wonder, or unusual thing, he never leaveth man without a remedy against the deceit, but doth control and confute the words of the deceiver; and usually he doth it but first to try the faith and steadfastness of men, and then to bring truth into the clearer light. And he controlleth false miracles these ways.

(1) He sealeth up the truth which the deceiver denieth, with a stream of most unquestionable miracles, and so showeth us that it cannot be a truth, and of God, which is said against such sealed verity, while all his miracles confute theirs. (2) Or, if it be a truth known to man by the common light of nature, that light confuteth the pretender's miracle. (3) If he do it to confirm a false prediction, it is confuted by the thing

---

not coming to pass. (4) In the case of Egyptian[23] magicians' wonders, God permitted them, that his power might triumph over them, and confute them; as he may permit a sophist to talk against the truth, that he may be silenced and shamed. In none of all this doth God become the world's deceiver. But the miracles of Christ, and his apostles and disciples, were never controlled by the light of nature, by more prevalent miracles, or any such means; but were the fullest signification of God's attestation that man can have to save him from deceit.

Q. 19. I confess if I had seen all these things myself, I should have made no doubt, but God and reason bound me to believe; but how can we at this distance be sure that all these words of Christ were spoken, and these works done?

A. Let us first consider how they were sure of it that lived in that age with the apostles, and then how we may be also sure. And (I). That age, (1) Had the common evidences of the best credibility of men. (2) They had most infallible perception of it by their senses. And (3) They had an immediate testimony from God themselves. Of these let us consider in order.

Q. 20. (I) What credible human testimony do you mean they had?

A. It is supposed that some persons are to believed much above others,[24] else all human trust and conversation would cease. He that will believe nobody, cannot expect to be himself believed.

And (1) The witnesses of Christ's words and works were not strangers to him, that took it by report, but those that had accompanied him, and heard and seen them.

(2) They spake to men of the same generation, time, and country, and mentioned things done before multitudes of spectators; so that had it been a false report, it had been most easy to confute it, and turn it all, as a lie, unto their scorn.

(3) They sharply reproved the rulers and teachers for rejecting Christ, and provoked all their rage against them; so that no doubt they would do their best to have searched out all deceit in the reprovers.

---

[23] Acts 8; Simon Magus's Case.

[24] John 19:35; and 20:31; 1 John 5:13; 1 Cor 15:6.

(4) They were men of no carnal interest, to tempt them into a deceiving plot; but were foretold that they must be hated, persecuted, and killed for their testimony.

(5) They were purposely chosen from among the meaner unlearned sort, that there might be no suspicion that it was a work of carnal craft or power.

(6) Though they heard and saw, so far were they from plotting it, that they understood it not themselves, nor believed that Christ must die for sin, rise the third day, and ascend into heaven, and gather a Catholic church, and reign spiritually, till the time that Christ was risen, and the Holy Ghost came down upon them. And yet Christ over and over foretold it them.

(7) They taught not one another, nor came to it by study and degrees; but, in the main, by sudden, common inspiration, and such as Christ had before promised them.[25]

(8) Paul was called by a glory and a voice of Christ from heaven, in the sight of other persecuting company.

(9) Their testimony all agreed, and all spake the same truth.

(10) Their enemies never wrote a confutation of them, nor decried most of the matters of fact, but imputed it to Beelzebub.

(11) None of them ever repented of his testimony; whereas had they confederated to deceive the world, some one's conscience, living or dying, would sure have forced him to confess it.

(12) Yea, they sealed it with their great labour, sufferings, and blood.

(13) When false teachers turned some of their followers to heresies, and to forsake them, they still appealed for the matters of fact, even to those dissenters or opposers.[26]

(14) Their doctrine, by its fore-described light and goodness, testified of itself that it was of God; and that those men that at so dear a rate divulged it, in design to sanctify and save mankind, were no such wicked knaves as to plot the world's delusion. These were evidences of more than human credibility.

---

[25] Gal 1 and 2.

[26] Gal 3:3, 5.

(II) And the disciples in Judea heard and saw Christ and his miracles, and so had as much certainty of the matter of fact as sense could give them.

(III) And they had God's immediate testimony in themselves; even his Spirit's internal revelation, illumination, and sanctifying work; and the wonderful gifts of healing, tongues, miracles, by which they convinced others.

Q. 21. Proceed to show me how their followers were certain?

A. (1) They were persons present, and, therefore, their senses assured them what was said and done; they were the men that heard the use of languages given by inspiration; that heard the triumphant praises of God; that saw them that were miraculously healed, and some raised from the dead; could those doubt of the miracles that saw the lame man that begged at the temple cured by Peter and John; and that saw multitudes cured by the very shadow and clothes of the apostles; when they that saw the lame man healed, (Acts 14,) would have sacrificed to Paul and Barnabas as gods?[27]

(2) They kept constant church meetings; and the use of languages, and other extraordinary gifts of the Spirit, were the ordinary exercises of those assemblies; so that they could not be unknown.[28]

(3) It was not a few apostles only that had this extraordinary spirit, but in one sort or other the generality of the persons converted by them; sometimes as the apostles were preaching, the Spirit came upon the hearers, as it did on Cornelius and his assembly. (Acts 10.) Usually by the laying on of the apostles' hands the Holy Ghost was given; and this not only to the sincere Christians, but to some unsound ones that fell away; all that did miracles in Christ's name were not saved.

(4) Yea, those that accused Christ, as casting out devils by devils, might have seen their own children cast them out. (Matt. 12.) And those that were seduced, and quarrelled with the apostles, could not deny but they themselves had received the Spirit, by their preaching. Paul appealeth to themselves when the Galatians were perverted: "O foolish Galatians! who hath bewitched you, that you should not obey the truth,

---

[27] Acts 2; 3, and 4.

[28] 1 Cor 14 and 12; Rev 1:9, 10.

before whose eyes Jesus Christ hath been evidently set forth crucified among you. This only would I learn of you: received ye the Spirit by the works of the law, or by the hearing of faith? Are ye so foolish, having begun in the Spirit, are ye now made perfect by the flesh? He that ministereth to you the Spirit, and worketh miracles among you, doth he it by the works of the law, or by the hearing of faith?" (Gal. 3:1–3.)

If these Galatians had not the Spirit, and such as worked miracles among them, would not this argument have turned to Paul's reproach, rather than to their conviction? Even Simon Magus was so convinced by the Spirit falling on the Samaritans, that he was baptised, and would have bought the power of giving the Holy Ghost with money. (Acts 8.) Their sense convinced them, and they that had the Spirit themselves must needs be sure of it.

Q. 22. Now tell me, how we may be certain that all this history is true, and that these things are not misreported by the Scripture?

A. I will speak first of the Gospel as such, and then of the book.

(1) You must first know, that the Gospel, in the strict sense, is the history and doctrine of Christ, necessary to be believed to our salvation; which is summarily contained in the baptismal covenant. For men were Christians when they were baptised: and they were not adult Christians till they believed the Gospel.

(2) You must know, that this Gospel was long preached and believed before it was written, St. Matthew began and wrote eight years after Christ's resurrection; and the Revelation of St. John was written about ninety-four years after Christ's birth; Luke's Gospel, about fifty; and Mark's, about fifty-nine; and St. John's, about ninety-nine from the birth of Christ.[29]

(3) You must know, that all the aforesaid miracles were wrought to confirm this gospel preached before it was written.

(4) And that while the apostles lived their preaching had as much authority as their writing. But they being to die, were moved by the Spirit to write what they had preached, that it might be, certainly without change, delivered to posterity to the end of the world; for had it

---

[29] Mark 16:20; Acts 4:16, 22; 6:8; 8:6, 13; 15:12; 19:11.

been left only to the memory of man, it would soon have been variously reported and corrupted.

(5) And you must know, that this Scripture is so far from being insufficient, as to the matter of our faith, as that it containeth not only the essentials, but the integrals, and useful accidents of the Gospel; as a complete body hath every part, and the very ornament of hair and colour. So that a man may be a Christian, that knoweth not many hundred words in the Scripture, but not unless he know and believe the essentials of the Gospel.

(6) And you must note, therefore, that the aforesaid miracles were wrought primarily, to confirm the Gospel; and that they do confirm all the accidental passages in the Bible but by consequence, because the same persons, by the same Spirit, wrote them.

Q. 23. Proceed now to show me the proof, which you promised.

A. (1) That there have been, from that time, Christians in the world, is, past all doubt, acknowledged by the history of their enemies that persecuted them. And all these Christians were baptised, for baptism was their solemn christening. And every one that was baptised at age did openly profess to receive this same Gospel: even to believe in God the Father, the Son, and the Holy Ghost, renouncing the devil, the lusts of the flesh, and the vanities of the world.[30]

(2) Yes, all that were baptised, were before taught this Gospel by teachers or catechizers, who had all but one gospel, one faith, and baptism.

(3) And they were all tried how they understood the aforesaid general words; and therefore they were opened in more words, which we call the creed: which, in substance and sense, was still the same, though two or three words be added since the first forming of it. So that every Christian, being instructed by the Gospel, and professing the essence of it in the creed and baptism, we have as many witnesses that this Gospel was then delivered, as there have been Christians.

(4) And no man doubteth but there have been ministers as long. And what was a minister but a preacher of this same Gospel, and a baptiser and guide of them that believe it?

---

[30] The Acts of the historical tradition of the Gospel.

(5) And none can doubt but there have been christian assemblies from that time; and what were those assemblies, but for the preaching, professing, and practising this Gospel?

(6) And none doubteth but they celebrated the Lord's supper in those assemblies: and the celebration of that sacrament containeth practically the profession of all the Gospel of Christ.

(7) And none can doubt but that the Lord's day hath ever since been constantly kept by Christians, in commemoration of Christ's resurrection, and in the performance of the aforesaid exercises. And therefore the very use of that day assureth us, that the Gospel hath been certainly delivered us.

(8) And all grant that these churches had still the use of discipline, which was, the censuring of such as corrupted this sacred doctrine by heresy, or sinned against it by wicked lives. And this could not have been, if the Gospel had not been then received by them.

(9) Yea, the numbers and opinions of heretics then are left on record; and they tell us what the Gospel then was, by telling us wherein they departed from it.

(10) Yea, the history of the persecutors and enemies tell us, that this Gospel was then extant which they persecuted.

(11) The Old Testament was long before in the common possession and use of the Jews. They read it every Sabbath-day. And in that we see Christ foretold, and abundance of prophecies, which in him are since fulfilled.

(12) Lastly, the sacred Scriptures, which contain all that God thought needful to be transmitted to posterity for history and doctrine, have been most certainly kept and delivered to us; so sure and full is our tradition.

Q. 24. That Christianity hath been propagated, none can doubt; but how are we sure that those Christians of the first age did indeed see, or believe, that they saw and heard those miracles?

A. (1) To be a Christian, was to be one that believed them. It was half their belief in Christ, and in the Holy Ghost, and so the very essence of Christianity, to believe that Christ wrought his miracles and rose again, and that the apostles, by the holy Spirit, did work theirs, and that believers received the Spirit by their ministry.

(2) They had not been made Christians but by these miracles. They all professed that it was the gifts of the Spirit that convinced and converted them.

(3) All the forementioned professions of their Christianity contained a profession that they believed these miracles. As the use of the Lord's day, Baptism, the Eucharist, showed their belief of Christ's life, death, and resurrection.

(4) They suffered persecution and martyrdom, in the profession of that belief.

(5) They pleaded these miracles in all their defences against their adversaries.

(6) The writings of their adversaries commonly acknowledge this plea; yea, and deny not the most of the miracles themselves.

(7) But most fully their receiving the sacred Scriptures as the word of God, as indited by the Holy Ghost in the apostles, showeth that they believed the miracles recorded in that book.

Q. 25. You are come up to the last part of the doubt in the history: how are we sure that these Christians then commonly believed the book as now we have it, and that it is the very same?

A. We have for this full, infallible, historical proof, premising that some parcels of the book (the Revelations, the Epistle of Jude, the Second of Peter, the Epistle to the Hebrews, and that of James) were longer unknown to some particular churches than the rest.

(1) The constancy of christian assemblies and public worship is a full proof, seeing that the reading, expounding, and applying of these books was a great part of their public work, as all history of friends and enemies agree.

(2) The very office of the ministry is full proof, which lay most in reading, expounding, and applying these same books. And therefore they were as much by office concerned to keep them, as judges and lawyers are to keep the statute-book.

(3) These ministers and churches, which so used this book, were dispersed over a great part of the world. If therefore they had changed it by adding or diminishing, they must have done it by confederacy, or by single men's error or abuse. It was impossible that all countries should agree in such a confederacy, but the meeting, motives, and treaties, would have been known. But no history of friend or foe hath any such

thing, but the clean contrary. And that it should be done by all single persons in the christian world, agreeing by chance in the same changes, is a mad supposition.

(4) And it is the belief of all Christians, that it is a damnable sin to add or alter in this book; and the book itself so concludeth. Therefore if some had agreed so to do, the rest would have detected and decried it.

(5) They took this book to be the charter for their salvation, and therefore would never agree to alter it; when men keep the deeds, evidences, leases, and charters of their estates, and worldly privileges unaltered.

(6) When a few heretics rose up, that forged some new books as apostolical, and rejected some that were such indeed, the christian churches condemned and rejected them, and appealed to the churches that had received the apostles' own epistles, and kept them.

(7) The many heresies that rose up did so divide men, and set them in cross interests and jealousies against each other, that it was impossible for any one sect to have altered the Scripture, but the rest would have fallen upon them with the loudest accusations. But all sorts of adversaries are agreed, that these are the same books.

And though the weakness and negligence of scribes have made many little words uncertain, (for God promised not infallibility to every scribe or printer,) yet these are not such as alter any article of faith or practice, but show that no corruption hath been designedly made, but that the book is the same.

For instance, let it be questioned, whether our statute-book contained really the same statutes that are there pretended? and you will see that the historical certainty amounteth even to a natural certainty, the contrary being a mere impossibility. For, (1) they are the king's laws, and the king would not bear a fraudulent alteration. (2) Parliaments would not bear it. (3) Judges that successively judge by these laws would soon discover it. (4) So would all justices and magistrates. (5) Men's lives and estates are held by them, and therefore multitudes would decry the fraud. (6) Enemies have daily suits, which are tried by these laws, and each party pleads them for himself; and their advocates and lawyers plead them against each other, and would soon detect the forgery. So that to suppose such a change is, (1) To suppose an effect that hath no cause in nature. (2) And that is against a stream of causes moral and natural, and so impossible.

And to feign such forgeries in the book that all Christians have taken for God's laws, is just such another case, and somewhat beyond it. That is but moral evidence, which dependeth only on men's honesty, or any free unnecessary acts of man's will. But man's will hath also of natural necessity, such as the love of ourselves, and our felicity, &c. And it is a natural impossibility that all men, or many, should agree in a lie, which is against these acts of natural necessity. But so they must do, if all men of cross interests, principles, and dispositions, should knowingly agree; *e. g.* that all our statutes are counterfeit, that there is no such place as Rome, Paris, or other such lies. And so the Gospel history hath such testimony of necessary truth.

Q. 26. You have made the case plainer to me than I thought it had been. But you yet seem to intimate that some words, yea some books of Scripture, have not the same evidence as the rest: can a man be saved that believeth not all the Scripture?

A. All truth is equally true, and so is all God's word; but all is not equally evident. He that taketh any word to be God's word, and yet to be false, believeth nothing as God's word; for he hath not the formal, essentiating act and object of faith. If God could lie, we had no certainty of faith. But he that erroneously thinketh that this or that word, yea epistle, or text, or book in the Bible, is not God's, but came in by mistake, may be saved, if he believe that which containeth the essentials of Christianity. A lame faith may be a saving faith; and he may see how miracles sealed the Gospel, that cannot see how they sealed every book, text, or word, in the Bible.[31]

Q. 27. Though we have been long on this, it is of so great importance to us living or dying, to be sure of the foundations of our faith, that I will yet ask you, have you any more proof?

A. I have told you of four proofs already: (I) The antecedent testimony of the Spirit in the Old Testament. (II) The inherent constitutive testimony in Christ and the Gospel. (III) The concomitant testimony of miracles. (IV) The consequent testimony of the Spirit to, and by, the

---

[31] Rom 14. and 15.

apostles' miracles and gifts. But there is yet that behind which to us is of the greatest moment; and that is,

(V) The sanctifying testimony of the Holy Spirit in all true Christians, in all ages and places on the earth.[32]

Here you must remember, (1) That the common experience of the world assureth us, that man's nature is greatly vitiated, inclined to known evil for some inferior good, and averse to the greatest good by the prevalency of the lesser; hardly brought to necessary knowledge, and more hardly to the love, delight, and practice of that which is certainly the best. And that hence the world is kept in confusion and misery by sin.[33]

(2) Experience assureth us that there is no hope of any great cure of this, by the common helps of nature and human reason; for it is that reason that is diseased, and blinded, and therefore unapt to cure itself, as an infant or fool is to teach himself. And as philosophers are a small part of the world, (for few will be at the cost of getting such knowledge,) so they are wofully dark themselves in the greatest things, and of a multitude of sects, contradicting one another, and few of them have hearts and lives that are answerable to that which they teach others; and the wisest confess that they must expect few approvers, much less followers. And every man's own experience tells him, how hard it is to inform the judgment about holy things, and to conform the will to them, and to reform the life to a holy and heavenly state.[34]

(3) The multitude of temptations makes this the more difficult, and so doth the nature of a vicious habit, and the privation of a good one; the self-defending and propagating nature of sin, and the experience of the world, tell us how wicked the world is, and how little the labours of the wisest philosophers, divines, or princes, do to reform it, and to make men better: and especially how hard it is to get a heavenly mind, and joy, and conversation: and all this being sure, it is as sure that the renovation of souls is a great work, well beseeming God. (4) And it must be added, that this is the most necessary work for us, and the most

---

[32] Rom 3:10–12.

[33] Rom 8:5–9; John 12:39, 40; Acts 28:26, 27.

[34] Luke 18:34; 1 Cor 2:14; 13:11; Isa 17:11; Jer 13:23.

excellent: Paul tells us but what reason tells us in that, (1 Cor. 13,) how much holy love (which is the divine nature and real sanctity) excelleth all knowledge, gifts, and miracles: this is the soul's health and well-being: no man can be miserable so far as he is good and holy; and no man can choose but be miserable that is not so: many shall lie in hell that cast out devils, and wrought miracles in Christ's name; but none that loved God, and are holy. Christ wrought miracles but in order to work holiness; (as St. Paul, 1 Cor. 1:14.) tells them, that strange languages are below edifying plainness;) his work, as a Saviour, is to destroy the works of the devil. Holiness is incomparably better than the gift of working miracles.[35]

This being considered, further think, (1) That all true Christians are saints: hypocrites have but the name and image: no one soundly and practically believeth in Christ, and consenteth to his covenant, but he is renewed by the Holy Ghost.

(2) Consider how great and excellent a work this is; to set a man's hope and heart on heaven; to live by faith on an unseen world; to place our chiefest love and pleasure on God, holiness, and heaven; to mortify fleshly lusts, and be above the power of the love of the world, and natural life; to love others as ourselves in the measure that appeareth in them; to love our enemies, and to make it the work of our lives to do the most good we can in the world; to bring every true believer to this in all ages and countries, which neither princes nor persuasions alone can do, this is above all miracles. And this is a standing witness which every true Christian hath in himself.[36]

(3) And note, also, that it is by the foresaid gospel or sealed word of Christ, that all this is wrought on all true Christians; and the divine effect proveth a divine cause. God would never bless a lie, to be the greatest means of the holiness, reformation, and happiness of the world. And were not the cause fitted to it, it would never produce such effects. Q. 28. Is this it that is called, the witness of the Spirit in us?

---

[35] 1 John 3:24, and 6:12, 15, 16; Matt 7:21, 22, 25, 26; Heb 12:14.

[36] Ezek 36:26; 1 John 5:10; 2 Tim 1:7; Rom 8:3, 4, 13, 15, 26, 33; 1 Cor 2:10–12; 6:10, 11, 17; and 12:11, 13; 2 Cor 3:3, 17; Gal 4:6, and 5:5, 16–18, 25; Eph 2:18, 22; 4:3, 4, 23, and 5:9; 2 Thess 2:13; 1 Pet 1:2, 3; 1 John 3:24, and 4:13.

A. Besides all the foresaid witnessings of the Spirit without us, the Spirit within us, (1) Causeth us to understand and believe the Scripture. (2) Maketh it powerful to sanctify us. (3) And therein giveth us a connaturality and special love to it, and sense of its inherent, divine excellency; which is writing it in our hearts. (4) And causeth us to live by it. (5) And confuteth the objections made against it. (6) And causeth us to fetch our comfort from it; in a word, imprinteth the image of it on us; and this is the inward witness.

Q. 29. But when we see so much ignorance, wickedness, confusion and cruelty, pride, lust, and worldliness among Christians, and how they live in malicious tearing one another, how can we know that their goodness is any proof of the truth of Christianity?

A. I told you, hypocrites have but the name, and picture, and art of Christianity. If custom, prosperity, laws, or carnal interest, bring the world into the visible Church, and make men say,[37] they believe, when they do not, is Christianity to be judged of by dissemblers and enemies? Mark any that are serious believers, and you will find them all seriously sober, just, and godly; and though weak believers have but weak grace, and many failings, they are sincerely, though imperfectly, such as I have described. And though the blind, malignant enemies can see no excellency in a saint, he that hath either known faith and holiness in himself, or hath but impartially observed mankind, will see that Christians indeed are quite another sort of men than the unbelievers, and that Christ maketh men such as he teacheth them to be, and the sanctifying Spirit is the sure witness of Christ, dwelling in all true Christians, (Rom. 8:9,) as Christ's agent and advocate, witnessing that he is true, and that we are his, interceding from Christ to us, by communicating his grace, and in us toward Christ, by holy love and desires; and is God's name and mark on us, and our pledge, earnest, and first-fruits of life eternal: and though we were in doubt of old historical proofs, yet, (I) The Old Testament fulfilled in the New. (II) The divine impress discernible on the gospel. (III) And the most excellent effect of sanctification

---

[37] 1 Cor 1:1, 2; Acts 20:32; and 26:18.

on all true believers, are evidences of the truth of Christianity and the Scriptures, which all true Christians have still at hand.[38]

Q. 30. But there are things in the Scripture of exceeding difficulty to believe; especially that God should become man.

A. (1) It is folly to be stalled at the believing of any thing, which we once are sure that God revealeth, considering how unmeet our shallow wit is to judge of the things of infinite wisdom, to us unseen.[39]

(2) To holy, illuminated, prepared souls, belief is not so hard: it is blindness and vice that make it difficult.

(3) God did not become man by any change of his Godhead, nor by confining his essence to the manhood of Christ: but, (1) by taking the human nature into a special aptitude for his operations. (2) And so relating it nearly to himself; and operating peculiarly in and on it, as he doth not on any other creature. And when all are agreed that God is essentially every where, and is as near us as we are ourselves, and more the cause of all good which we do than we ourselves are; it will be harder to show, that he is not hypostatically united to every man, than that he is so to Christ (though the aforesaid aptitude of Christ's human nature, and the relation and operation of the divine, indeed, make that vast difference). If God can so peculiarly operate in and by our human nature, where lieth the incredibility?

Q. 31. But is it so transcendently above all the works of nature, that such condescension of God is hard to be believed?

A. Great works best beseem the infinite God: is not the make of the whole world as wonderful, and yet certain? God's love and goodness must have wonderful products, as well as his power.

But is it not very congruous to nature and reason, that God should have mercy on lapsed man? And that he should restore depraved human nature? And that he should do this great work like his greatness and goodness, and above man's shallow reach? And that polluted souls should not have immediate access to the most Holy, but by a Holy Mediator? And that mankind should have one universal head and monarch in our own nature? And that when even heathens are conscious of

---

[38] John 17:17, 19; Eph 5:26; 1 Thess 5:23; Heb 2:11; and 10:10, 14.

[39] Prov 8:9, and 14:6.

the great need of some divine revelations, besides the light of nature, and therefore consult their oracles and augurs, that God should give us a certain messenger from heaven to teach us necessary truth? Many such congruities I have opened in the 'Reasons of the Christian Religion,' Part II. Chap. 5.

The sum of all that is said, is this: (I) If any history in the world be sure, the history of the gospel is sure. (II) And if the history be sure, the doctrine must needs be sure. (III) The continued evidences: (1) In the holiness of the doctrine; and, (2) In the holiness of all true, serious believers, are a standing proof of both, as the miracles were to all the beholders, who did not blaspheme the Holy Ghost.

Q. 32. But how comes it to be so hard then to the most to become serious believers and godly, when the evidence is so clear?

A. A blind, dead, worldly, fleshly heart doth undispose them, and they will not consider such things, nor use the means.

Yea, they so wilfully sin against knowledge and conscience, and will not obey that which they know, that they forfeit further grace. I will name you briefly many things, which every man's natural reason might know, and ask you whether you ever knew any unbeliever that was not false to this light of nature.

(1) Doth not sense and reason tell men, how vile a thing that flesh is which they prefer before their souls? (2) Doth it not certify them that they must die, and so that fleshly pleasure is short? (3) Doth it not tell them of the vanity and vexation of this world? (4) And that greatest prosperity is usually parted with with greatest sorrow? (5) Doth it not tell them, that man's nature can hardly choose but fear what will follow after death? (6) Doth it not tell them, that there is a God that made them, and ruleth all? (7) And that he is infinitely great, and wise, and good, and therefore should be obeyed, loved, and trusted above all? (8) And that their lives, and souls, and all, are his, and at his will? (9) And that man hath faculties which can mind a God and life to come, which brutes have not; and that God doth not make such natures in vain? (10) Doth not experience tell them, that human nature seeth a vast difference between moral good and evil, and that all government, laws, and converse show it; and no man would be counted false and bad? (11) And that good men are the blessing of the world, and bad men the plagues? (12) And that there is a conscience in man, that condemneth sin, and

approveth goodness? (13) And that most men when they die, cry out against that which worldly, fleshly men prefer; and wish that they had lived the life of saints, and might die their death? Are not these easily knowable to all? And yet all the ungodly live as if they believed none of this: and can you wonder, if all such men understand not, or believe not, the heavenly things: have no experience of the[40] sanctifying work and witness of the Holy Spirit, and have no delight in God and goodness, no strength against sin and temptations, no trust in God in their necessity, no suitableness to the gospel, nor the heavenly glory; but as they lived in sin, do die in a stupid or despairing state of soul?

---

[40] John 3:7, 8; Rom 1:19, 20; Acts 14:17.

PART II

7

Of the Christian Religion, What it is, and of the Creed

Q. 1. Now you have laid so good a foundation, by showing the certain truth of the gospel, I would better know what Christianity is? And what it is to be a true Christian.

A. First I must tell you what religion is in general, and then what the christian religion is. Religion is a word that signifieth either that which is without us, the rule of our religion, or that which is within us, our conformity to that rule.

The doctrinal, regulating religion, is the signification of God's will, concerning man's duty to God, and his hopes from God. The inward religion of our souls is our conformity to this revealed, regulating will of God, even our absolute resignation to God, as being his own; our absolute subjection to him, as our absolute sovereign Ruler; and our prevailing love to him, as our chief Benefactor, and as love and goodness itself. Thus religion is our duty to God, and hope from God.

Q. 2. Now what is the christian religion?

Obj. A. The christian religion, as doctrinal, is, the revelation of God's will concerning his kingdom, as our Redeemer; or the redeeming and saving sinful, miserable man by Jesus Christ.

Subj. And the christian religion as it is in us, is the true conformity of our understanding, will, and practice, to this doctrine, or the true belief of the mind, the thankful love and consent of the will, and the sincere obedience of our lives to God, as our reconciled Father in Christ, and to Jesus Christ, as our Saviour, and to the Holy Ghost, as our Sanctifier, to deliver us from the guilt and power of sin, from the flesh, the world, and the devil, from the revenging justice of God, and from everlasting damnation, giving us here a union with Christ, the pardon of our sins, and sanctifying grace, and hereafter everlasting, heavenly glory.[1]

Q. 3. Is there any other religion besides the christian religion?

A. There be many errors of men, which they call their religion.

Q. 4. Is there any true religion, besides Christianity?

A. There be divers that have some part of the truth, mixed with error. (1) The heathens acknowledge God, and most of his attributes and perfections, as we do; but they have no knowledge of his will, but what mere nature teacheth them; and they worship many idols, if not devils, as an under sort of Gods.

(2) The Jews own only the law of nature and the Old Testament, but believe not in Jesus Christ our Redeemer.

(3) The Sadducees, and all Brutists, worship God as the Governor of man in this world, but they believe not a life to come for man.

(4) The Pythagorean heathens look for no reward or punishment after death, but by the passing of the soul into some other body on earth, in which it shall be rewarded or punished.

(5) The Mahomedans acknowledge one God, as we do: but they believe not in Jesus Christ, as man's Redeemer, but only take him for an excellent, holy prophet; and they believe in Mahomet, a deceiver, as a prophet greater than he.

(6) The mere deists believe in God, but not in Jesus Christ, and have only the natural knowledge of his will, as other heathens, but worship not idols, as they do.

Q. 5. Is there but one christian religion?

A. No: true Christianity is one certain thing.

Q. 6. How then are Christians said to be of divers religions?

A. Sound Christians hold to christian religion alone, as Christ did institute it: but many others corrupt it; some by denying some parts of it, while they own the rest; and some by adding many corrupting

---

[1] John 1:11, 12, and 3:16, 21; Acts 26:18; Matt 28:19, 20; John 14:5, and 15:10; 1 John 2:3, and 5:2, 3; Rev 14:12.

inventions of man, and making those a part of their religion, as the papists do.

Q. 7. Where is the true christian religion, doctrinal, to be found, that we may certainly know which is it indeed?

A. The christian religion containeth, (I) The light and law of nature, and that is common to them with others, and is to be found in the nature of all things, as the significations of God's will. (II) Supernatural revelation, clearing the law of nature, and giving us the knowledge of the Redeemer, and his grace.[2]

And this is contained, (I) Most fully in the holy Bible. (II) Briefly and summarily in the creed, Lord's prayer, and commandments. (III) Most briefly of all in the sacraments of baptism and the Lord's supper, and the covenant made and sealed by them.

Q. 8. But are not the articles of our church, and the confessions of churches, their religion?

A. Only God's word is our religion as the divine rule: but our confessions, and books, and words, and lives, show how we understand it.

Q. 9. What is the protestant religion?

A. The religion of protestants is mere Christianity: they are called protestants but accidentally, because they protest for mere Scripture Christianity, against the corruptions of popery.

Q. 10. What sorts of false religions are there among Christians?

A. There are more corruptions of religion than can easily be named. The chief of them are of these following sorts:

(I) Some of them deny some essential article of faith or practice, as the immortality of the soul, the Godhead, or manhood, or offices, of Christ, or the Holy Ghost, or the Scripture, &c.

(II) Some of them pretend new revelations falsely, and set their pretences of the Spirit's inspirations against the sealed word of God.

(III) Some of them set up an usurped power of their own, against the office, authority, or sufficiency of the said sealed Scriptures, pretending that they are successors to the apostles, in the power and office of making laws for the universal church, and being the judges of the sense of Scripture; yea, and what is to be taken for God's word, and

---

[2] Matt 5:17, and 23:23; Rom 2:14; 8:4, 7, and 13:8, 10.

what not, and judges of all controversies about it. Of these, the papists pretend that the pope and a general council are supreme, visible governors under Christ of all the christian world, and that none may appeal from them to God, to Christ, to the Scripture, or to the day of judgment. Others pretend to such a power in every patriarchal, national, or provincial church. And all of them, instead of a humble, helping, guiding ministry, set up a church leviathan, a silencing Abaddon, and Apollyon, a destroying office, setting up their usurped power above, or equal in effect with, God's word.

Q. 11. How come the Scriptures to be God's word, when the bishops' canons are not; and to be so far above their laws?

A. You must know, that God hath two different sort of works to do for the government of his church: the first is legislation, or giving new doctrines and laws: the other is the teaching and guiding the church by the explication and application of these same laws. God is not still making new laws for man, but he is still teaching and ruling them by his laws.[3]

Accordingly, God hath had two sorts of ministers: one sort for legislation, to reveal new doctrines and laws; and such was Moses under the old administration, and Christ and his commissioned apostles under the new. These were eminent prophets inspired by God infallibly to record his laws, and God attested their office and work by multitudes of evident, uncontrolled miracles. But the laws being sealed, the second sort of ministers are only to teach and apply these same laws and doctrines, and not to reveal new ones. And such were the priests and Levites under Moses, and all the succeeding ministers and bishops of the churches under Christ and the apostles, who are the foundation on which the church is built. And though all church guides may determine of the undetermined circumstances of holy things, by the general laws which God hath given therein, yet to arrogate a power of making a new word of God, or a law that shall suspend our obedience to his laws, or any law for the universal church, whether it be by pope or council, is treasonable usurpation of a government which none but Christ is capable of: and as if one king or council should claim the civil sovereignty of all the earth, which is most unknown to them.

---

[3] Isa 8:20; Isa 33:22; Jas 4:12; Mal 2:7, 8; Matt 28:20.

Q. 12. But I pray you tell me how the creed comes to be of so great authority, seeing I find it not in the Bible?

A. It is the very sum and kernel of the doctrine of the New Testament, and there you may find it all, with much more: but it is older than the writing of the New Testament, save that two or three words were added since.

I told you before, (1) That Christ himself did make the nature and terms of Christianity, commissioning his apostles to make all nations his disciples, baptising them into the name of the Father, the Son, and the Holy Ghost: this is the sum of the creed first made by Christ himself.

(2) The apostles were inspired and commissioned to teach men all that Christ commanded. (Matt. 28:19, 20.)

(3) To say these three words, 'I believe in the Father, Son, and Holy Ghost,' without understanding them, was easy, but would make no true Christians; therefore, if we had never read more of the apostles' practice, we might justly conclude that those inspired teachers, before they baptised men at age, taught them the meaning of those three articles, and brought them, accordingly, to confess their faith, and this is the creed. And though a man might speak his profession in more or various words, the matter was still the same, and the words made necessary must not be too many, nor left too much at men's liberty to alter, lest corruption should creep into the common faith. For the baptismal confession was the very symbol, badge, or test by which all Christians were visibly to pass for Christians, and as Christianity must be a known, certain thing, so must its symbol be.

(4) And infallible historical tradition assureth us, that accordingly, ever since the apostles' days, before any adults were baptised, they were catechised, and brought to understand and profess these same articles of the faith. And if the Greeks and the Latins used not the same words, they used words of the same signification (two or three words being added since).

Q. 13. Do you not by this set the creed above the Bible?

A. No otherwise than I set the head, heart, liver, and stomach of a man above the whole body, which containeth them and all the rest; or than I set the ten commandments above the whole law of Moses, which includeth them: or than Christ did set, loving God above all, and our neighbour as ourselves, above all that law of which they were the sum.

We must not take those for no Christians, nor deny them baptism, who understand and believe not particularly every word in the Bible; as we must those that understand not and believe not the creed.

8

Of Believing, what it Signifieth in the Creed

Q. 1. I understand by what you have said, that as man's soul hath three powers, the understanding, the will, and the executive, so religion, being but the true qualifying and guidance of these three powers, must needs consist of three parts. (I) Things to be known and believed. (II) Things to be willed, loved, and chosen. And (III) Things to be done in the practice of our lives; and that the creed is the symbol or sum of so much as is necessary to our Christianity, of the first sort; and the Lord's prayer the rule and summary of the second; and the ten commandments of the third.[1]

I entreat you, therefore, first to expound the creed to me, and first the first word of it "I believe," as it belongs to all that followeth.

A. You must first know what the word signifieth in common use. To believe another, signifieth to trust him as true or trusty; and to believe a thing, signifieth to believe that it is true, because a trusty person speaketh it. The things that you must believe to be true, are called the matter, or material object of your faith. The person's trustiness that you believe or trust to, is called the formal object of your faith, for which you trust the person, and believe the thing. The matter is as the body of faith, and the form as its soul. The matter which the church hath believed, hath by God had alterations, and to this day more is revealed to some

---

[1] Heb 11:6.

than to others. But the formal reason of your faith is still and in all the same, even God's fidelity, who, because of his perfection, cannot lie.[2]

Q. 2. How may I be sure that God cannot lie, who is under no law?

A. His perfection is more than a law. (1) We see that God, who made man in his own image, and reneweth them to it, making lying a hateful vice to human nature and conversation: no man would be counted a liar, and the better any man is, the more he hateth it.[3]

(2) No man lieth but either for want of wisdom to know the truth, or for want of perfect goodness, or for want of power to attain his ends by better means. But the infinite, most perfect God hath none of these defects.

Q. 3. But God speaketh to the world by angels and men, and who knows but they may be permitted to lie?

A. When they speak to man as sent by God, and God attested their credibility by uncontrolled miracles or other evidence, if then they should lie, it would be imputable to God, that attesteth their word: of which I said enough to you before.

Q. 4. Proceed to open the formal act of faith, which you call trust?

A. As you have noted, that man's soul hath three powers, understanding, will, and executive, so our affiance, or trust in God, extendeth to them all: and so it is in one an assenting trust, a consenting trust, and a practical trust. By the first, we believe the word to be true, because we trust the fidelity of God. By the second, we consent to God's covenant, and accept his gifts, by trusting to the truth and goodness of the promiser. By the third, we trustingly venture on the costliest duty.[4]

Q. 5. I pray you open it to me by some familiar similitude?

A. Suppose you are a poor man, in danger of a prison, and a king from India sends his son hither, proclaiming to all the poor in England, that if they will come over with his son, he will make them all princes. Some say, he is a deceiver, and not to be believed: others say, a little

---

[2] Titus 1:2; Rom 3:4; Num 23:29.

[3] Prov 12:22; 6:17; 19:5, 9, and 13:5; John 8:44, 55; 1 John 5:10; Rev 21:8; Prov 14:5; Col 3:9; Heb 6:18.

[4] Ps 112:7; Matt 27:43; Heb 11; Eph 1:12, 13; 2 Tim 1:12; 1 Tim 3:16; Titus 3:8; 1 Pet 1:21; Heb 11:39; Acts 27:25.

in hand with our old acquaintance is better than uncertainty in an unknown land: another saith, I know not but a leaky vessel, storms, or pirates, may prevent my hopes. Here are now three questions: (1) Do you believe that he saith true? (2) Do you so far trust him as to consent to go with him? (3) When it comes to it, do you so far trust him as to venture on all the difficulties, and go?

Again, suppose you have a deadly sickness. There are many unable and deceitful physicians in the world; there is one only that can cure you, and offereth to do it for nothing, but with a medicine made of his own blood. Many tell you he is a deceiver; some say others can do it as well; and some say the medicine is intolerable, or improbable. Here are three questions: (1) Do you trust his word by believing him? (2) Do you trust him so as to consent and take him for your physician? (3) Do you trust him so as to come to him, and take his medicine, forsaking all others? I need not apply it; you can easily do it.

Trust, then, or affiance, is the vital, or formal, act of faith; and assenting, consenting, and practice, are the inseparable effects, in which, as it is a saving grace, it is always found.

Q. 6. But is all this meant in the Creed?

A. Yes: (1) The Creed containeth the necessary matter revealed by God, which we must believe. (2) And it mentioneth him to whom we must trust, in our assent, consent, and practice, even God the Father, the Son, and the Holy Ghost.

Q. 7. But is this the faith by which we are justified? Are we justified by believing in God the Father and the Holy Ghost, and the rest of the articles? Some say it is only by believing in Christ's righteousness as imputed to us.

A. Justification is to be spoken of hereafter. But this one entire christian faith, is it which God hath made the necessary qualification, or condition, of such as he will justify by and for the merits of Christ's righteousness.

Q. 8. Doth not "I believe," signify that I believe that this God is my God, my Saviour, and my Sanctifier, in particular?

A. It is an applying faith. It signifieth, (1) That you believe his right to be your God. (2) And his offer to be your God. (3) And that you consent to this right and offer, that he may, by special relation, be yours. (4) But it doth not signify that every believer is sure of the sincerity of

9

Of the First Article—"I believe in God the Father Almighty, Maker of Heaven and Earth"

Q. 1. Seeing that you before proved that there is a God, from the light of nature, and heathens know it, why is it made an article of faith?

A. The understanding of man is so darkened and corrupted now by sin, that it doth but grope after God, and knoweth him not as revealed in his works alone, so clearly and surely as is needful to bring home the soul to God, in holy love, obedience, and delight: but he is more fully revealed to us in the sacred Scripture by Christ and his Spirit, which, therefore, must be herein believed.[1]

Q. 2. What of God doth the Scripture make known better than nature?

A. That there is a God, and what God is, and what are his relations to us, and what are his works, and what are our duties to him, and our hopes from him.[2]

Q. 3. That there is a God, none but a madman, sure, can doubt: but what of God is so clearly revealed in Scripture?

A. (1) His essential attributes; and, (2) The Trinity in one essence.

Q. 4. Which call you his essential attributes?

---

[1] John 17:3.

[2] Heb 11:6; 1 Tim 2:5.

A. God is, essentially, life, understanding, and will, or vital power, wisdom, and goodness, or love, in one substance, and this in absolute perfection.[3]

Q. 5. But are not all the rest of his attributes essential?

A. Yes; but they are but these same named variously, from their various respects to the creatures; such are his truth, his justice, and his mercy, as he is our Governor; his bounty, as our Benefactor; and his self-sufficiency, eternity, immensity, or infiniteness, his immutability, immortality, invisibility, and very many such respective names, are comprehended in his Perfection.[4]

Q. 6. I have oft heard of three persons and one God, and I could never understand what it meant, how three can be but one?

A. It is like that is, because you take the word "person" amiss, as if it signified a distinct substance, as it doth of men.

Q. 7. If it doth not so, doth it not tend to deceive us that never heard of any other kind of person?

A. The Scripture tells us that there are three, and yet but one God;[5] but it giveth us not a name which may notify clearly so great a mystery, for it is unsearchable and incomprehensible. We are to be baptised into the name of the Father, Son, and Holy Ghost. (Matt. 28:19.) And there are three that bear record in heaven, the Father, the Word, and the Holy Spirit, and these three are one. (1 John 5:7.) But the custom of the Church having used the word "person," having none that clearly expresseth the mystery, it is our part rather to labour to understand it, how a divine person differs from a human, than to quarrel with an improper word. God is one infinite, undivided Spirit; and yet that he is Father, Son, and Holy Ghost, must be believed.

And God hath made so marvellous an impression on all the natures of active beings, of three in one, as to me doth make this mystery of our religion the more easy to be believed; so far is it from seeming a contradiction.

Q. 8. I pray show me some such instances?

---

[3] John 14:24; Ps 90:2.

[4] Mal 3:6; Ps 86:5, and 145:17; Prov 15:3; Ps 139:4, 5, 12, 23; Jer 23:24; Deut 32:4.

[5] Matt 28:19; 1 John 5:7.

A. (I) The sun and all true fire is one substance, having three essential powers, the moving power, the enlightening power, and the heating power. Motion is not light, light is not heat, and heat is not motion, or light, yet all are one substance, and, radically, one virtue or power, and yet three as operative.

(II) Every plant hath one vegetative principle, which hath essentially a power discretive, as discerning its own nutriment, appetitive, desiring or drawing it in, and motive, and so digestive and assimilative.

(III) Every brute hath one sensitive soul, which essentially hath a power of vital, sensitive motion, perception, and appetite.

(IV) Every man hath one soul in substance, which hath the powers of vegetation, sense, and intellection, or reasoning.

(V) The soul of man, as intellective, hath essentially a threefold power, or virtue, mental life for motion and execution, understanding, and will. All active beings are three virtues in one substance.

Q. 9. But these do none of them make three persons?

A. (1) But if all these be undeniable in nature, and prove in God active life, understanding, and will, it shows you that three essentials in one substantial essence is no contradiction. And why may not the same be as true of the divine persons.

(2) And in God, who is an infinite, undivided Spirit, little can we conceive what personality signifieth, and how far those school-men are right or wrong, who say that God's essential self-living, self-knowing, and self-loving, are the Trinity of the persons as in eternal existence; and that the operations and appearances in power, wisdom, and love in creation, incarnation for redemption, and renovation in nature, grace and initial glory, or communion, are the three persons in the second notion as outwardly operative. And how much more than this soever there is, it is no wonder that we comprehend it not; yea, I believe there is yet more in the mystery of the Trinity, because this much is so intelligible.

Q. 10. But is it not strange that God will lay our salvation on the belief of that which we cannot understand; yea, is it not on the bare saying of a word, whose meaning none can know?

A. The doctrine of the Trinity in unity is the very sum of all the christian religion, as the baptismal covenant assureth us; and can we think that Christianity saveth men as a charm, by words not understood? No;

the belief of the Trinity is a practical belief. Far be it from us to think that every plain Christian shall be damned, who knoweth not what a person in the Trinity is, as eternally inexistent, when all the divines and school wits as good as confess, after tedious disputes with unintelligible words, that they know not: it is the Trinity, as related to us, and operative, and therein notified, that we must necessarily understand and believe, even as our Creator, Redeemer, and Sanctifier, that the love of God the Father, and the grace of the Son, and the communion of the Holy Ghost, may be believed, received, and enjoyed: as there are diversities of gifts, but the same Spirit; and differences of administrations, but the same Lord; and diversities of operations, but the same God which worketh all in all. (1 Cor. 12:4-6; 2 Cor. 13:14.) Even as it is not our understanding the essence of the sun, but our reception of its communicated motion, light, and heat, that our nature liveth by.[6]

Q. 11. But how can any man love him above all, of whom we can have no true conception? I cannot conceive what God is?

A. It may be you think that you know nothing but what you see or feel by sense; for so men's long use of bodies and sense is apt to abuse them: or you think you know nothing, which you know not fully; and so no angel knoweth God by an adequate, comprehensive knowledge. How far are we from knowing fully what sun, and moon, and stars are, and what is in them, and how they are ordered, and move! And yet nothing is more easily and surely known, than that there is a sun and stars, and that they are substances that have the power of motion, light, and heat. Yea, philosophers cannot yet agree what light and heat are; and yet we know enough of them for our necessary use. And can it be expected, then, that man give a proper definition of the infinite God? And yet nothing is more certain than that there is a God, and that he is such as I have before described: and we may know as much of him as our duty and happiness requireth.[7]

Q. 12. But what is the best conception I can have of God?

---

[6] Ps 16:8, and 125:2; Matt 28:19; 1 John 5:7, 10; 1 Cor 12:4-6; 2 Cor 13:14. The doctrine of the Trinity is ever proposed relatively, and practically to our faith.

[7] John 17:3; 2 Tim 1:12; 1 John 4:6, 7; John 8:19, and 14:7, 9, and 10:14; 1 Cor 8:3; Gal 4:9; 1 John 2:13, 14.

A. I partly told you in the third chapter, and the second. I now tell you further, that we see God here but as in a glass: his image on man's soul is the nearest glass: how do you conceive of your own soul? You cannot doubt but you have a soul, while you perceive its constant acts; yet you see it not: you find clearly that it is a spiritual substance, that hath essentially the power of vital activity, understanding, and will. By this you perceive what a spirit is: and by this you have some perception what God is. All the world is far less to God than a body to its soul; and God is infinitely more than a soul to all the world; but by the similitude of a soul you may most easily conceive of him.

10

Of God's Almightiness and Creation

Q. 1. Why is God here called "the Father," in whom we believe?

A. (1) As he is the first person in the eternal Trinity, and so called, the Father of the eternal word, or wisdom, as his Son.

(2) As he is the Father of Jesus Christ, as incarnate.[1]

(3) As he is the Maker of the whole creation, and, as a common Father, giveth being to all that is.

(4) As he is our reconciled father by Christ; and hath adopted us as his sons, and bound us to love, and trust, and obey him, as our Father. But the two first are the chief sense.

Q. 2. What is God's "Almightiness?"

A. His infinite power by which he can do all things which are works of power: he cannot lie, nor die, nor be the cause of sin, for these are no effects of power, but of impotency.

Q. 3. Why is his Almightiness to be believed by us?

A. We do not else believe him to be God: and we cannot else reverence, admire, trust him, and obey him as we ought.[2]

Q. 4. Why is his Almightiness only named, and no other properties?

---

[1] 2 Cor 1:3, and 11:31; 1 Cor 8:6, and 15:24; Gal 1:1, 3, 4; Eph 1:3, 17; 4:6, and 6:23; Phil 2:11; Col 2:2, and 3:17; 2 Tim 1:2; Jas 3:9.

[2] Gen 17:1; Rev 1:8; 2 Cor 6:18; Ps 91:1, 2; Matt 8:2.

A. All the rest are supposed when we call him God; but this is named, because he is first to be believed in as the Creator; and his creation doth eminently manifest his power. And though the Son and the Holy Ghost are Almighty, the Scripture eminently attributeth power to the Father, wisdom to the Son, and love and perfective operations to the Holy Ghost.

Q. 5. Is the creation named to notify to us God's Almightiness?

A. Yes; and it is a great part of our duty when we look up to the heavens, and daily see so far as our short sight can reach, of this wonderful world, to think, with most reverend admiration, 'O what a God have we to serve and trust!'[3]

Q. 6. How did God make all things?

A. He gave them all their being, order, and well-being, by the power of his will and word.[4]

Q. 7. When did he make all things?

A. It is not yet six thousand years since he made this world, even as much as belongs to us to know.

Q. 8. How long was God making this world?

A. It pleased him to make it the work of six days; and he consecrated the seventh day, a Sabbath, for the commemoration of it, and for the solemn worshipping him as our Creator.

Q. 9. For whom, and for what use did God make the world?

A. God made all things for himself; not as having need of them, but to please his own will, which is the beginning and the end of all his works; and to shine in the glory of the greatness, order, and goodness of the world, as in a glass to understanding creatures, and to communicate goodness variously to his works.[5]

Q. 10. What did God with the world when he had made it?

A. By the same power, wisdom, and will, he still continueth it; or else it would presently return into nothing.[6]

Q. 11. What further must we learn from God's creating us?

---

[3] Gen 1:31; Rev 4:11, and 10:6; Isa 11:28; 42:5, and 45:12, 18; Ps 8:1, 3; 19:1; 89:5, 11; 104:1, 2, and 115:16.

[4] Gen 1:2, 3.

[5] Prov 16:4; Rev 4:11.

[6] Heb 1:3; Ezek 18:4; 1 Cor 6:20; Ps 10:16.

A. We certainly learn that he is our Owner, our Ruler, and our Benefactor, or Father, and that we are his own, and his subjects, and his benefitted children.

Q. 12. What mean you by the first, that he is our Owner?

A. He that maketh us of nothing, must needs be our absolute Lord or Owner; and therefore may do with all things what he will, and cannot possibly do any wrong, however he useth us. And we must needs be wholly his own, and therefore should wholly resign ourselves to his disposing will.[7]

Q. 13. What mean you by the second, that God is our Ruler?

A. He that by creation is our absolute Owner, and hath made us reasonable, and with free-will, must needs have the only right and fitness to be our Ruler by his laws and doctrine: and we are bound, as his subjects, to obey him absolutely in all things.[8]

Q. 14. How gather you that he is our Father, or Benefactor?

A. If we have our very being from him, and all the good that the whole creation enjoyeth is his free gift, then as he is love itself, so he is the great Benefactor of the world, but specially to his chosen, faithful people: and no man or angel hath any thing that is good by way of merited exchange from God, but all is of free gift: and we owe him our superlative love, and thanks, and praise.

Q. 15. Why are heaven and earth named as the parts of his creation?

A. They are all that we are concerned to know: we partly see the difference between them, and God's word tells us of more than we see: earth is the place of our present abode in our life of trials in corruptible flesh; heaven is the place where God doth manifest his glory, and from whence he sendeth down those influences which maintain nature, and which communicate his grace, and prepare us for the glory which we shall enjoy in heaven. By heaven and earth is meant all creatures, both spirits and corporeal.[9]

Q. 16. Were there no more worlds made and dissolved before this? It seems unlikely that God, from all eternity, should make nothing till

---

[7] Ps 119:94; Acts 27:23; 1 Cor 6:19; John 17:6, 9, 10; Isa 63:19; 1 Chron. 29:11.

[8] Ps 59:13; 66:7, and 103:19; Dan 4:17, 25, 32; 1 Tim 6:15, and 1:17; Rev 17:14, and 19:6.

[9] Gen 1:1.

less than six thousand years ago; when he is a communicative good, and delighteth to do good in his works?

A. It is dangerous presumption so much as to put such a question with our thought or tongue, and to pry into God's secrets, of which we are utterly incapable (unless it be to shame it, or suppress it). God hath, by Christ and the Holy Ghost, in Scripture, set up a ladder, by which you may ascend to the heaven that you are made for; but if you will climb above the top of the ladder, you may fall down to hell.[10]

---

[10] Deut 29:29.

11

Of the Person of Jesus Christ, the only Son of God

Q. 1. Who is Jesus Christ?

A. He is God and man, and the Mediator between God and man.[1]

Q. 2. When did he begin to be God?

A. He is the eternal God that had no temporal beginning?

Q. 3. When did he begin to be a man?

A. About one thousand six hundred and eighty-one years ago.[2]

Q. 4. If he be God, why is he called the Son of God? Are there more Gods than one? And how doth God beget a son?

A. There is but one God: I before opened to you the mystery of the Trinity in unity, to which you must look back. Begetting is a word that we must not take carnally; and a son in the Deity signifieth not another substance. If the sun be said to beget its own light, that maketh it not another substance.

But Christ is also, as man, begotten of God, in a virgin's womb.[3]

Q. 5. Was Christ God in his low condition on earth?

A. Yes, but the Godhead appeared not as in heavenly glory.

Q. 6. Is Christ a man now he is in heaven?

---

[1] 1 Tim 2:5; Heb 12:24; 8:6, and 9:15.

[2] John 1:1–3, &c.; 1 Tim 3:16; Rom 9:5; Titus 2:13.

[3] Phil 2:7–10.

A. Yes, he is still God and man: but his glorified manhood is not like our corruptible flesh, and narrow souls.[4]

Q. 7. Hath Christ a soul besides his Godhead?

A. Yes, for he is a perfect man, which he could not be without a soul.

Q. 8. Then Christ hath two parts: one part is God, and the other man?

A. The name of part, or whole, is not fit for God: God is no part of any thing, no, not of the universe of being; for to be a part is to be less than the whole, and so to be imperfect: and every whole consisteth of parts; but so doth not God.[5]

Q. 9. Is Jesus Christ one person or two, viz. a divine and human?

A. It is dangerous laying too great a stress on words, that are either not in Scripture, or are applied to God as borrowed from similitude in man; as the word person signifieth the eternal word, the second in the Trinity, Christ is but one person. And though his human soul and body assumed be substances, they are not another person, but another nature united to his eternal person; yet not as a part of it, but by an union which we have no proper words to express. Christ hath two natures, and but one person. But if you take the word person only for a relation, (as of a king, a judge, &c.,) so Christ, as Mediator, is a person distinct from the same Christ, as the eternal, second person in the Trinity.[6]

Q. 10. It seems then Christ had three natures, a divine, a soul, and a body?

A. This is a question about mere names, he hath only the nature of God and of man. But if you go to anatomise man, you may find in him on earth, perhaps, more natures than two, spirit, fire, air, water, and earth: but this is a frivolous dispute.

Q. 11. In what nature did Christ appear of old before his incarnation?

A. If it were not by an angel, as his agent, it must be by some body, light, or voice, made or assumed for that present time.

Q. 12. I hear some say, that Christ is not one God with the Father, but a kind of under God, his first creature above angels.

---

[4] Acts 3:21; John 2:17, and 6:62; Eph 4:8–10

[5] Gal 3:20.

[6] 1 John 5:7; 1 Tim 2:5; Eph 4:5, 6; Rom 5:17, 18.

A. The Scriptures fully prove Christ to be God, and one God with the Father: the form of baptism proveth it. There be some learned men that to reconcile this controversy say, that Christ hath three natures, (1) The divine: (2) A super-angelical: (3) A human. And that God, the Eternal Word, did first of all produce the most perfect of all his creatures, above angels, like an universal soul, and the Godhead uniting itself to this, did, by this, produce all other creatures; and, at last, did in and by this unite itself hypostatically to the human nature of Christ. They think divers texts do favour this threefold nature; and that the Arians erred only by noting the super-angelical nature, and not noting the divine united to it. But I dare not own so great a point, which I find not that the universal church ever owned; nor do I see any cogent proof of it in the Scripture.[7]

Q. 13. But God doth all his works in order: and he made angels far nobler than man: and is it like then that he setteth a man so far above all angels as personal union doth import?

A. It is not like, if we might judge by the conjectures of our reason: but God's lower works are none of them perfectly known here to us; much less the most mysterious, even the glorious person of the Son of God. If God will thus glorify his mercy to man, by setting him above all the angels, who shall say to him, 'What doest thou?' And if there be in Jesus Christ a first created superangelical nature, besides the divine and human, we shall know it when we see as face to face. In the mean time, he will save those that truly believe in him as God and man.[8]

Q. 14. Why is Christ called "our Lord?"

A. Because he is God; and also, as Mediator, all power in heaven and earth is given him, and he is made Head over all things to his church. (Matt. 28:18; Eph. 1:22, 23.)

Q. 15. What do his names "Jesus Christ" signify.

A. Jesus signifieth a Saviour, and Christ, anointed of God. He being anointed by God to the office of a Mediator, as the great Prophet, Priest, and King of the church.

---

[7] John 1:1, 2; Matt 28:19; Col 1:15–18; Heb 1:2–4; Rev 1:5, 8.

[8] Heb 1 and 2.

12

How Christ Was Conceived by the Holy Ghost, and Born of the Virgin Mary

Q. 1. Doth it not seem impossible, that Christ should be begotten on a virgin without a man?

A. There is no contradiction in it: and what is impossible to him that made all the world of nothing?[1]

Q. 2. But it seems incredible that God should be made man?

A. God was not at all changed by Christ's incarnation. The Godhead was not turned into flesh or soul, but united itself thereto.[2]

Q. 3. But it seemeth an incredible condescension in God to unite the nature of man to himself, in personal union.

A. When you understand what it is, it will not seem incredible to you, though wonderful. Consider, (1) That it doth not turn the human nature into divine. (2) Nor doth it give it any of that part or work which was proper to the divine nature, and second person in the Trinity, from eternity. (3) The divine nature is united to the human, only to advance this to the excellent office of mediation, and that Christ in it may be Head over all things to the church. (4) And it will abate your wonder if you consider, that God is as near to every creature as the soul is to the

---

[1] Matt 8:20; Luke 1:35.

[2] Rom 1:3; John 1:14; 1 Tim 3:16; Gal 4:4.

body: in him we live, move, and have our being. And he is more to us than our souls are to our bodies.

Q 4. You now make me think that God is one with every man and creature, as well as with Christ. I pray you wherein is the difference?

A. God's essence is every where alike; but he doth not appear or work every where alike: as he is more in heaven than on earth, because he there operateth and appeareth in glory, and as he is more in saints than in the ungodly, because in them he operateth his grace; so he is in Jesus Christ, otherwise than he is in any other creature: (1) In that he by the divine power qualified him as he never did any other creature. (2) And designeth him to that work which he never did any other creature. (3) And fixeth him in the honourable relation to that work. (4) And communicateth to him, by an uniting act, the glory which he doth not to any other creature: and though it is like there is yet more unknown and incomprehensible to us, yet these singular operations express a singular, operative union. The sun, by shining on a wall, becomes not one with it: but by its influence on plants, it becometh one with them, and is their generical life.

Q. 5. But how is the second person in the Trinity more united to the human nature, than the Father and the Holy Ghost? Are they divided?

A. You may as well ask, why God is said to make[3] the world by his word, and by his Son: though the persons are undivided in their works on the creature, yet creation is eminently ascribed to the Father, incarnation and redemption to the Son, and sanctification to the Holy Ghost. The sun's power of motion, light, and heat are inseparable: and yet it is the light, as such, that with our eye doth cause the same act of light, as united to it. But the perfect answer to this doubt is reserved for heaven.

Q. 6. But how was he conceived by the Holy Ghost, the second person by the third, when it is only the second that was incarnate?

A. The Holy Ghost is not said to operate on the second person in the Trinity, or the Godhead, for Christ's conception, but on the virgin's body, and by miraculously causing a human soul and body, and their union with the eternal Word. God's perfecting operations are usually

---

[3] John 1:3, 10.

ascribed to the Holy Ghost: but the Father and Son are still supposed operating by the Holy Spirit.

Q. 7. Was Christ's flesh made of the substance of his mother?

A. Yes: else he had be been the Son of Man?[4]

Q. 8. Was Christ's soul begotten by his mother?

A. It is certain that man begetteth man: but how souls are generated is not fully known by man: some say they are not generated, but created: some say, that they are not created, but generated: and I think that there is such a concurrence of God's act and man's, as may be called a conjunction of creation and generation; that is, that as the sunbeams by a burning-glass may light a candle, and that candle light another, and another; yet so that the light and heat that doth it, is only from the sun's continual communication; but will not light another, but as contracted and made forcible by the burning-glass, or the candle. So all the substance of new souls is from the divine efflux, or communication of it, which yet will not ordinarily beget a soul, but as it is first received in the generative, natural faculty, and so operateth by it, as its appointed natural means. Thus it seems all human souls are caused (pardon the defects of the similitude). But the soul of Christ miraculously, not without all operation of the mother's, (for then he had not been the Son of Man,) but without a human father; the Holy Ghost more than supplying that defect.

Q. 9. If Christ was Mary's son, how escaped he original guilt?

A. By being conceived by the Holy Ghost, and so in his human nature made the Son of God, and not generated, as other men are.

Q. 10. Had Mary any children after Jesus Christ?

A. It goes for a tradition with most, that she had none: but it is uncertain, and concerneth not our faith or salvation.[5]

Q. 11. Why was Christ born of a Jew?

A. God had made a special promise to Abraham first, that[6] Christ should be his seed, in whom all nations should be blessed: and to David after, that he should be his offspring, and everlasting King.

---

[4] Gal 4:4.

[5] Heb 7:26; Matt 12:46; Mark 3:31; John 2:12, and 7:3, 5, 10; Gal 1:19.

[6] Gen 22:18, and 26:4; Ps 89:29, 36; Rom 1:3, and 4:16; 2 Tim 2:8.

Q. 12. Why was not Christ born till about four thousand years after the fall?

A. It is dangerous asking reasons of God's councils, which he hath not revealed. But this much we may know, that Christ was man's Redeemer, by undertaking what he after did, before his incarnation. And that he revealed the grace of redemption, by promises, types, and prophecies, and so saved the faithful: and that God's works are usually progressive perfection, and ripest at last: and therefore when he had first sent his prophets, he lastly sent his Son to perform his undertaking, and bring life and immortality more fully to light, and bring in a better covenant, and gather a more excellent, universal church.

Q. 13. Were any saved by Christ before he was made man

A. Yes: they had the love of the Father, the grace of Christ and the necessary communion of the Holy Ghost, and the promise. And in every age and nation, he that feared God, and worked righteousness, was accepted of him.[7]

---

[7] See Heb 11.

13

"Suffered under Pontius Pilate, was Crucified, Dead and Buried; He Descended into Hell"

Q. 1. Why is there nothing said in the Creed, (1) Of Christ's overcoming the temptations of the devil and the world?[1] Or, (2) Of his fulfilling the law, his perfect holiness, obedience and righteousness? (3) Nor of his miracles?

A. (1) You must know that the Creed at first when Christ made it the symbol of Christianity, had but the three baptismal articles:[2] to be baptised into the name of the Father, Son, and Holy Ghost. (2) And that the rest were added, for the exposition of these three. (3) And that the errors that rose up occasioned the additions. Some denied Christ's real humanity, and some his death, and said, that it was another in his shape that died: and this occasioned these expository articles. (4) But the Apostles, and other preachers, expounded more to those whom they catechised than is put into the Creed: and more is implied in that which is expressed: and had any heretics then denied Christ's perfect righteousness, and victory in temptation, it is like it would have occasioned an article for these. (5) But Christ would not have his Apostles put more into the Creed than was needful to be a part of the test of Christianity. And he that understandingly, consentingly, and practically believeth

---

[1] Matt 4.

[2] Matt 28:19.

in God the Father, Son, and Holy Ghost, shall be saved. (6) And as to Christ's miracles; yea, and his holiness, they are contained in the true meaning of believing in the Holy Ghost, as I shall after show.

Q. 2. But why is none of Christ's sufferings mentioned before that of his being crucified?

A. This, which is the consummation, implieth the humiliation of his life: his mean[3] birth and education, his mean estate in the world, his temptations, accusations, reproaches, buffeting, scourging, his agony, his betraying, his condemnation as a malefactor, by false witness, and the people's clamour, and the rulers' malice and injustice: his whole life was a state of humiliation, finished in his crucifixion, death, and burial.

Q. 3. What made the Jews so to hate and crucify him?[4]

A. Partly a base fear of Cæsar, lest he should destroy them, in jealousy of Jesus, as a king: and having long revolted from sincerity in religion, and become ceremonious hypocrites, God left them to the blindness and hardness of their hearts, resolving to use them for the sacrificing of Christ, the redemption of the world, and the great enlargement of his church.

Q. 4. Why is Pontius Pilate named in the Creed?

A. Historically, to keep the remembrance of the time when Christ suffered: and to leave a just shame on the name of an unjust judge.[5]

Q. 5. Why was crucifying the manner of Christ's death?

A. (1) It was the Roman manner of putting vile malefactors to death. (2) And it was a death especially cursed by God; and Christ foretold it of himself.

Q. 6. Was it only Christ's body that suffered, or also his soul and Godhead?

A. The Godhead could not suffer; but he that was God suffered in body and soul.[6]

Q. 7. What did Christ's soul suffer?

---

[3] Phil 2:7–9; Heb 12:2–4.

[4] Job. 11:48, 50.

[5] 1 Tim 6:13; Col 1:20, and 2:14; Eph 2:16; Gal 3:13.

[6] Matt 26:38; John 12:27.

A. It suffered not by any sinful passion, but by natural, lawful fear of what he was to undergo, and feeling of pain, and especially of God's just displeasure with man's sin, for which he suffered; which God did express by such withholdings of joy, and by such inward, deep sense of his punishing justice as belonged to one that consented to stand in the place of so many sinners, and to suffer so much in their stead.[7]

Q. 8. Did Christ suffer the pains of hell, which the damned suffer?

A. The pains of hell are God's just punishment of man for sin, and so were Christ's sufferings, upon his consent. But, (1) The damned in hell are hated of God, and so was not Christ. (2) They are forsaken of God's Holy Spirit and grace, and so was not Christ. (3) They are under the power of sin, and so was not Christ. (4) They hate God and holiness, and so did not Christ. (5) They are tormented by the conscience of their personal guilt, and so was not Christ. Christ's sufferings and the damned's vastly differ.

Q. 9. Why must Christ suffer what he did?

A. (1) To be an expiatory sacrifice for sin. God thought it not meet, as he was the just and holy Ruler of the world, to forgive sin, without such a demonstration of his holiness and justice as might serve as well to the ends of his government as if the sinners had suffered themselves. (2) And he suffered to teach man what sin deserveth, and what a God we serve, and that we owe him the most costly obedience, even to the death, and that this body, life, and world, are to be denied, contemned, and forsaken, for the sake of souls, and of life everlasting, and of God, when he requireth it. The cross of Christ is much of the Christian's book.[8]

Q. 10. What sorts of sin did Christ die for?

A. For all sorts, except men's not performing those conditions which he requireth of all that he will pardon and save.

Q. 11. For whose sins did Christ suffer?

A. All men's sins were instead of a meritorious cause of Christ's sufferings; he suffered for mankind as the Saviour of the world: and as to the effect, his suffering purchased a conditional gift of free pardon

---

[7] Luke 22:44.

[8] Heb 9:26, and 10:12; 1 Cor 5:7; Luke 14:33; 1 Cor 2:2; Gal 2:2; 3:1; 5:24, and 6:14; Phil 2:8; and 3:7–9.

and life to all that will believingly accept it, according to the nature of the things given. But it was the will of the Father and the Son not to leave his death to uncertain success, but infallibly to cause the elect to believe and be saved.[9]

Q. 12. Was it just with God to punish the innocent?

A. Yes, when it was Christ's own undertaking, by consent, to stand as a sufferer in the room of the guilty.

Q. 13. How far were our sins imputed to Christ?

A. So far as that his consent made it just that he suffered for them. He is said to be made sin for us, who knew no sin, which is, to be made a curse or sacrifice for our sin. But God never took him to be really, or in his esteem, a sinner: he took not our fault to become his fault, but only the punishment for our faults to be due to him. Else sin itself had been made his own, and he had been relatively and properly a sinner, and God must have hated him as such, and he must have died for his own sin when ours was made his own: but none of this is to be imagined.[10]

Q. 14. How far are Christ's sufferings imputed to us?

A. So far as that we are reputed to be justly forgiven and saved by his grace, because he made an expiation by his sacrifice for our sins: but not so as if God mistook us to have suffered in Christ, or that he or his law did judge that we ourselves have made satisfaction or expiation, by Christ.[11]

Q. 15. Was not that penal law "In the day that thou eatest thereof, thou shalt die," and "The soul that sinneth shall die," fulfilled by execution for us all in Christ, and now justifieth us as so fulfilled?

A. No: that law condemned none but the sinner himself, and is not fulfilled unless the person suffer that sinned. That law never said, "Either the sinner, or another for him, shall die." Christ was given us by God as above his law, and that he might justly and mercifully forgive sin, though he executed not that law: that law did but make punishment our due, and not Christ's, but not bind God to inflict it on us,

---

[9] Rom 5:6, 8, and 14:9, 15; 2 Cor 5:14, 15; Heb 2:9; 1 Tim 2:6; 1 John 2:2; John 1:29; 3:16, 18, 19; 4:42, and 6:51.

[10] 1 Pet 2:22.

[11] 1 Pet 3:18; Acts 26:18.

when his wisdom knew a better way. It is not that law as fulfilled that justifieth us, but another, even the law of grace. Satisfaction is not the fulfilling of the penal law.[12]

Q. 16. Did not Christ fulfil the commands of the law for us by his holiness and perfect righteousness? What need was there that he suffer for us?

A. The law, or covenant, laid on him by his Father was, that he should do both; and therefore both is the performance of that condition on which God gave us to him to be pardoned and saved by him. If he had fulfilled the commands of the law by perfect holiness and righteousness, in our legal persons, so as that God and his law would have reputed us to have done it by him, then, indeed, being reputed perfect obeyers, we could not have been reputed sinners, that needed suffering or pardon. But Christ's habitual, active, and passive righteousness, were (all the parts of his one condition) performed by him, to be the meritorious cause of our justification.[13]

Q. 17. Why is Christ's death and burial named besides his crucifixion?

A. Those words have been since added, to obviate their error who thought Christ died not on the cross.

Q. 18. What is meant by his descending into hell?

A. Those words were not of some hundred years in the Creed, and since they were put in, have been diversely understood. There is no more certain nor necessary to be believed, but that (1) Christ's soul was, and so ours are, immortal, and remained when separated from the body. (2) And that as death (being the separation of soul and body) was threatened by God, as a punishment to both, so the soul of Christ submitted to this penal separation, and went to the place of separated souls, as his body did to the grave.[14]

Q. 19. Of what use is this article to us?

A. Of great and unspeakable use. (1) We learn hence what sin deserveth. Shall we play with that which must have such a sacrifice?[15]

---

[12] Rom 3:19, 20, 21, 28; 4:13, 15, and 10:4; Gal 2:16, 21, and 3:11, 13, 18, 19, 24.

[13] Matt 3:15, and 5:17; Isa 53:11; 1 Cor 1:30; 2 Cor 5:21.

[14] 1 Cor 15:4, 5; Ps 16:9, 10; 1 Pet 3:18–21.

[15] Heb 9:21; 1 Cor 1:20; Eph 1:7; 1 Pet 1:2, 19; Rom 3:25; Heb 2:14; 1 John 2:1–3, and 4:10;

(2) We learn hence that a sufficient expiatory sacrifice is made for sin, and therefore that God is reconciled, and we need not despair, nor are put to make expiation ourselves, or by any other.

(3) We learn that death and the grave, and the state of separate souls, are sanctified, and Satan conquered, as he had the power of death, as God's executioner; and therefore that we may boldly die in faith, and commit soul and body into the hand of him that died for them.

Q. 20. But did not Christ go to Paradise, and can that be penal?

A. Yes, and so do faithful souls. But the soul and body are a perfect man, and nature is against a separation: and as the union of Christ's soul and glorified body now in heaven is a more perfect state than that was of his separated soul, so the deprivation of that union and perfection was a degree of penalty, and therefore it was the extraordinary privilege of Enoch and Elias not to die.

Heb 9:14; Eph 2:13; Rev 1:5; 5:9; 7:14, and 14:20.

CHAPTER

14

"The Third Day He Rose Again from the Dead"

Q. 1. How was Christ said to be three days in the grave?

A. He was there part of the sixth day, all the seventh, and part of the first.[1]

Q. 2. Is it certain that Christ rose from the dead the third day?

A. As certain as any article of our faith: angels witnessed it. Mary first saw him, and spake with him. Two disciples, going to Emmaus, saw him, to whom he opened the Scriptures concerning him. Peter, and others fishing, saw him, and spake, and eat with him. The eleven assembled saw him. Thomas, that would not else believe, was called to see the print of the nails, and put his finger into his pierced side. He was seen of above five hundred brethren at once. He gave the apostles their commission, and instructions, and his blessing, and ascended bodily to heaven in their sight; and afterwards appeared in glory to Stephen and Paul. But I have before given you the proof of the gospel, and must not repeat it.[2]

Q. 3. Was it foreknown that Christ would rise?

---

[1] Matt 12:39, 40; 16:4; John 20; Matt 28.

[2] 1 Cor 15:5, 6.

A. Yes; it was foretold by the prophets, and expressly and often by himself, to his apostles and the Jews, and therefore they set a sealed stone, with a guard of soldiers, on the sepulchre, to watch it.[3]

Q. 4. It is a wonder that the Jews then believed not in him,

A. The rulers were now more afraid than before that Christ would by the people be proclaimed their King, and then the Romans destroy their city and nation, for they feared men more than God: and withal they had put him to death on that account, as if his making himself a King had been rebellion against Cæsar, and King of the Jews was written, as his crime, by Pilate on his cross, and so they were engaged against him as a rebel, though he told them his kingdom was not a worldly one: and they seemed to believe that he did all his miracles by the devil, as a conjurer, and therefore that he was raised by that devil:[4] which was the blasphemy against the Holy Ghost. And as for the common people, they deceived them by hiring the soldiers to say, that his disciples stole his body while they slept.[5]

Q. 5. But why would Christ appear to none but his disciples?

A. We are not fit to give God a law: his works are done in infinite wisdom. But we may see, (1) That they who had hardened their hearts against all his doctrine, and the miracles of his life, and maliciously put him to death as a blasphemer, a conjurer, and a traitor to Cæsar, were unworthy and unmeet to be the witnesses of his resurrection: and it is like it would but have excited their rage to have tried a new persecution. His resurrection being the first act of his triumphant exaltation, none were so fit to see him as those that had followed him to his sufferings: even as wicked men are not meet (as Paul was) to be rapt up into Paradise and the third heavens, and hear the unutterable things.[6]

(2) The witnesses whom he chose were enow, and fit persons for that office, being to be sent abroad to proclaim it to the world.

---

[3] Acts 26:23; Matt 20:19; Mark 8:31; 9:31, and 10:34; Luke 24:7, 46; John 20:9; Rom 14:9; 1 Thess 4:14.

[4] Matt 12.

[5] Matt 28:3.

[6] Acts 10:41; 1:2–5, 22; 4:2, 33, and 17:18; Heb 6:2.

And God confirmed their testimony by such abundant miracles, of which you heard before.[7]

(3) And yet he left not the infidels without convincing means: as he before told them that he would raise in three days the temple of his body, when they destroyed it, so they saw the earth quake, the sun darkened, the veil of the temple rent at his death, and their soldiers saw the angels that terrified them, and told the rulers what they saw: and, after all, it was to Paul, a persecutor, (and partly to his company,) that Christ appeared.[8]

Q. 6. Why must Christ rise from the dead?

A. You may as well ask why he must be our Saviour?

(1) If he had not risen, death had conquered him, and how could he have saved us that was overcome and lost himself?[9]

(2) He could not have received his own promised reward, even his kingdom and glory: it was for the joy that was set before him, that he endured the cross and despised the shame; therefore God gave him a name above every name, to which every created knee must bow.[10]

(3) His resurrection was to be the chief of all those miracles by which God witnessed that he was his Son, and the chief evidence by which the world was to be convinced of his truth,[11] and so was used in their preaching by the apostles. That Christ rose from the dead, is the chief argument that makes us Christians.

(4) The great executive parts of Christ's saving office were to be performed in heaven, which a dead man could not do. How else should he have interceded for us, as our heavenly High Priest? How should he have sent down the Holy Ghost to renew us? How should he, as King, have governed and protected his church on earth unto the end? How should he have come again in glory to judge the world? And how should

---

[7] 1 Cor 15:4, 6; Heb 2:3–5.

[8] Matt 26, and 27; Luke 23; Acts 9.

[9] 1 Cor 15:13, 14, 20.

[10] Heb 12:3, 4; Phil 2:7, 8.

[11] Rom 1:4; 1 Pet 1:3, 4, and 3:21; John 11:24, 25.

we have seen his glory (as the Mediator of fruition) in the heavenly kingdom?[12]

Q. 7. I perceive, then, that Christ's resurrection is to us an article of the greatest use. What use must we make of it?

A. You may gather it by what is said. (1) By this you may be sure that he is the Son of God, and his gospel true. (2) By this you may be sure that his sacrifice on the cross was accepted as sufficient. (3) By this you may be sure that death is conquered, and we may boldly trust our Saviour, who tasted and overcame death, with our departing souls. (4) By this we may be sure that we have a powerful High Priest and Intercessor in heaven, by whom we may come with reverend boldness unto God. (5) By this we may know that we have a powerful King, both to obey and to trust with the church's interest and our own. (6) By this we may know that we have a Head still living, who will send down his Spirit to gather his chosen, to help his ministers, to sanctify and comfort his people, and prepare them for glory. (7) By this we are assured of: our own resurrection, and taught to hope for our final justification and glory. (8) And by this we are taught that we must rise to holiness of life.[13]

---

[12] 1 Pet 1:3, 4, and 3:21; Phil 3:10, 11, 19, 20, 21; Rom 6:5; Heb 4:14, 15; 6:20; 7:16–18; 8:1–3, and 10:21, 22.

[13] Rom 8:34; Col 2:12, 15; Col 3:1–5.

15

"He Ascended into Heaven, and Sitteth on the Right Hand of God, the Father Almighty"

Q. 1. How long was it between Christ's resurrection and his ascension?

A. Forty days: he rose on the day which we call Easter day, and he ascended on that which we call Ascension day, or Holy Thursday.[1]

Q. 2. Did Christ stay all this while among his disciples visibly?

A. No; but appeared to them at such seasons as he saw meet.[2]

Q. 3. Where was he all the rest of the forty days?

A. God hath not told us, and therefore it concerneth us not to know.

Q. 4. He showed them that he had flesh and blood, how then was he to them invisible the most part of the forty days?

A. The divine power that raised Christ, could make those alterations on his body which we are unacquainted with.

Q. 5. How was Christ taken up to heaven?

A. While he was speaking to his apostles of the things concerning the kingdom of God, and answering them that hoped it would presently be, and had given their commission, and the promise of the Holy Ghost, and commanded them to wait for it at Jerusalem, he was taken up as they gazed after him, till a cloud took him out of their sight: and two angels, like two men in white, stood by them, and asked them why

---

[1] Acts 1:3, 4; Matt 28.

[2] John 20, and 21.

they stood gazing up to heaven, telling them that Jesus, who was taken up, should so come again.[3]

Q. 6. Had it not been better for us that he had staid on earth?

A. No: He is many ways more useful to us in heaven.[4] (1) He is now no more confined, in presence, to that small country of Judea, above the rest of the world, as a candle to one room, but, as the sun in his glory, shineth to all his church on earth. (2) He is possessed of his full power and glory (by which he is fit to protect and glorify us.) (3) He intercedeth for us where our highest concerns and interest are. (4) He sendeth his Spirit on earth to do his work on all believers' souls.

Q. 7. What is meant by his sitting on the right hand of God?

A. Not that God hath hands, or is confined to a place as man is. But it signifieth that the glorified man, Jesus, is next to God in dignity, power and glory; and, as the lieutenant under a king, is now the universal Administrator, or Governor, of all the world, under God, the Father Almighty.[5]

Q. 8. I thought he had been only the Lord of his church?

A. He is Head over all things to his church. All power and things in heaven and earth are given him: even the frame of nature dependeth on him; he is Lord of all; but it is his church that he sanctifieth by his Spirit, and will glorify.

Q. 9. If Christ have all power, why doth he let Satan and sin still reign over the far greatest part of the earth?

A. Satan reigneth but over volunteers that wilfully and obstinately choose that condition; and he reigneth but as the jailer in the prison, as God's executioner on the wilful refusers of his grace.[6] And his reign is far from absolute; he crosseth none of the decrees of God, nor overcometh his power, but doth what God seeth meet to permit him to do. He shall destroy none of God's elect, nor any that are truly willing of

---

[3] Acts 1:4, 5.

[4] Acts 1:10, 11; John 16:17; 15:26, and 14:16, 26; Gal 4:4, 6.

[5] Matt 26:64; Acts 7:55, 56; Rom 8:34; Eph 1:20–23; Col 3:1; Heb 1:3, 13; 8:1, and 10:12; Eph 1:23; Matt 28:18.

[6] Rev 12:9, and 13:14.

saving grace. And as for the fewness of the elect, I shall speak of it after, about the catholic church.

Q. 10. But is not Christ's body present on earth, and in the sacrament?

A. We are sure he is in heaven, and we are sure that their doctrine is a fiction contrary to sense, reason, and Scripture, that say the consecrated bread and wine are substantially turned into the very body and blood of Christ, and are no longer bread and wine. But how far the presence of Christ's soul and body extendeth, is a question unfit for man's determination, unless we better knew what glorified souls and bodies are: we see that the sun is eminently in the heaven: and yet, whether its lucid beams be a real part of its substance, which are here on earth, or how far they extend, we know not; nor know we how the sun differeth, in greatness or glory, from the soul and body of Christ: nor know when an angel is in the room with us, and when not: these things are unfit for our inquiry and decision.[7]

---

[7] Acts 3:21; 1 Cor 15:44, 45.

16

"From Thence He Shall Again Come to Judge the Quick and the Dead"

Q. 1. What is meant by the quick and the dead?

A. Those that are found alive at Christ's coming, and those that were dead before.[1]

Q. 2. Are not the souls of men judged when men die?

A. In part they are: but as it is soul and body that make a man, so it is the judgment upon soul and body which is the full judgment of the man. God's execution is the principal part of his judgment; and as souls have not the fulness of glory or misery, till the resurrection, so they are not fully judged till then; and societies must be then judged, and persons in their sociable relations, together.[2]

Q. 3. Whither is it that Christ will come, and where will he judge the world?

A. Not in heaven, for the wicked shall not come thither: but Paul tells us, (1 Thes. 4:16,) "That the Lord himself shall descend from heaven, with a shout, with the voice of the arch-angel, and with the trump of God, and the dead in Christ shall rise first, and then they that are alive and remain shall he caught up together with them in the clouds, to meet the Lord in the air, and so shall we ever be with the Lord." By which it

---

[1] 1 Thess 4:15–17.

[2] Matt 25; 2 Thess 1:6, 7, 10, 11; John 5:22, 25.

appeareth that the place of judgment will be in the air, between heaven and earth.

Q. 4. In what manner will Christ come to judgment?

A. Christ tells us, (Matt. 25:31,) "That the Son of Man (that is, Christ as man) shall come in his glory, and all the holy angels with him, and shall sit on the throne of his glory, and before him shall be gathered all nations, and he shall separate them one from another, as a shepherd divideth his sheep from the goats." And St. Paul saith, 2 Thess. 1:7, 8. "The Lord Jesus shall be revealed from heaven, with his mighty angels, in flaming fire, taking vengeance on them that know not God, and that obey not the gospel of our Lord Jesus Christ; who shall be punished with everlasting destruction from the presence of the Lord, and from the glory of his power, when he shall come to be glorified in his saints, and to be admired in all them that believe."

Q. 5. Where are the souls of the dead before the day of judgment?

A. The souls of the faithful are with Christ in heaven, and the souls of the wicked are with devils in misery.

Q. 6. Where is it that the devils and wicked are in misery?

A. They are shut out from the glory of God; and wherever it be that they are, it is as God's prison, till the judgment of the great day. But the Scripture calleth the devil, "the Prince of the power of the air." (Eph. 2:2.) Yet is he on earth, "for he worketh in the children of disobedience," and is ready with his temptations with all men: and he is said to "go to and fro in the earth." (Job. 1:7, and 2:2.) And he is said to "walk in dry places, seeking rest, and dwelling in the wicked." (Matt. 12:43, 44.)

Q. 7. But are the souls of the wicked in no other hell than the devils are?

A. The Scripture tells us of no other; but it tells us not of their tempting and possessing men as devils do, but of their suffering.

Q. 8. Are devils and wicked souls in the same hell that they shall be in after the day of judgment, and have they the same punishment?

A. Whether there shall be any change of the place, it is not needful for us to know; but the punishment is of the same kind, but it will be greater after judgment; were it but because the body joined to the soul, and the multitude of the damned joined in the suffering, will make every one more receptive of it.

Q. 9. Is there no middle place between heaven and hell? or a middle state of souls that are in hope of deliverance from their pain?

A. Hell itself is not all one place,[3] seeing devils are both in the air and in the earth, and where else we know not. And in Job 1:11, 12, "Satan was among the sons of God." But as for any hope of deliverance to them that die unpardoned, the Scripture tells us of none, but saith, that "the night cometh when none can work," and that "This is the accepted time, this is the day of salvation." And that "every man shall be judged according to what he had done in the body, whether it be good or evil." It is therefore mad presumption for any one to neglect this day of salvation, upon a hope of his own making, that they that die the slaves of the devil may repent and be delivered in their airy life, and be made the children of God; or that any purgatory fire shall refine them, or any prayers of the saints in heaven or earth deliver them.[4]

Q. 10. But it seems by their pleading, described by Christ, "that they will not be past hope till the sentence be passed on them." (Matt. 25.)

A. But the same text tells you what sentence certainly shall pass; and, therefore, that if they keep any hope, it is not of God's making, but their own, and will be all in vain; but indeed those words seem rather to express their fervent desire to escape damnation than their hope. The wicked may cry for mercy when it is too late, but shall not obtain it. "Dives" (Luke 16) may beg for a drop of water, but not get it.

Q. 11. But will it not be a long work to judge all that ever lived, from the beginning of the world unto the end?

A. God's judgment is not like man's, by long talk and wordy trial, though Christ open the reasons of it after the manner of men: God's judgment consisteth of full conviction and execution. And he can convince all men in a moment by his light, shining at once into every one's conscience; as the sun can enlighten at once the millions of eyes all over the earth. And God's execution (casting all the wicked into utter darkness and misery) needs no long time, though its continuance will be for ever.[5]

Q. 12. May we know in this life what judgment Christ will then pass on us?

---

[3] Luke 16:9, 22.

[4] Matt 5:25, 26; Mark 9:43–46.

[5] 2 Tim 4:1.

A. All men, or most men, do not know it. Nor will it be known by a slight and sudden thought; nor by blinded or self-flattering sinners; nor by the worser sort of true believers, that sin as much as will stand with sincerity; nor yet by such ignorant Christians who understand not well the terms of the covenant of grace, or have true grace, and know it not to be true; nor yet by such timorous Christians, whose fear doth hinder faith and reason. But there is no doubt but we may know, and ought to use all diligence to know, what sentence Christ will pass upon us.[6]

For, (1) The difference between heaven and hell is so great that there must needs be a great difference between them that shall go to each; and therefore it may be known. Christ's Spirit is not an undiscernible mark and pledge to them that have it. (2) And we are commanded to search and try ourselves; and many marks of difference are told us, and the persons plainly described that shall be justified and condemned; and they are already here justified and condemned by that law by which they shall be judged. (3) And what comfort could we have in all the redemption and grace of Christ, and all the promises of salvation, if we could not come to know our title by them?[7]

Q. 13. Who be they that Christ will then justify, or condemn?

A. I must not here answer that question, because its proper place is afterward, under some of the following articles.

Q. 14. But I find some Scriptures saying, "That we are not justified by works, but by faith in Christ;" and yet, in Matt. 25, Christ passeth the sentence upon men's works as the cause; and it is said, "We shall be judged according to our works."

A. By works, Paul meaneth[8] all works that are conceived to make the reward to be, not of grace, but of debt; all works which are set in competition, or opposition, to justification by faith in Christ. The question between him and the Jews was, whether the divine excellency of Moses's law was such as that it was given to justify the doers of it as such; or whether it was but an index to point them to Christ, the end

---

[6] John 12:47, 48; Rom 2:12, 13; Acts 17:31; Mark 16:16.

[7] Mal 3:17, 18; Matt 13, and 25; Rom 8:30; John 17:2, 3; Heb 6:2; 9:27; 2 Cor 5:10.

[8] Acts 24:25; Jas 2:13; Acts 17:31; Rom 3:27; Gal 2:16, 17, and 3:2, 5, 10; Eph 2:7; Titus 3:5, 6; Rom 4:4, and 2:2, 3, 5; Eccl. 12:14.

of the law, by whom they must be justified. But it is not believing in Christ, nor begging his grace, nor thankfully accepting it, that Paul meaneth by works in his exclusion: it is this that he sets against these works. And as we are here made justified persons by mere grace, giving us repentance and faith in Christ, (that is, making us Christians,) so this obligeth us to live and die as Christians, if we will be saved. And therefore, the final, justifying sentence at judgment, doth pass on us according to such works only as are the performance of our covenant with Christ, without which we shall not be saved, and therefore not then justified: our justification then being the justifying of our title to salvation, and therefore hath the same conditions.

Q. 15. What may we further learn by this article of Christ's coming?[9]

A. (1) We must learn to fear and obey him, that must judge us, and to live as we would then hear of it, and to make it all the work of our lives to prepare for that day and final doom; and diligently to try our hearts and lives, that we may be sure to be then justified.

(2) We must not be discouraged that we see not Christ, but remember that we shall shortly see him in his glory: in the sacrament, and all his worship, let us do it, as expectants of his coming.

(3) We have no cause to be dismayed at the prosperity of the wicked, nor at our persecutions, or any sufferings, while we forsee, by faith, that glorious day.

(4) We should live in the joyful hopes of that day when he that died for us, and sanctified us, shall be our Judge, and justify us, and finally judge us to endless life: and we must love, and long, and pray for this glorious coming of Christ. Come Lord Jesus, come quickly. Amen.

---

[9] Rom 14:10; Rev 20:12, 13, and 22:14, Jas 2:14, &c.; Matt 12:36, 37; 2 Pet 3:11, 12.

17

"I Believe in the Holy Ghost"

Q. 1. What is meant by believing in the Holy Ghost?[1]

A. It meaneth our believing what he is, and what he doth; and our trusting to himself, and to his works.

Q. 2. What must we believe of himself?

A. That he is God, the Third Person in the Trinity, One in essence with the Father and the Son.

Q. 3. What must we believe of his works?

A. We must believe, (1) That the Holy Ghost is the great Agent and Advocate of Jesus Christ on earth, by his works to be his witness, and to plead his cause, and communicate his grace.

(2) That the Holy Ghost was the Author of those many uncontrolled miracles by which the gospel of Christ was scaled to the world; and therefore that those miracles were the certain attestation of God.[2]

(3) That the Holy Ghost was given by Christ to his apostles and evangelists, to enable them to perform the extraordinary office to which they were commissioned, to teach the nations to observe all things that

---

[1] Matt 12:31, 32, and 28:1, 19; John 5:7; Acts 5:3.

[2] John 14:15–17, 26; 15:16, and 16:7–11, 13–15; Mark 1:8; Acts 1:5, 8; 2:4, 33, 38; 4:31; 6:3, 5; 8:17; 10:44, 45; 11:15, 16, and 19:2, 6; Rom 15:13, 16; 1 Cor 12 and 6:11, 19; 2 Cor 13:14; Titus 3:5, 6; Heb 2:3, 4; 2 Pet 1:21; Rom 8:9, 15, 16; Jude 20;Luke 11:13; Eph 1:13, and 4:30; 1 Thess 4:8.

Christ had commanded, and to lead them into all truth, and bring all things to their remembrance.

(4) That therefore the doctrine of the said apostles and evangelists, first preached by them, and after recorded in the sacred Scriptures, for the use of the church to the end of the world, as the full doctrine and law of Christ, is to be received as the word of God, indited by the Spirit.

(5) That is the work of the Holy Ghost to sanctify all God's elect; that is, to illuminate their understandings, to convert their wills to God, and to strengthen and quicken them to do their duty, and conquer sin, and save them from the devil, the world, and the flesh; and to be in them a Spirit of power and love, and a sound mind; and so that the Holy Ghost is an Intercessor within us, to communicate life, light, and love, from the Father and the Son, and excite in us those holy desires, thanks, and praise, which are meet for God's acceptance. All this is contained in our believing in the Holy Ghost.

Q. 4. If all this be in it, it seemeth a most necessary part of faith?

A. The perfective works of God are used to be ascribed to the Holy Ghost. This is so weighty and necessary a part of faith, that all the rest are insufficient without it. Millions perish that God created, and that Christ, in a general sort, as aforesaid, died for; but those that are sanctified by the Holy Ghost are saved. It is the work of the Holy Ghost to communicate to us the grace of Christ, that the work of creation and redemption may attain their ends.

Q. 5. How is it proved that the Holy Ghost is God?

A. In that we are baptised into the belief of him, as of the Father and the Son; and in that he doth the works proper to God, and hath the attributes of God in Scripture, which also expressly saith, "There are three which bear record in heaven, the Father, the Word, and the Holy Spirit; and these three are one." (1 John 5:7.)

Q. 6. I have oft marvelled that the Creed left out, (1) The authority of the apostles. (2) And their miracles and Christ's. (3) And the authority of the Scriptures. And, now, I perceive that all these are contained in our believing in the Holy Ghost.

A. No doubt but it is a practical article of faith,[3] in which we profess to believe in the Holy Ghost, in his relation and works on man; and

---

[3] John 16:13.

therefore, as Christ's agent in gathering his church, by the apostolical power, preaching, writings, and miracles; and in the sanctifying and helping all true believers.

Q. 7. By this it seems there are many ways of denying the Holy Ghost?

A. Yes; (1) They deny him, who deny his Godhead as the Third Person in the blessed Trinity.

(2) They deny him, who deny that the miracles of Christ and his apostles were God's testimony to Christ, being convinced of the truth of the facts.

(3) They deny him, who deny the extraordinary qualifications of the apostles, and suppose them to have had but the prudence of ordinary, honest men.

(4) They deny the Holy Ghost, who deny the sacred Scriptures to be indited by him, and to be true.

(5) They deny him, who deny him to be the Sanctifier of God's elect, and feign holiness to be but conceit, deceit, or common virtue.

Q. 8. But are all these the unpardonable sin against the Holy Ghost?

A. The unpardonable sin is called "the blasphemy against the Holy Ghost." (Matt. 12.) And it is when men are convinced that those miracles were done, and those gifts given, which are God's attestation to Christ and his gospel; but they fixedly believe, and say, that they were all done by the power of the devil, by conjuration, and not by God; and therefore, notwithstanding them, Christ was but a deceiver. And this sin is unpardonable, because it rejecteth the only remedy, the Spirit's witness to the truth of Christ. He that will not believe this witness shall have no other.

Q. 9. But how may we know that we are sanctified by the Spirit?

A. By that holiness which he causeth. (1) When our understandings so know and believe the truth and goodness of the gospel and its grace, as that we practically esteem and prefer the love of the Father, the grace of the Son, and the communion of the Holy Ghost, and the heavenly glory, before all the pleasures, profits, and honours of this world, that stand against them, sad before life itself.

(2) When our wills do, with habitual inclination and resolution, love and choose the same, before all the said things that stand in competition.

(3) When in the course of our lives, we seek them first, and hold them fastest in a time of trial, forsaking the flesh, the world, and the

devil, so far as they are against them, and living in sincere, though not perfect, obedience to God.[4]

Q. 10. Is the Spirit, or the Scripture, higher than the role of faith and life?

A. The Spirit, as the Author of the Scripture, is greater than the Scripture; and the Scripture, as the word of the Spirit, is the rule of our faith and lives, and greater than our spiritual gifts. The Spirit in the apostles was given them to write (when they had preached) that doctrine which is our rule: but the Spirit is not given to us to make a new law, or rule, but to believe, love, and obey that already made. As under the law of Moses, God, that made the law, was greater than the law. But when God had made that law their rule, he did not, after that, teach good men to make another law, but to understand and obey that.

Q. 11. There are many that boast of the Spirit and revelations. How shall we try such, whether their spirits be of God?

A. (1) If they pretend to do that which is fully done by the Spirit already, that is, to preach or write another gospel, or make a new law for the universal church, seeing this was the prophetical extraordinary office of Christ, and the Spirit in the apostles, such imply an accusation of insufficiency on Christ's and the Spirit's law, or rule, and arrogate a power never given them, and so are false prophets.

(2) If they contradict the written word of God, which is certainly sealed by God's Spirit already, it must needs be by an evil spirit; for God's Spirit doth not contradict itself.[5]

Q. 12. But had not the priests, under the law, the Spirit of God, as well as Moses, that gave them the law?

A. Moses only, and Aaron under him, had God's revelation to make the law; and the priests only to keep it, teach it, and rule by it. And so it is as to the apostles of Christ, and the succeeding ministry.

Q. 13. But might not kings, then, make religious laws?

---

[4] Acts 26:18; Eph 1:18; Col 1:9, 10; 2 Cor 5:17; Matt 18:2; John 3:3, 5, 6; Heb 12:14; Matt 6:33; 2 Thess 2:13; 1 Pet 1:1, 2; 2 Thess 2:2; 1 John 4:1–3.

[5] Gal 2:7, 8.

A. Yes; to determine such circumstances as God had only given them a general law for, and left to be determined by them, but not to make new laws of the same kind with God's, nor to add to, or alter them.

Q. 14. But were there not prophets, after Moses, that had the Spirit?

A. Yes; but they were not legislators, but sent with particular mandates, reproofs, or consolations, save only David and Solomon, who had directions from God himself, not to make a new law of God, but to order things about the temple and its worship.

So if any man now pretend to a prophetical revelation, it must not be legislative to the catholic church, nor against Scripture, but about particular persons, acts, and events; and it must be proved by miracle, or by success, before another is bound to believe him.

Q. 15. Must I take every motion in me to be by the Holy Ghost, which is agreeable to the word of God, or for doing what is there commanded?

A. Yes; if it be according to that word, for the matter, end, manner, time, and other circumstances. But Satan can transform himself into an angel of light,[6] and mind us of some text or truth to misapply it, and put us on meditation, prayer, or other duty, at an unseasonable time, when it would do more hurt than good; or in an ill manner, or to ill ends. He can move men to be fervent reprovers, or preachers, or rulers, that were never called to it, but are urged by him, and the passion and pride of their own hearts: and good men, in some mistakes, know not what manner of spirit they are of.

---

[6] 2 Cor 11:14.

18

"The Holy Catholic Church"

Q. How is this article joined to the former?

A. This article hath not always been in the Creed, in the same order and words as now. But the belief of a holy church was long before it was called "catholic;" and it is joined as part of our belief of the work of the Holy Ghost, and the redemption wrought by Christ. Christ, by his death, purchaseth, and the Holy Ghost gathereth, the "holy catholic church." It were defective to believe Christ's purchase, and the Holy Ghost's sanctification, and not know for whom, and on whom, it is done. To sanctify, is to sanctify some persons; and so to make them the holy society, or christian church.

Q. 2. What is a church?

A. The name is applied to many sorts of assemblies which we need not name to you; but here it signifieth the christian society.

Q. 3. Why is it called catholic?

A. Catholic is a Greek word, and signifieth universal. It is called catholic, because, (1) It is not, as the Jews' church, confined to one nation, but comprehendeth all true Christians in the world: and, (2) Because it consisteth of persons that have everywhere in the world the same essentiating qualifications summed up, (Eph. 4:3-6,) one body, one spirit, one hope of our calling, one Lord, one faith, one baptism, one God and Father of all, though in various measures of grace. And so the concordant churches of Christ throughout the world, were called the catholic church, as distinct from the sects and heresies that broke from it.

Q. 4. How comes the Pope of Rome to call only his subjects catholics?

A. The greatest part of the church on earth, by far, was long in the Roman empire, and when emperors turned Christians, they gave the churches power for the honour of Christianity, to form the churches much like the civil state: and so a general council of all the churches in that empire was their supreme church power. And three patriarchs first, and five after, were in their several provinces, over all the rest of the archbishops and bishops: and so the orthodox party at first were called the catholics, because they were the greater concordant part; but quickly the Arians became far greater, and carried it in councils, and then they called themselves the catholics. After that, the orthodox, under wiser emperors, got up again, and then they were the greater part called catholics. Then the Nestorians a little while, and the Eutychians after, and the Monothelites after them, got the major vote in councils, and called themselves the catholic church: and so, since then, they that had the greatest countenance from princes, and the greatest number of bishops in councils, claimed the name of the catholic church: and the Pope, that was the first patriarch in the empire, first called himself the head of the catholic church in that empire; and when the empire was broke, extended his claim to the whole christian world, partly by the abuse of the word "catholic church," and partly by the abuse of the name "general councils;" falsely pretending to men that what was called catholic and general, as to the empire, had been so called as to all the world. And thus his church was called catholic.

Q. 5. Why is the catholic church called holy?

A. (1) To notify the work of our Saviour, who came to save us from our sins, and gather a peculiar people, a holy society, who are separated from the unbelieving, ungodly world.

(2) To notify the work of the Holy Ghost, who is given to make such a holy people.

(3) Yea, to notify the holiness of God the Father, who will be sanctified in all that draw near him, and hateth the impure and unholy, and will have all his children holy as he is holy.

(4) And to tell us the fitness of all God's children for his favour and salvation.

Q. 6. Wherein consisteth the holiness of the church?

A. (1) Christ their Head is perfectly holy. (2) The gospel and law of Christ, which is our objective faith and rule, are holy. (3) The founders of the church were eminently holy. (4) All sincere Christians are truly holy, and marked out as such for salvation. (5) The common ministers have a holy office. (6) The church worship, as God's ordinances, are holy works. (7) All that are baptised, and profess Christianity, are holy as to profession, and so far separated from the infidel world, though not sincerely to salvation.

Q. 7. What is it now that you call The Holy Catholic Church?

A. It is the universality of Christians, headed by Jesus Christ.

Or, it is a holy kingdom, consisting of Jesus Christ,[1] the Head, and all sincere Christians, the sincere members, and all professed Christians, the professing members; first founded and gathered by the Holy Ghost, eminently working in the apostles and evangelists, recording the doctrine and laws of Christ for their government to the end, and guided by his ministers, and sanctifying Spirit, according to those laws and doctrine in various degrees of grace and gifts.

Q. 8. What is it that makes all churches to be one?

A. (1) Materially their concord in their same qualifications, which is called, (Eph. 4:3,) "the unity of the Spirit." They are all that are sincere, sanctified by the same Spirit, and have the same essentials of faith, hope, baptismal covenant, and love:[2] and the hypocrites profess the same.

(2) Formally their common union with, and relation to, God the Father, Son, and Holy Ghost, that is, to Jesus Christ their Head, bringing them home to God the Father by the Spirit.

Q. 9. Is there no one ministerial head of all the church on earth?

A. No: neither one man, nor one council, or collection of men. For, (1) None are naturally capable of being one supreme pastor, teacher, priest, and ruler over all the nations of the earth, nor can so much as know them, or have human converse with them. And a council gathered equally out of all the world, as one such supreme, is a more gross fiction of impossibles than that of a Pope.

---

[1] Eph 1:22, 23, and 5:23, 24; Col 1:18, 19, 24; Matt 16:18; 1 Cor 12:28–30; Acts 2:47.

[2] John 17:21, 23; 1 Cor 12:5, 27–29; Eph 4:5–7; Matt 28:19.

(2) And Christ, that never so qualified any, never gave any such power. But all pastors are like the judges, justices, and mayors that rule subordinately under one king, in their several precincts, and not like an universal viceroy, lieutenant, or aristocracy, or parliament.

Q. 10. But is not monarchy the best form of government, and should not the church have the best?

A. (1) Yes: and therefore Christ is its monarch, who is capable of it.

(2) But a human, universal monarchy of all the world is not best. Nor was ever an Alexander, a Cæsar, or any man, so mad, as soberly to pretend to it. Who is the man that you would have to be king at the antipodes, and over all the kings on earth?

(3) Yea, the case of the church is liker that of schools and colleges, that rule volunteers in order to teaching them. And did ever papist think that all the schools on earth of grammarians, philosophers, physicians, &c., should have one human, supreme schoolmaster, or a council or college of such to rule them?

Q. 11. But Christ is not a visible Head, and the church is visible?

A. We deny not the visibility of the church, but we must not feign it to be more visible than it is.[3] (1) It consisteth of visible subjects. (2) Their profession is visible, and their worship. (3) They have visible pastors in all the particular churches, as every school hath its schoolmaster. (4) Christ was visible in the flesh on earth. (5) He was after seen of Stephen and Paul. (6) He is now visible in heaven, as the king in his court. (7) And he will come in glorious visibility shortly, to judge the world. (8) And his laws are visible by which he ruleth us and will judge us. If all this visibility will not satisfy men, Christ will not approve of usurpation for more visibility.

Q. 12. Of what use is this article to us?

A. (1) To tell us that Christ died not in vain, but will certainly have a holy church which he will save.[4]

---

[3] 1 Cor 11:3; Eph 5:23; Col 2:10, 18, and 2:19; Acts 14:23; Titus 1:5; Eph 2:20; Acts 8:36; 9, and 22:14; Rev 1:7; Matt 25:40.

[4] Eph 5:27; Acts 2:47, and 20:28; 1 Cor 10:32; Eph 3:10; Col 1:18, 24; Eph 3:21; Heb 2:12; 1 Thess 5:12, 13; Eph 4:16; 1 Tim 3:15.

(2) To show us, in the blessed effect, that the sanctification of the Spirit is not a fancy, but a holy church is renewed and saved by it.

(3) To tell us that God forsaketh not the earth, though he permit ignorance, infidelity, and wickedness to abound, and malice to persecute the truth: still God hath a holy church which he will preserve and save. And though this or that church may apostatise, and cease, there shall be still a catholic church on earth.

(4) To mind us of the wonderful providence of God, which so continueth and preserveth a holy people, hated by open enemies, and wicked hypocrites, by Satan and all his instruments on earth.

(5) To teach us to love the unity of Christians, and carefully maintain it, and not to tear the church by the engines of proud men's needless snares, nor to be rashly censorious of any, or excommunicate them unjustly, nor to separate from any, further than they separate from Christ, but to rejoice in our common union in christian faith and love, and not let wrongs, or infirmities of Christians, or carnal interests, or pride or passion, nor different opinions about things not necessary to our unity, destroy our love or peace, or break this holy bond.

19

"The Communion of Saints"

Q. 1. How is this article joined to the former?

A. As it belongs to our belief in the Holy Ghost, it tells us the effect of his sanctification: and as it belongs to our belief of the holy catholic church, it tells us the end of church relation, that saints may live in holy communion.

Q. 2. What is it to be a saint?

A. To be separated from a common and unclean conversation unto God, and to be absolutely devoted to him, to love, serve and trust him, and hope for his salvation.

Q. 3. Are all saints that are members of the catholic church?

A. Yes, by profession, if not in sincerity: all that are sincere and living members of the church, are really devoted to God by heart-consent; and the rest are devoted by baptism, and outward profession, and are hypocrites, pretending falsely to be real saints.[1]

Q. 4. Why then doth the Church of Rome canonize some few, and call them saints, if all Christians be saints?

A. By saints they mean extraordinary saints: but their appropriating the name to such, much tendeth to delude the people, as if they might be saved though they be not saints.[2]

---

[1] 1 Cor 1:1, 2; Rom 1:7; 12:15, and 15:25, 26, 31; 1 Cor 14:33, and 16:1, 15.

[2] 2 Cor 1:1; Eph 1:1; 5:3, and 6:18; Phil 1:1; Col 1:2; Heb 13:24; Acts 4.

Q. 5. What is meant by the Communion of Saints?

A. Such a frame and practice of heart and life towards one another as supposeth union, such as is between the members of the body.

Q. 6. Wherein doth this communion consist?

A. (1) In their common love to God, faith in Christ, and sanctification by the Spirit. (2) In their love to one another as themselves.[3] (3) In their care for one another's welfare, and endeavour to promote it as their own:[4] and when love makes all their goods so far common to all Christians within their converse, as that they do to their power supply their wants in the order and measure that God's providence, and their relations and acquaintance direct them; preferring the relief of others necessities, before their own superfluity or fulness. (4) In their joining, as with one mind and soul and mouth, in God's public worship, and that in the holy order under their respective pastors, which Christ, by his Spirit in the apostles, hath instituted.[5]

Q. 7. Why is our joining in the Lord's supper called our communion?

A. Because it is a special symbol, badge, and expression of it instituted by Christ, to signify our communion with him and one another.

Q. 8. Is that to be only a communion of saints?

A. Yes, that in a special manner is appropriated to saints: other parts of communion, (as eating together, relieving each other, duties of religion, &c.,) are so far to be used toward unbelievers, that they are not so meet to be the distinguishing symbols of Christians: but the two sacraments, baptism for entrance, and the Lord's supper, for continuance of communion, Christ hath purposely appointed for such badges or signs of his people as separate from the world.[6]

Q. 9. By what order are others to be kept from church communion?

A. Christ hath instituted the office of the sacred ministry for this end, that when they have made disciples to him, they may be entrusted with the keys of his church, that is, especially the administration of these

---

[3] Col 1:4; 1 Peter 1:22.

[4] Heb 13:2, 3; 1 Tim 6:18.

[5] 1 Cor 10:16; 2 Cor 6:14; Heb 10:22, 24; John 13:34, 35; 1 Thess 5:12, 13.

[6] Matt 26:26; 1 Cor 11:21, 22, 24, &c.; Acts 20:7; 1 Cor 10:10; Acts 2:42, 46.

sacraments, first judging who is fit to be entered by baptism, and then who is fit for continued communion.[7]

Q. 10. May not the pastors, by this means, become church tyrants?

A. We must not put down all government for fear of tyranny; else kingdoms, armies, colleges, schools, must be all dissolved, as well as churches: somebody must be trusted with this power; and who is fitter than they who are called to it as their office, and therefore supposed best qualified for it.

Q. 11. What if none were trusted with it, and sacraments left free to all?

A. Then sacraments would be no sacraments, and the church would be no church: if any man or woman that would, might baptise whom, and when, they would, they might baptise Turks and heathens, and that over and over, who come in scorn; and they might baptise without a profession of true faith; or upon a false profession. And if every man might give the Lord's supper to another, it might be brought into ale-houses and taverns, in merriment, or as a charm, or every infidel or enemy might in scorn profane it: do you think that if baptism and the Lord's supper were thus administered, that they would be any symbols or badges of Christianity, or of a church, or any means of salvation? No Christians ever dreamt of such profanation.

Q. 12. But why may not the pastors themselves give them to all that will?

A. Either you would have[8] them forced to do so, or to do it freely. If forced, they are no judges who is fit; and who then shall be judge? If the magistrate, you make him a pastor; and oblige him to teach, examine, hear, and try all the people's knowledge, faith, and lives, which will find them work enough: and this is not to depose the ministers' power, but to put it on another that hath more already than he can do: and a pastor then that delivereth the sacrament to every one that the magistrate bids him shall be a slave and not a free performer of the acts of his own office, unless that magistrate try and judge, and the minister be but a deacon, that must give account for no more than the bare delivering it. But if it be the receivers of baptism, or the Lord's supper, that shall

---

[7] Matt 16:19, and 24:45, 46; 1 Cor 4:1, 2; Acts 20:20, 28; 1 Thess 5:12, 13; Heb13:7, 17, 24.

[8] 1 Cor 5; 2 Thess 3; Titus 3:10; 2 Cor 6:16, 17; 1 Cor 1:1, 2, and 2 Cor 1:1; Eph 1:1, 2.

be judges, and may force the pastor to give it them; I have showed you already the profanation will make it no sacrament nor church.

And if pastors, that are judges, shall freely give them to all, they will be the profaners, and such ministration will confound the church and the world.

Q. 13. I do not mean that they should give them to heathens, but to all that profess the christian faith.

A. Therefore they must judge whether they profess the christian faith or not; and whether they speak as parrots, or understand what they say: and withal, christian love, and a christian life must be professed, as well as christian faith.

Q. 14. What are the terms on which they must receive men to communion?

A. They must baptise them and their infants, who, with competent understanding, and seeming seriousness, profess a practical belief in God the Father, Son, and Holy Ghost, and consent to that covenant, as expounded in the Creed, Lord's Prayer, and Ten Commandments. And they must admit all to communion in the Lord's supper, who continue in that profession, and nullify it not by proved apostasy, or inconsistent profession or practice.[9]

Q. 15. May not hypocrites make such professions, that are do saints?

A. Yes; and God only is the judge of hearts, not detected by proved contrary words or deeds: and these are saints by profession.

Q. 16. But it is on pretence of being the judge of church communion, that the pope hath got his power over the christian world.

A. And if tyrants, by false pretences, claim the dominions of other princes, or of mens' families, we must not therefore depose our kings or fathers.

Q. 17. But how shall we know what pastors they be that have this power of the keys, and judging men's fitness for communion?

A. All pastors, as such, have power, as all physicians have in judging of their patients, and all schoolmasters of their scholars. But great difference there is, who shall correct men's injurious administrations: whether the magistrate do it himself, or whether a bishop over many

---

[9]   Matt 28:19; Rev 22:17.

pastors do it; or many pastors in a synod do it, is no such great matter as will warrant the sad contentions that have been about it, so it be done. Or if none of these do it, a people intolerably injured may right themselves, by deserting such an injurious pastor. But the pastors must not be disabled, and the work undone, on pretence of restraining them from misdoing it.[10]

Q. 18. What is the need and benefit of this pastoral discipline?

A. (1) The honour of Christ (who, by so wonderful an incarnation, &c., came to save his people from their sins) must be preserved: which is profaned, if his church be not a communion of saints.[11]

(2) The difference between heaven and hell is so great, that God will have a visible difference between the way to each, and between the probable heirs of each. The church is the nursery for heaven, and the womb of eternal happiness. And dogs and swine are no heirs for heaven.

(3) It is necessary to the comfort of believers.

(4) And for the conviction and humbling of the unbelievers, and ungodly.

Q. 19. What further use should we make of this article?

A. (1) All Christians must carefully see that they be not hypocrites, but saints indeed, that they be meet for the communion of saints.

(2) All that administer holy things, and govern churches, should carefully see that they be a communion of saints, and not a swine-sty: not as the common world, but as the garden of Christ: that they promote and encourage holiness, and take heed of cherishing impiety.

(3) We must all be much against both that usurpation, and that neglect of necessary discipline, and differencing saints from wicked men, which hath corrupted most of the churches in the world.[12]

Q. 20. But when experience assureth us that few Christians can bear church discipline, should it be used when it will do hurt?

A. It is so tender, and yet so necessary, a discipline which Christ hath appointed, that he is unfit for the communion of saints who will not endure it. It is not to touch his purse or body: it is not to cast any man

---

[10] Phil 1:15–18.

[11] Titus 2:14; Eph 1:22, 23, and 5:25–29; Col 1:18, 24; Eph 4:14, 16.

[12] Matt 22:21, 22; 13:39, 41, and 7:21, 22; Luke 13:27.

out of the church for small infirmities: no, nor for gross sin, that repenteth of it, and forsakes it: it is not to call him, magisterially, to submit to the pastor's unproved accusation or assertions: but it is, with the spirit of meekness and fatherly love, to convince a sinner, and draw him to repentance, proving from God's word,[13] that the thing is a sin, and proving him guilty of it, and telling him the evil and danger of it, and the necessity of repentance, and confession, and amendment. And if he be stubborn, not making unnecessary haste, but praying for his repentance, and waiting a competent time, and joyfully absolving him upon his repentance: and if he continue impenitent, only declaring him unfit for church communion, and requiring the church accordingly to avoid him, and binding him to answer it at the bar of God, if he repent not.[14]

Q. 21. But if men will not submit to public confession, may not auricular, private confession to the priest serve turn?

A. In case the sin be private, a private confession may serve: but when it is known, the repentance must be known, or else it attaineth not the ends of its amendment: and the papists' auricular confession, in such cases, is but a trick to delude the church, and to keep up a party in it of wicked men, that will not submit to the discipline of Christ: it pretendeth strictness, but it is to avoid the displeasure of those that are too proud to stoop to open confession. Let such be never so many, they are not to be kept in the church on such terms: he that hath openly sinned against Christ, and scandalized the church, and dishonoured his profession, and will by no conviction and entreaty be brought to open confession, (in an evident case,) doth cast himself out of the communion of saints, and must be declared such by the pastors.

---

[13] Matt 18:21, 22; Luke 17:3; 2 Cor 2:7, 10, and 7:8; John 20:23.

[14] Mark 3:6; Luke 13:3, 5, and 17:3; Acts 2:37, 38, and 3:19; Luke 24:47; Jas 5:16; 1 John 1:9; Prov 28:13; Acts 19.

20

"The Forgiveness of Sins"

Q. 1. What is the dependence of this article on the former?

A. It is part of the description of the effects of Christ's redemption, and the Holy Ghost's application of it: his regeneration maketh us members of the Holy Catholic Church, where we must live in the communion of saints, and therewith we receive the forgiveness of sins: the same sacrament of baptism signifying and exhibiting both, as washing us from the filth or power of sin, and from the guilt of punishment.[1]

Q. 2. What is the forgiveness of sin?

A. It is God's acquitting us from the deserved punishment.[2]

Q. 3. How doth God do this?

A. By three several acts, which are three degrees of pardon: the first is, by his covenant, gift promise, or law of grace, by which, as his instrument or act of oblivion, he dissolveth the obligation to punishment which we were under, and giveth us lawful right to impunity, so that neither punishment by sense or by loss shall be our due.[3]

The second act is by his sentence as a Judge, pronouncing us forgiven, and justifying this our right against all that is or can be said against it.

---

[1] 1 John 1:9.

[2] Mat. 9:2, 5–7; Mark 2:7, 10.

[3] Ps 32:1, 2, and 85:2; Luke 5:20, and 7:48, 50; Jas 5:15; Eph 4:32; Heb 1:3; 2 Cor 5:18, 19; Ps 130:4.

The third act is by his execution, actually delivering us from deserved punishment of loss and sense.[4]

Q. 4. Doth not God forgive us the guilt of the fault as well as the dueness of punishment?

A. Yes, for these are all one in several words: to forgive the sin, and to acquit from dueness of punishment for that sin, are the same thing. God doth not repute or judge us to be such as never sinned, for that were to judge falsely; nor doth he judge that our sin is not related to us as the actors, for that is impossible; nor doth he judge that our sin did not deserve punishment; but only that the deserved punishment is forgiven, for the merits of Christ's righteousness and sacrifice.

Q. 5. Is not justification and forgiveness of sin all one?

A. To be justified: (1) Sometimes signifieth to be made just and justifiable in judgment; and then it sometimes includeth both the gift of saving faith and repentance, and the gift of pardon, and of right to life everlasting; and sometimes it pre-supposeth faith and repentance given, and signifieth the annexed gift of pardon and life.

(2) Sometimes it signifieth God's justifying us by his sentence in judgment, which containeth both the justifying of our right to impunity and salvation, and the justifying our faith and holiness as sincere, which are the conditions of our right.[5]

(3) And sometimes to justify us, is to use us as just men. And as long as we understand the matter thus signified by pardoning and justifying, we must not strive about words so variously used.[6]

Q. 6. But if Christ's perfect righteousness, habitual and actual, be our own righteousness by God's imputation, how can we need a pardon of sin, when we were perfectly obedient in Christ?

A. We could not possibly be pardoned as sinners, if God reputed us to have fulfilled all righteousness in Christ, and so to be no sinners; therefore it is no such imputation that must be affirmed. But God justly reputeth Christ's holiness and righteousness, active and passive,

---

[4] Acts 5:31; 13:38, and 26:18.

[5] Isa 53:11, and 45:25; 1 Cor 6:11; Titus 3:5, 7; Rev 22:12; Rom 4:2, 5; 2:13, and 3:20; Gal 2:16, 17; Rom 8:33; Jas 2:21, 24.

[6] Isa 1:8; 1 Kgs 8:32; Deut 25:1; Isa 5:23.

dignified by his divinity, to be fully meritorious of our pardon, justification, and salvation. And so it is ours, and imputed as the true meritorious cause of our righteousness, which consisteth in our right to pardon and salvation.[7]

Q. 7. Is pardon perfect in this life, and all punishment remitted at once?

A. No: (1) The punishment denounced in God's sentence of Eve and Adam is not wholly forgiven; the curse on the ground, the woman's sorrows, the pain and stroke of death. (2) Temporal, correcting punishments are not all forgiven. (3) Some measure of sin is penally permitted in us. (4) The want of more holiness and help of God's Spirit, and communion with God, is to all of us a sore punishment. (5) The permission of many temptations from devils and men are punishments, specially when they prevail to heinous sinning. (6) To be so long kept out of heaven, and to lie after in the grave, are punishments. Sure few men believe that pardon is here perfect, that feel any of these. (7) And it is not perfect, till we are justified before the world, and put in possession of salvation: that is the perfect pardon.[8]

Q. 8. But some say, that chastisements are no punishments.

A. They are not damning, destructive punishments, but they are chastising punishments; for they are evil to nature, inflicted by fatherly, correcting justice, for sin.

Q. 9. Is that an evil which always bringeth greater good?

A. It is no such evil as sinners should repine at. But ask any of that opinion, under the stone, or other tormenting disease, or if he must die as a malefactor, whether it be not a natural evil? If there be no evil in it, why doth he groan under it, why doth he pray against it, or use physic, or other remedies? Why is he offended at those that hurt him? Had he not rather have his holiness and salvation without torment, prisons, &c., than with them.

But it is not true, that all the punishments of such as are saved make them better; some are permitted to fall into heinous sin, and to decline

---

[7] Rom 3:22, 25, 26; Gal 3:6; Rom 4:5, 9, 22; 5:17–19; 6:13, 16, 18, and 8:4, 10.

[8] I think no man that felt what I feel, at the writing of this, in my flesh, and for my friends, can possibly think that pardon is perfect in this life. Jas 5:15; Luke 6:37; Matt 12:31; Josh 24:19; Matt 6:12, 14; 2 Kgs 23:26, 27; Matt 18:32.

in their faith, love, and obedience, and to die worse than once they were; and so to have a less degree of glory, when they have been hurtful scandals in the world. And is there no harm in all this? Nothing is perfect in this imperfect world.[9]

Q. 10. How are Christ's merits and satisfaction perfect then?

A. That is perfect which is perfectly fitted to its use; it was not a use that Christ ever intended, to pardon all temporal, correcting punishment, nor to make each believer perfect the first hour. That our greatest sins should go unpunished is against Christ's will and kingly government, and the nature of his salvation; and his righteousness and satisfaction are not intended against himself.[10]

Q. 11. What sins are pardoned? Is it all, or but some?

A. All sin is pardoned, though the pardon be not perfect at first, to all true penitent believers. But final impenitence, unbelief, and unholiness, never had a pardon purchased or offered; but that which is not final is forgiven; yea, no sin is actually forgiven, as to the everlasting punishment, to final impenitents and unbelievers.[11]

Q. 12. Are sins pardoned before they are committed?

A. If you call the mere purpose or purchase a pardon unfitly, or you speak but of the general act of oblivion, which pardoneth all men on condition that they penitently and believingly accept it, so sins to come are pardoned: but (not to strive about words) no one hath any actual, proper pardon for any sin before it is committed; for it is no sin, and so no pardoned sin.[12]

Q. 13. When is it that sin is pardoned?

A. God's purpose is eternal; the conditional pardon was made when the covenant of grace was made; some degrees of punishment God remitteth by common and preparatory grace. But saving pardon none receive (at age) till they believe, nor are they justified.[13]

---

[9] 2 Sam 7:14; Ps 73:14, and 118:18; 1 Cor 11:32; Jer 31:18; Heb 12:8–10; 2 Cor 2:6; Lam. 3:39; Job 31:11; Amos 3:2; Matt 16:23.

[10] Phil 3:12, 13; 1 Pet 5:10; 1 Cor 13:10; 2 Cor 7:1; Prov 8:36; 1 John 1:8, and 5:17.

[11] Matt 12:32; Exod 34:6, 7; Luke 13:3, 5; John 3:16; Mark 16:16.

[12] Matt 18:32; 2 Cor 5:19; Matt 6:12.

[13] Heb 1:3; John 3:16, 18, 25; Rom 4:2, and 5:1.

Q. 14. Why do we pray for pardon daily, when sin is already pardoned?

A. (1) I told you, sin is not pardoned when it is no sin; we sin daily, and, therefore, must have daily pardon. And this also proveth, that pardon and justification are not perfect before death, because there are more sins still to be pardoned. (2) And we pray for the continuance of the pardon we have, and for removal of punishments.

Q. 15. Is this the meaning of this article, that "I believe my own sins are actually forgiven," as a divine revelation?

A. The meaning is: (1) That by Christ a certain degree of punishment is taken off from all mankind, and they are not dealt with according to the rigour of the law of innocent nature. (2) And that a conditional pardon is given to all in the new covenant so far as it is revealed. (3) And that this pardon becometh actual to every one when he penitently and bellevingly consenteth to the (baptismal) covenant with Christ.[14] (4) And that this pardon is offered to me as well as others, and shall be mine if I be a sincere believer; this is all that the article containeth. (5) But while I profess to believe, it is supposed that I hope I do it sincerely, and, therefore, have some hope that I am pardoned. (6) But because a man may sincerely believe, and yet doubt of the sincerity, and God hath no where said in Scripture, that I or you are sincere believers, or are pardoned; therefore to believe this is no divine faith, save by participation; nor is it professed by all that profess the creed. But it is an effect of two acts: (1) Of our faith. (2) And of the conscience of our sincerity in believing; it is a conclusion that all should labour to make sure, though it be not the proper sense of the article.

Q. 16. Seeing all true believers are at first justified and pardoned as to the everlasting punishment, doth it not follow, that all God's children have afterward none but temporal chastisement to be forgiven?

A. (1) I told you that sin is not forgiven, even to stated believers, before it is committed; and when it is committed, the qualifying condition must be found in us; and though our first true faith and repentance qualify us for the pardon of all sin past, yet when more is committed, more is required in us to our pardon, that is, that we renew repentance and faith as far as sin is known, and that we beg pardon and forgive

---

[14] 2 Sam 12:12, 13; Ps 1 and 32.

others. (2) Yet the future punishment is not so much unforgiven to the faithful as to others, before renewed repentance; for they have the main qualification, and want but an act for which they are habituated, and have God's Spirit to assist them. (3) And though sins unknown, which are ordinary infirmities, are forgiven without express, particular repentance, yet, in order of nature, the desert of punishment goeth before the forgiveness; the very law of nature maketh durable punishment due to durable souls, till the dueness be remitted by forgiveness.[15]

Q. 17. Is my sin forgiven, as long as I believe it not forgiven?

A. If you believe not that God is a merciful, pardoning God, and Christ a pardoning Saviour, whose sacrifice and merits are sufficient, and God's promise of pardon to the penitent believer is true, and to be trusted, you are not pardoned; but if you believe this, and consent to Christ's pardoning covenant, you are pardoned, though you doubt of your own forgiveness.

Q. 18. How may I be sure that I am forgiven?

A. The everlasting punishment is forgiven, when you are one that God by his covenant pardoneth, and that is, when by true faith and repentance you consent to the covenant terms, and give up yourself to God, as your God, and Saviour, and Sanctifier. And when temporal punishments are remitted in soul or body, experience of their removal may tell you.[16]

Q. 19. What keepeth up doubts of forgiveness of sin?

A. (1) Ignorance of the terms of the pardoning covenant. (2) And ignorance of ourselves and our own sincerity. (3) Especially renewing our guilt by sin, and being so defective in our repentance, and other grace, as that we cannot be sure of our sincerity; above all, when frequent sinning after God's promises makes us not creditable to ourselves.

Q. 20. But is not the cure of a doubting soul to believe, though he find no evidence in himself; and that because he is commanded to believe, and so believing will be his evidence?

A. Believing is a word that signifieth divers acts. As I told you, it is every man's duty to believe God's mercy, and Christ's redemption and

---

[15]   Ps 32; 25, and 51; Matt 18:32, and 6:14, 15; 1 John 1:9; Acts 8:22.

[16]   John 3:16; Rom 10:14.

sufficiency, and the truth of the conditional promise,[17] and to accept pardon, as offered on the terms of that promise, and then not to cherish doubts of his sincerity. But it is not every man's duty to believe that he is sincere, or that his sin is pardoned; else most should be bound to believe an untruth that it may after become true. Presumption destroyeth far more than despair; for an ungodly, impenitent person to believe that he is godly, and justified by Christ, is to believe himself, who is a liar, and not to believe Christ; yea it is to believe himself against Christ, who saith the contrary.

Q. 21. What is the use of this article of the forgiveness of sin?

A. The use is exceeding great; not to embolden us in sin, because it is pardonable, nor to delay repentance and forsaking sin, for that were to cast away pardon by contempt. But, (1) to show us what a merciful God we serve. (2) And what a mercy it is to have a Redeemer,[18] and a pardoning Saviour. (3) And what a comfort to be under a pardoning covenant of grace. (4) And it tells in that the review of the sins of our unregenerate state, though they must keep us humble, should yet be still used to raise our hearts to joyful thankfulness to God, for the grace of a Redeemer. (5) And it should keep us from despair and discouragement in all our weaknesses, while we have the evidence of daily pardon. (6) Yea, it should make us hate sin the more, which is against so good a God. (7) We may come with reverent boldness to God, in meditation, prayer, and sacraments, when we know that sin is pardoned. (8) And we may taste the sweetness of all our mercies, when the doubt of our forgiveness doth not embitter them. (9) And we may much the easier bear all afflictions when the everlasting punishment is forgiven. (10) And we may die when God calls us, without horror, when we believe that we are pardoned through Christ. Nothing but sin can hurt or endanger us at Christ's tribunal; when that is forgiven, and there is no condemnation to us, being in Christ, how joyfully may we think of his appearing! (11) What peace of conscience may we have continually, while we can say that all our sins are forgiven us! For, as Psalm 32:1; "And blessed are

---

[17] Mark 3:28; Acts 5:31.

[18] Jer 31:34, and 36:3; Luke 7:12, 13; Acts 26:18; Eph 1:7; Col 1:14.

21

"The Resurrection of the Body"

Q. 1. I have oft wondered why there is nothing in the Creed of the immortality of the soul, and its state before the resurrection.

A. (1) The article of Christ's descent tells us, that his soul was among the separated souls, while his body was in the grave; as he told the thief, that he should be that day with him in Paradise.

(2) The resurrection of the body is a thing not known at all by nature, but only by supernatural revelation, and therefore is an article of mere belief. But the immortality, or future life of souls, is a point which the light of nature revealeth, and therefore was taken, both by Jews and sober heathens, as a truth of common notice. Even as the love of ourselves is not expressed in the Ten Commandments, but only the love of God and others, because it was a thing presupposed.

(3) The immortality of the soul is included in the article of the resurrection of the body; for if the soul continue not, the next at the resurrection would be another soul, and a new created one, and not the same. And then the body would not be the same soul's body, nor the man the same man, but another. Who was so unwise to think that God had so much more care of the body than of the soul, as that he would let the soul perish, and raise the body from the dust alone, and join it with another soul?

(4) Very learned and wise expositors think, that the Greek word, *anastasis*, used for resurrection, indeed signifieth the whole-life after this, both of the soul first, and body also after, oft in the New Testament.

It is a living again, or after this life, called a standing up again. And there is great probability of it in Christ's argument with the Sadducees, and some passages of Paul's, 1 Cor. 15.

Q. 2. What texts of Scripture do fully prove that the soul liveth when it is separated from the body?

A. Very many: (1) God breathing into man the breath of life, and making him a living soul, is said thereby to make him in the image of God, who is the living God; and so the soul is essentially life.

(2) God's calling himself the God of Abraham, Isaac, and Jacob, is by Christ expounded, as proving that he is the God of living Abraham.

(3) None ever dreamed that Enoch and Elijah had no company of human souls in heaven. For (Matt. 17.) Moses also appeared with them on the Mount, and showed that his soul did live.

(4) When Saul himself would have Samuel raised to speak with him, it plainly implieth that it was then the common belief of the Jews, that separated souls survive.

(5) When (1 Kings 17:22) Elijah raised the dead child of the widow of Zarephath; and (2 Kings 4.) Elisha raised the Shunamite's child; and (2 Kings 13:21) a dead man was raised; all these proved that the soul was the same that came again, else the persons had not been the same.

(6) When Christ raised Lazarus, and Jairus's daughter, (Mark 5:41, 42; Luke 8:55,) and another, (Luke 7:12, 14, 15,) the same souls came into them.

(7) Many of the dead rose and appeared at Christ's death. And Peter raised one from death, which was by a re-union of the same living soul to the same body.

(8) Christ tells us (Luke 12:4) that men cannot kill the soul.

(9) He tells us (Luke 16:9) that as the wise steward, when he was put out, was received by the persons whom he had obliged; so if we make us friends of the mammon of unrighteousness, when these things fail us, which is at death, we shall be received into the everlasting habitations.

(10) The parable of the sensual Rich Man and Lazarus: one going presently to hell, and the other to the bosom of Abraham in Paradise, fully prove that Christ would have this believed, and would have all men warned accordingly to prepare; and that Moses and the prophets were so sufficient for such notice, as that one from the dead would have been less credible herein. Though it be a parable, it is an instructing, and

not a deceiving parable, and very plain in this particular. The name of Abraham's bosom was according to the common sense of the Jews, who so called that state of the blessed, not doubting but that Abraham was then in happiness, and the blessed with him.

(11) Herod's thought, that John had been risen from the dead, and the Jews' conceit that Christ had been one of the old prophets risen, and the Pharisees' approbation of Christ's argument with the Sadducees do put it past doubt, that it was then taken for certain truth, that the souls of the faithful do survive by all, except such as the heretical Sadducees.

(12) Christ saith, "This is life eternal, to know thee the only true God, and Jesus Christ whom thou hast sent." (John 17:3.) How is it eternal, if it have as long an interruption as from death till the day of judgment?

(13) It is the sum of God's Gospel, that "Whosoever believeth in Christ shall not perish, but have everlasting life." (John 3:16.) Therefore they perish not till the day of judgment.

(14) Christ hath promised, that whoever drinketh of the water which he will give him, (the Spirit,) "it shall be in him a well of water springing up to everlasting life." (John 4:14.) But if the soul perish, that water perisheth to that soul.

(15) To be born again of the Spirit fitteth a man to enter into the kingdom of God. But if the soul perish, all that new birth is lost to that soul, and profiteth the dust only.

(16) "He that believeth on the Son, hath everlasting life." (John 3:36.) "He is passed from death to life." (John 5:24.) "He giveth meat, which endureth to everlasting life." (John 6:27.) "He shall never hunger or thirst (that is, be empty) that cometh to Christ." (Ver. 35.) "Of all that cometh to him he will lose nothing;" therefore will not lose all their souls. (Ver. 39.) "They have everlasting life." (Ver. 40, 47.) "He dwelleth in Christ, and Christ in him," and therefore is not extinct. (Ver. 54, 56, 58.) "Verily, verily, I say unto you, if a man keep my sayings, he shall never see death." (John 8:51.) "I give unto them eternal life, and they shall never perish, neither shall any pluck them out of my hand." (John 10:28.)

(17) "Whosoever liveth and believeth in me shall never die." (John 11:26.)

(18) "The Comforter shall abide with you for ever," (John 14:26.) "For he dwelleth with you, and shall be in you." (Ver. 17.)

(19) "I will that they whom thou hast given me, be with me where I am, that they may behold my glory." (John 17:24.) If the soul perish, it is not they that shall be with him, but others.

(20) "Today shalt thou be with me in Paradise." (Luke 23:43.)

(21) "Father, into thy hands I commend my Spirit." (Luke 23:46.)

(22) "Where I am, there shall my servant be." (John 12:26.) But Christ is not perished.

(23) "Stephen called on God, saying, Lord Jesus receive my spirit." (Acts 7:59.) Therefore it perished not.

(24) "If children, then heirs." (Rom. 8:17.) "We groan, waiting for the adoption." (Ver. 23.) "Whom he justified, them he glorified." (Ver. 30.) In short, all the whole Gospel, that promiseth life to be sanctified, doth prove the immortality of the soul: for if the soul perish, no man that lived upon earth is saved: for if the soul be not the man, it is most certainly the prime, essential part of the man. The dust of the carcass is not the man; and if another soul, and not the same, come into it, it will be another man, and so all the promises fail.

(25) So all the texts that speak of resurrection, judgment, that we shall all be judged according to our works, and what we did in the body. If it be another soul that must be judged, which never was in that body before, nor ever did any thing in that body, how shall it be judged for that which it never did? All the texts that threaten hell, or future punishment, and promise heaven, prove it. "I was hungry and ye fed me, naked and ye clothed me," &c. (Matt. 25.) Ye did it, or did it not to me, might they not say, 'We never did it, nor ever lived till now?' "The angels shall gather out of his kingdom all things that offend, and them that work iniquity, and cast them into the lake of fire." (Matt. 13.) And all the Scripture which threateneth damnation to them that obey not the truth, and promiseth salvation to the faithful; which is never performed, if all done on another soul. (2 Thes. 1:6–10, and 2:12.)

(26) And all the texts that speak of God's justice and mercy hereafter. Is it justice to damn a new-made soul that never sinned?

(27) Paul knew not whether he were in or out of the body, when he was in Paradise. (2 Cor. 12:2–4.) The separated soul then may be in Paradise.

(28) How can the hope of unseen things make affliction and death easy to that soul that shall never be saved? And how can we be comforted or saved by such hope? (2 Cor. 4:16–18.)

(29) "We know that if our earthly house of this tabernacle were dissolved, we have a building of God." (2 Cor. 5:1.) "For in this we groan earnestly, desiring to be clothed upon with our house which is from heaven." (Ver. 2.) "He that hath wrought us for the self-same thing is God, who also hath given us the earnest of the Spirit." (Ver. 5.) "Therefore we are always confident, knowing that whilst we are at home in the body we are absent from the Lord; we are confident and willing rather to be absent from the body and present with the Lord. Wherefore we labour, that whether present or absent we may be accepted of him. For we must all appear before the judgment-seat of Christ, that every one may receive the things done in his body, whether it be good or bad." (Ver. 6.)

(30) "To me to live is Christ, and to die is gain. What I shall choose I know not: for I am in a strait between two, having a desire to depart and be with Christ, which is far better." (Phil. 1:21–23.)

(31) "Blessed are the dead that die in the Lord," &c. (Rev. 14:13.)

(32) "We are come to Mount Zion, the city of the living God, &c., the spirits of the just made perfect." (Heb. 12:22, 23.)

Abundance more might be added. And I have been so large on this, because it is of most unspeakable importance, as that which all our comfort and our religion lieth on; and though the light of nature have taught it philosophers, and almost all the world in all ages, yet the devil is most busy to make men doubt of it, or deny it.

Religion lieth on three grand articles. (1) To believe in God; and this is so evident in the whole frame of nature, that there is a God, that he is worse than mad that will deny it. (2) To believe the immortality of the soul, and the life hereafter. And, (3) To believe in Christ. And though it be this third that is known only by supernatural Revelation, yet to him that believeth the immortality of the soul, and the life hereafter, Christianity will appear so exceeding congruous, that it will much the more easily be believed. And experience tells us, that the devil's main game, for the debauching and damning of fleshly, worldly, ungodly men, and for troubling and discomforting believers, lieth in raising doubts of the soul's immortality, and the future life of reward and punishment.

Q. 3. But what good will a resurrection of the body do us, if the soul be in happiness before?

A. (1) It will be for God's glory to make and bless a perfect man. (2) It will be our perfection: a whole man is more perfect than a soul alone. (3) It will be the soul's delight.[1] As God, that is perfectly blessed in himself, yet made and maintaineth a world, of which he is more than the soul, because he is a communicative good, and pregnant, and delighteth to do good; so the soul is made like God in his image, and is communicative, and would have a body to act on. As the sun, if there were nothing in the world but itself, would be the same that it now is; but nothing would receive its motion, light, or heat, or be the better for it. And if you did imagine it to have understanding, you must think that it would be much more pleased to enlighten and enliven so many millions of creatures, and cause the flourishing of all the earth, than to shine to nothing. So may you think of the soul of man; it is by God inclined to actuate a body.

Q. 4. If that be so, it is till then imperfect, and deprived of its desire, and so in pain and punishment.

A. It is not in its full perfection; and it is a degree of punishment to be in a state of separation. But you cannot call it a pain as to sense, because it hath an unspeakable glory, though not the most perfect. Nor hath the will of the blessed any trouble and striving against the will of God, but takes that for best which God willeth. And so the separated state is best, while God willeth it, though the united state will be beat (as more perfect) in its time.

Q. 5. But the dust in a grave is so vile a thing, that one would think the raising it should not be very desirable to the soul.

A. It shall not be raised in the shape of ugly dust, or filth, nor of corruptible flesh and blood; but a glorious and spiritual body, and a meet companion for a glorified soul. And even now, as vile as the body is, you feel that the soul is loth to part with it.[2]

Q. 6. But there are so many difficulties and improbabilities about the resurrection, as make the belief of it very hard.

---

[1] Rev 21 and 22.

[2] 1 Cor 15.

A. What is hard to God, that made heaven and earth of nothing, and maintains all things in their state and course? What was that body a while ago? Was it not as unlikely as dust to be what it now is?

It is folly to object difficulties to omnipotency.

Q. 7. But the body is in continual flux, or change; we have not the same flesh this year that we had the last; and a man in a consumption loseth before death the mass of flesh in which he did good or evil; shall all that rise again, which every day vanisheth? And shall the new flesh be punished for that which it never did?

A. It is a foolish thing, from our ignorance and uncertainties, to dispute against God, and certain truth: will you know nothing, unless you know all things? Will you doubt of the plain matter, because, in your darkness, you understand not the manner or circumstances of it? The soul hath a body consisting of various parts; the fiery part in the spirits is its most immediate vehicle or body; the seminal, tenacious humour, and air, is the immediate vehicle of the fiery part; whether the spirits do any of them depart, as its vehicle or body, with the soul; or, if not, whether they be the identifying part, that the soul shall be re-united to first; or what, or how much, of the rest, even the aqueous and earthy matter, which we had from our birth, shall be re-assumed, are things past our understanding. You know not how you were generated in the womb, and yet you know that you were there made; and must God teach you how you shall be raised before you will believe it? Must he answer all your doubts of the flesh that is vanished, or the bodies eaten by other bodies, and teach you all his unsearchable skill, before you will take his word for true?

He that maketh the rising sun to end the darkness of the night, and the flourishing spring to renew the face of millions of plants, which seemed in the winter to be dead, and the buried little seed to spring up to a beautiful plant and flower, or a strong and goodly tree, hath power and skill enough to raise our bodies, by ways unknown to foolish man.

Q. 8. What should a man do that he may live in a comfortable hope of the resurrection, and the soul's immortality, and the life to come?

A. We have three great things to do for this end. (1) To get as full a certainty as is possible, that there is such a life to come. And this is done by strengthening a sound belief. (2) To get a suitableness of soul to that blessed life; and this is by the increase of love and holiness, and by a spiritual, heavenly conversation. And, (3) To get and exercise a joyful hope and assurance that it shall be ours; and this is done by a life of careful obedience to God, and the conscious notice of our sincerity and title, and by the increase and exercise of the foresaid faith and love; daily dwelling on the thoughts of God's infinite goodness, and fatherly love; of Christ's office and grace, and the seals of the Spirit, and the blessed state of triumphant souls, in the heavenly Jerusalem, and living as in familiarity with them.

Q. 9. But when doubting thoughts return, would it not be a great help to faith if you could prove the soul's immortality by reason?

A. I have done that largely in other books; I will now say but this: if there be no life of retribution after this, it would follow that not only Scripture, but religion, piety, and conscience, were all the most odious abuses of mankind; to set man's heart and care upon seeking, all his days, a life which he can never obtain, and to live honestly, and avoid sin, for fear of an impossible punishment, and to deny fleshly pleasure and lust, upon mere deceit, what an injury would religion, conscience, and honesty be? Men that are not restrained by any fear or hopes of another life, from tyranny, treason, murder, perjury, lying, deceit, or any wickedness, but only by present interest, would be the wisest men. When yet God hath taught nature to abhor these evils, and bound man to be religious and conscionable by common reason, were it but for the probability of another life. And can you believe that wickedness is wisdom, and all conscionable goodness is folly and deceit?

22

Of the "Life Everlasting"

Q. 1. Where is it that we shall live when we go hence?

A. With Christ in heaven, called Paradise, and the Jerusalem above.

Q. 2. How is it, then, that the souls of men are said sometimes to appear on earth? Is it such souls, or is it devils?

A. Either is possible: for souls are in no other hell than devils are, who are said to be in the air, and to go to and fro, and tempt men, and afflict them here on earth: but when it is a soul that appeareth, and when a devil, we have not acquaintance enough to know. But though God can for just causes let a blessed soul appear, as Moses and Elias did on the Mount, and perhaps Samuel to Saul, yet we have reason to suspect, that it is the miserable souls of the wicked that oftenest appear.

Q. 3. But how come devils or souls to be visible, being spirits?

A. Spirits are powerful, and dwell in airy and other elementary matter, in which they can appear to us as easily as we can put on our clothes. Fire is invisible in its simple unclothed substance, and yet when it hath kindled the air, it is visible light.

Q. 4. Why then do they appear so seldom?

A. God restraineth evil spirits, and keepeth them within their bounds, that they may not either deceive or trouble mankind: and the spirits of the just are more inclined to their higher, nobler region and work: and God will have us here live by faith, and not by seeing either the heavenly glory, or its inhabitants.

Q. 5. But it seems that we shall live again on earth; for it is said that the new Jerusalem cometh down from above, and we look for a new heaven, and a new earth, wherein dwelleth righteousness?

A. It greatly concerneth us to difference certainties from uncertainties. It is certain that the faithful have a promise of a great reward in heaven, and of being with Christ, and being conveyed into Paradise by angels, and are commanded to lay up a treasure in heaven, and there to set their hearts and affections, and to seek the things that are above, where Christ is at God's right hand; and they desire to depart and be with Christ, as far better than to be here; and to be absent from the body, and be present with the Lord; so that the inheritance of the saints in heavenly light and glory is certain. But as to the rest, whether the new earth shall be for new inhabitants, or for us; and whether the descending Hierusalem shall be only for a thousand years, before the final judgment, or after for perpetuity; or whether it shall come no lower than the air, where it is said, that we shall be taken up to meet the Lord, and so shall ever be with him; or whether earth shall be made as glorious to us as heaven, and heaven and earth be laid together in common, when separating sin is gone: these matters being to us less certain, must not be set against that which is certain. And the new Jerusalem coming down from heaven, doth imply that it was first in heaven; and it is said that it is now above, and we are come to it in relation and foretaste, where are the perfected spirits of the just, as it is described, Heb. 12:22–24.

Q. 6. But some think that souls sleep till the resurrection, or are in an unactive potentiality, for want of bodies?

A. Reason and Scripture confute this dream. The soul is essential life, naturally inclined to action, intellection, and love or volition, and it will be in the midst of objects enow on which to operate: and is it not absurd to think that God will continue so noble a nature in a state of idleness, and continue all its essential faculties in vain, and never to be exercised? As if he would continue the sun without light, heat, or motion. What then is it a sun for? and why is it not annihilated? The soul cannot lose its faculties of vitality, intellection, and volition, without losing its essence, and being turned into some other thing. And why it cannot act out of a body, what reason can be given? If it could not, yet that it taketh not hence with it a body of those corporeal spirits which it acted in, or that it cannot as well have a body of light for its own action, as it can take a body (as Moses on the Mount) to appear to man, is that which we have no reason to suspect.

But Scripture puts all out of doubt, by telling us, that to die is gain, and that it is better to be with Christ, and that Lazarus was comforted in Abraham's bosom, and the converted thief was with Christ in Paradise, and that the souls under the altar and in heaven pray and praise God, and that the spirits of the just are there made perfect; and this is not a state of sleep. It is a world of life, and light, and love, that we are going to, more active than this earthy, heavy world, than fire is more active than a clod. And shall we suspect any sleepy unactivity there? This is the dead and sleepy world: and heaven is the place of life itself.

Q. 7. What is the nature of that heavenly, everlasting life?

A. It is the perfect activity and perfect fruition of divine communicated glory, by perfected spirits, and spiritual men, in a perfect glorious society, in a perfect place, or region, and this everlasting.

Q. 8. Here are many things set together, I pray you tell them me distinctly?

A. (1) Heaven is a perfect, glorious place, and earth to it is a dungeon. The sun which we see is a glorious place in comparison of this.

(2) The whole society of angels and saints will be perfect and glorious. And our joy and glory will be as much in participation by union and communion with theirs, as the life and health of the eye or hand is, in and by union and communion with the body: we must not dream of any glory to ourselves, but in a state of that union and communion with the glorious body of Christ. And Christ himself, the glorified Head, is the chief part of this society, whose glory we shall behold.

(3) Angels and men are themselves there perfect. If our being and nature were not perfect, our action and fruition could not be perfect.

(4) The objects of all our action are most perfect: it is the blessed God, and a glorious Saviour and society, that we shall see, and love, and praise.

(5) All our action will be perfect: our sight and knowledge, our love, our joy, our praise, will be all perfect there.

(6) Our reception and fruition will all be perfect. We shall be perfectly loved by God, and one another, and perfectly pleasing to him, and each other; and he will communicate to us and all the society as much glorious life, light, and joyful love, as we are capable of receiving.

(7) And all this will be perfect in duration, being everlasting.

Q. 9. O what manner of persons should we be, if all this were well believed! Is it possible that they should truly believe all this, who do not earnestly desire and seek it, and live in joyful, longing hope to be put into possession of it?

A. Whoever truly believeth it, will prefer it before all earthly treasure and pleasure, and make it the chief end, and motive, and comfort of his soul and life, and forsake all that stands against it, rather than forsake his hopes of this. But while our faith, hope, and love, are all imperfect, and we dwell in flesh, where present and sensible things are still diverting and affecting us, and we are so used to sight and sense that we look strangely towards that which is above them, and out of their reach, it is no wonder if we have imperfect desires and joy, abated by diversions, and by griefs and fears, and if in this darkness unseen things seem strange to us; and if a soul united to a body be loth to leave it, and be unclothed, and have somewhat dark thoughts of that state without it, which it never tried.

Q. 10. But when we cannot conceive how souls act out of the body, how can the thought of it be pleasant and satisfying to us?

A. (1) We that can conceive what it is to live, and understand, and will, to love and rejoice in the body, may understand what these acts are in themselves, whether out of a body, or in a more glorious body: and we can know that nothing doth nothing, and therefore that the soul that doth these acts is a noble substance, and we find that it is invisible. But of this I spake in the beginning.

(2) When we know in general all before mentioned, that we shall be in that described blessedness with Christ and the heavenly society, we must implicitly trust Christ with all the rest, who knoweth for us what we know not, and stay till possession give us that clear, distinct conception of the manner, and all the circumstances, which they that possess it not can no more have than we can conceive of the sweetness of a meat or drink which we never tasted of, and we should long the more for that possession which will give us that sweet experience.

Q. 11. Is not God the only glory and joy of the blessed? Why then do you tell us so much of angels and saints, and the city of God?

A. God is all in all things; of him, and through him, and to him are all things, and the glory of all is to him for ever. But God made not any single creature to be happy in him alone, as separate from the rest, but an universe, which hath its union and communion. I told you, as the eye and hand have no separated life or pleasure, but only in communion with the whole body, so neither shall we in heaven. God is infinitely above us, and if you think of him alone, without mediate objects for the ascent and access of your thoughts, you may as well think to climb up without a ladder. We are not the noblest creatures next to God, nor yet the most innocent: we have no access to him but by a Mediator, and that Mediator worketh and conveyeth his grace to us by other subordinate means. He is the Saviour of his body, which is the fulness of him that filleth all. If we think not of the heavenly Jerusalem, the glorious city of God, the heavenly society and joyful choir that praise Jehovah and the Lamb, and live together in perfect knowledge, love, and concord, in whose communion only we have all our joy; to whom in this unity God communicateth his glory; and if we think not of the glorious Head of the church, who will then be our Mediator of fruition, as he was of acquisition; nay, if we think not of those loving, blessed angels that rejoiced at our conversion, and were here the servants, and will be for ever the companions of our joy; and if we think not of all our old, dear friends and companions in the flesh, and of all the faithful who, since Adam's days, are gone before us; and if we think not of the attractive love, union, and joy of that society and state, we shall not have sufficient familiarity above, but make God as inaccessible to us. Delight and desire suppose attractive suitableness: inaccessible excellency draws not up the heart. I thank God for the pleasure that I have in thinking of the blessed society, which will shortly entertain me with joyful love.

Q. 12. But may not "everlasting" signify only a long time, as it oft doth in the Scripture, and so all may be in mutable revolutions, as the Stoics and some others thought?

A. (1) What reason have we to extort a forced sense against our own interest and comfort, without any warrant from God? (2) The nature of the soul being so far immortal as to have no inclination to its own death, why should we think it strange that its felicity should be also everlasting. (3) It can hardly be conceived how that soul can possibly revolt from God and perish, who is once confirmed with that sight of his glory, and the full fruition of his love. Whether nature be so bad as to allow such a revolt. If the devils had been as near God, and as much

PART III

23

What is the True Use of the Lord's Prayer

Q. 1. What is Prayer?

A. It is holy desires expressed, or actuated, to God, (with heart alone, or also with the tongue,) including our penitent confession of sin, and its deserts, and our thankful acknowledgment of his mercies, and our praising God's works and his perfections.

Q. 2. What is the use of prayer? Seeing God cannot be changed and moved by us, what good can it do to us, and how can it attain our ends?

A. You may as wisely ask, what good any thing will do towards our benefit or salvation, which we can do, seeing nothing changeth God. As God, who is one, maketh multitudes of creatures; so God, who is unchangeable, maketh changeable creatures; and the effect is wrought by changing us, and not by changing God. You must understand these great philosophical truths, that, (1) All things effect according to the capacity of the receiver. (2) Therefore, the various effects in the world proceed from the great variety of receptive capacities. The same sun-beams do cause a nettle, a thorn, a rose, a cedar, according to the seminal capacity of the various receivers. The same sun enlighteneth the eye, that doth not so by the hand or foot, or by a tree, or stone: and it shineth into the house whose windows are open, which doth not so when the windows are shut; and this without any change in itself. The boatman layeth hold on the bank, and pulls as if he would draw it to the boat, when he doth but draw the boat to it. Two ways prayer procureth the blessing without making any change in God. First, by our performing the condition on which God promiseth his mercy. Secondly, by disposing our souls to receive it. He that doth not penitently confess his sin, is unmeet for pardon; and he that desireth not Christ and mercy, is unmeet to be partaker of them: and he that is utterly unthankful for what he hath received, is unmeet for more.

Q. 3. Who made the Lord's Prayer?

A. The Lord Jesus Christ himself, as he made the gospel; some of the matter being necessary yet before his incarnation.

Q. 4. To whom and on what occasion did he make it?

A. To his disciples, (to whom also he first delivered his commands) upon their request that he would teach them to pray.

Q. 5. To what use did Christ make it them?

A. First, to be a directory for the matter and method of their love, desires, hope, and voluntary choice and endeavours; and, secondly, to be used in the same words when their case required it.

As man hath three essential faculties, the intellect, will, and vital, executive power; so religion hath three essential parts, viz., to direct our understandings to believe, our will to desire, and our lives in practice.

Q. 6. What is the matter of the Lord's Prayer in general?

A. It containeth, first, what we must desire as our end: And, secondly, what we must desire as the means; premising the necessary preface, and concluding with a suitable conclusion.

Q. 7. What is the method of the Lord's Prayer?

A. (I) The preface speaks, (1) To God, as God. (2) As our reconciled Father in Christ, described in his attributes, by the words "which art in Heaven," which signify the perfection of his power, knowledge, and goodness; and the word "Father" signifieth that he is supreme Owner, Ruler, and Benefactor.

(3) The word "our" implieth our common relation to him, as his creatures, his redeemed and sanctified ones, his own, his subjects, and his beneficiaries, or children.

(II) The petitions are of two sorts (as the commandments have two tables): the first proceed according to the order of intention, beginning at the highest notion of the ultimate end, and descending to the lowest. The second part is according to the order of execution and assecution, beginning at the lowest means, and ascending to the highest.

(III) The conclusion enumerateth the parts of the ultimate end by way of praise, beginning at the lowest, and ascending to the highest. The method throughout is more perfect than any of the philosophers' writings.

Q. 8. Why do we not read that the apostles after used this prayer?

A. (1) It is enough to read that Christ prescribed it them, and that they were obedient to him. We read not of all that the apostles did.

(2) This is a comprehensive summary of all prayer, and therefore must needs be brief in the several parts: but the apostles had occasion sometimes for one branch, and sometimes for another, on which they particularly enlarged, and seldom put up the whole matter of prayer all at once.

(3) They formed their desires according to the method of this prayer, though they expressed those desires as various occasions did require.

Q. 9. Is every Christian bound to say the words of the Lord's prayer?

A. The same answer may serve as to the last. Every Christian is bound to make it the rule of his desires and hopes, both for matter and order; but not to express them all in every prayer. But the words themselves are apt, and must have their due reverence, and are very fit to sum up our scattered, less ordered requests.

Q. 10. But few persons can understand what such generals comprehend?

A. (1) Generals are useful to those that cannot distinctly comprehend all the particulars in them. As the general knowledge, that we shall be happy in holy and heavenly joy with Christ, may comfort them that know not all in heaven that makes up that happiness, so a general desire may be effectual to our receiving many particulars. (2) And it is not so general as "God be merciful to me a sinner," an accepted prayer of the publican, by Christ's own testimony. There are six particular heads there plainly expressed.

24

"Our Father Which Art in Heaven," Expounded

Q. 1. Who is it that we pray to, whom we call "our Father?"

A. God himself.

Q. 2. May we not pray to creatures?

A. Yes, for that which it belongeth to those creatures to give us upon our request, supposing they hear us: but not for that which is God's, and not their own to give; nor yet in a manner unsuitable to the creature's capacity or place. A child may petition his father, and a subject his prince, and all men one another.

Q. 3. May we not pray to the Son, and the Holy Ghost, as well as to the Father?

A. As the word "Father" signifieth God as God, it comprehendeth the Son, and the Holy Ghost: and as it signifieth the first Person in the Trinity, it excludeth not, but implieth, the second and the third.

Q. 4. What doth the word "Father" signify?

A. That as a Father, by generation, is the owner, the ruler, and the loving benefactor to his child, so is God, eminently and transcendently, to us.

Q. 5. To whom is God a Father, and on what fundamental account?

A. He is a Father to all men by creation; to all lapsed mankind, by the price of a sufficient redemption: but only to the regenerate by regeneration and adoption, and that effective redemption which actually delivereth men from guilt, wrath, sin, and hell, and justifieth and sanctifieth them, and makes them heirs of glory.

Q. 6. What is included, then, in our child-like relation to this Father?

A. That we are his own, to be absolutely at his disposal, his subjects, to be absolutely ruled by him, and his beloved to depend on his bounty, and to love him above all, and be happy in his love.

Q. 7. What is meant by the words "which art in heaven?"

A. They signify, (I) God's real substantiality: he is existent.

(II) God's incomprehensible perfection in power, knowledge, and goodness, and so his absolute sufficiency and fitness to hear and help us. (1) The vastness, sublimity, and glory of the heavens tell us, that he who reigneth there over all the world, must needs be omnipotent, and want no power to do his will, and help us in our need.

(2) The glory and sublimity tell us, that he that is there above the sun, which shineth upon all the earth, doth behold all creatures, and see all the ways of the sons of men, and therefore knoweth all our sins, wants, and dangers, and heareth all our prayers.

(3) Heaven is that most perfect region whence all good floweth down to earth; our life is thence, our light is thence; all our good and fore-taste of felicity and joy is thence: and therefore the Lord of heaven must needs be the best; the fountain of all good, and the most amiable end of all just desire and love. Yet heaven is above our sight and comprehension; and so much more is God.

(III) And the word "art" signifieth God's eternity in heavenly glory: it is not "who wast," or "who wilt be." Eternity indivisible.

Q. 8. Is not God every where? Is he more in heaven than any where else?

A. All places and all things are in God; he is absent from none; nor is his essence divisible or commensurate by place, or limited, or more here than there; but to us God is known by his works and appearances, and therefore said to be most where he worketh most: and so we say, that God dwelleth in him who dwelleth in love: that he walketh in his church; that we are his habitation by the Spirit; that Christ and the Holy Spirit dwell in believers, because they operate extraordinarily in them; and so God is said to be in heaven, because he there manifesteth his glory to the felicity of all the blessed, and hath made heaven that throne of his Majesty, from whence all light, and life, and goodness, all mercy, and all justice, are communicated to, and exercised on, men. And so we that cannot see God himself, must look up to the throne of the Heavenly Glory in our prayers, hopes, and joys: even as a man's soul is undivided in all his body, and yet it worketh not alike in all its parts, but is in the head, that it useth reason, sight, &c., and doth most notably appear to others in the face, and is almost visible in the eye: and therefore when you talk to a man, you look him in the face; and as you talk not to his flesh, but to his sensitive and intellectual soul, so you look to that part where it most apparently showeth its sense and intellection.

Q. 9. Is there no other reason for the naming of heaven here?

A. Yes: it teacheth us whither to direct our own desires, and whence to expect all good, and where our own hope and felicity is. It is in heaven that God is to be seen and enjoyed in glory, and in perfect love and joy: though God be on earth, he will not be our felicity here on earth: every prayer, therefore, should be the soul's aspiring and ascending towards heaven, and the believing exercise of a heavenly mind and desire. For a man of true prayer to be unwilling to come to heaven, and to love earth better, is a contradiction.

Q. 10. But do we not pray that on earth he may use us as a Father?

A. Yes: that he will give us all mercies on earth, conducing to heavenly felicity.

Q. 11. What else is implied in the words, "our Father?"

A. Our redemption and reconciliation by Christ, and, to the regenerate, our regeneration by the Holy Ghost, and so our adoption; by all which, of the enemies and the heirs of hell, we are made the sons of God, and heirs of heaven. It is by Christ and his Spirit that we are the children of God.

Q. 12. Why say we "our Father," and not "my Father?"

A. (1) To signify that all Christians must pray as members of one body, and look for all their good, comfort, and blessedness, in union with the whole, and not as in a separate state. Nor must we come to God with selfish, narrow minds, as thinking only of our own ease and good, nor put up any prayer or praise to God but as members of the universal church in one choir, all seen and heard at once by God, though they see not, and hear not one another: and therefore that we must abhor the pregnant, comprehensive sin of selfishness; by which wicked men care only for themselves, and are affected with little but their personal concerns, as if they were all the world to themselves, insensible of the world's or the church's state, and how it goeth with all others. (2) And therefore that all Christians must love their brethren and neighbours, as themselves, and must abhor the sin of schism, much more of malignant enmity, envy, and persecution, and must be so far from disowning the prayers of other Christians, on pretence of their various circumstances and imperfections, and from separating in heart from them on any account, for which God will not reject them, as that they must never put up a prayer or praise, but as in concord with all the Christians on earth, desiring a part in the prayers of all, and offering up hearty prayers for all: the imperfections of all men's prayers we must disown, and most of our own; but not for that disown their prayers, nor our own. They that hate, or persecute, or separate from God's children, for not praying in their mode, or by their book, or in the words that they write down for them, or for not worshipping God with their forms, ceremonies, or rites, or that silence Christ's ministers, and scatter the flocks, and confound kingdoms, that they may be lords of God's heritage, and have all men sing in their commanded tune, or worship God in their unnecessary, commanded mode, do condemn themselves when they say "our Father." And to repeat the Lord's prayer many times in their liturgy, while they are tormenting his children in their prisons and inquisitions, is to worship God by repeating their own condemnation.

Q. 13. It seems this particle "our," and "us," is of great importance.

A. The Lord's prayer is the summary and rule of man's love and just desires; it directeth him what to will, ask, and seek. And therefore must needs contain that duty of love which is the heart of the new creature, and the fulfilling of the law: the will is the man; the love is the will. What man wills and loves, that he is in God's account, or that he shall attain. And therefore the love of God, as God, and of the church, as the church, and of saints, as saints, of friends, as friends, and of neighbours, as neighbours, and of men, (though enemies and sinners,) as men, must needs be the very spring of acceptable prayer, as well as the love of ourselves, as ourselves. And to pray without this love, is to offer God a carrion for sacrifice, or a lifeless sort of service. And love to all makes all men's mercies and comforts to be ours, to our great joy, and that we may be thankful for all.

25

"Hallowed be Thy Name"

Q. 1. Why is this made the first petition in our prayers?

A. Because it containeth the highest notion of our ultimate end; and so must be the very top or chief of our desires.

Q. 2. What is meant by God's Name here?

A. The proper notices or appearances of God to man; and God himself as so notified and appearing to us. So that here we must see that we separate not any of these three: (1) The objective signs, whether words or works, by which God is known to us.

(2) The inward conceptions of God received by these signs.

(3) God himself so notified and conceived of.

Q. 3. And what is the hallowing of God's Name?

A. To use it holily: that is, in that manner as is proper to God as he is God, infinitely above all the creatures, that is sanctified which is appropriated to God by separation from all common use.

Q. 4. What doth this hallowing particularly include?

A. (1) That we know God, what he is. (2) That our souls be accordingly affected towards him. (3) That our lives and actions be accordingly managed. (4) And that the signs which notify God to us be accordingly reverenced, and used to these holy ends.

Q. 5. Tell us now, particularly, what these signs or names of God are, and how each of them is to be hallowed?

A. God's name is either, (1) His sensible or intelligible works objectively considered. (2) Or those words which signify God, or any thing proper to God. And the inward light or conception, or notice of God, in the mind. And all these must be sanctified.

Q. 6. What Are God's works which must be so sanctified, as notifying God?

A. All that are within the reach of our knowledge. But especially those which he hath designed most notably for this use, and most legibly, as it were written his name or perfections upon.[1]

Q. 7. Which are those?

A. (1) The glorious, wonderful frame of heaven and earth.

(2) The wonderful work of man's redemption by Jesus Christ.

(3) The planting of his nature, image, and kingdom in man, by his Spirit.

(4) The marvellous providence exercised for the world, the church, and each of ourselves, notifying the disposal and government of God.

(5) The glory of the heavenly society, known by faith, and hoped for.

Q. 8. How must the first, God's creation, be sanctified.

A. When we look on, or think of the incomprehensible glory of the sun, it's wonderful greatness, motion, light, and quickening heat;[2] of the multitude and magnitude of the glorious stairs, of the vast heavenly regions, the incomprehensible invisible spirits or powers that actuate and rule them all; when we come downward and think of the air and its inhabitants, and of this earth, a vast body to us, but as one inch or point in the whole creation; of the many nations, animals, plants of wonderful variety, the terrible depths of the ocean, and its numerous inhabitants, &c. All these must be to us but as the glass which showeth somewhat of the face of God, or as the letters of this great book, of which God is the sense; or as the actions of a living body by which the invisible soul is known. And as we study arts for our corporeal use, we must study the whole world, even the works of God, to this purposed use, that we may see, love, reverence, and admire God in all: and this is the only true philosophy, astronomy, cosmography, &c.

Q. 9. What is the sin which is contrary to this?

---

[1] Exod 9:16; Ps 8:1.

[2] Ps 19:1, &c.; Rom 1:19, 20.

A. Profaneness; that is, using God's name as a common thing:[3] and, in this instance, to study philosophy, astronomy, or any science, or any creature whatsoever, only to know the thing itself, to delight our mind with the creature knowledge, and to be able to talk as knowing men, or the better to serve our worldly ends, and not to know and glorify God, is to profane the works of God. And, alas, then, how common is profaneness in the world!

Q. 10. What is it to sanctify God's Name as in our redemption?

A. Redemption is such a wonderful work of God, to make him known to sinners for their sanctification and salvation, as no tongue of man can fully utter. To think of God, the Eternal Word, first undertaking man's redemption, and then taking the nature of man, dwelling in so mean a tabernacle, fulfilling all righteousness for us, teaching man the knowledge of God, and bringing life and immortality to light, dying for us as a malefactor, to save us from the curse, rising the third day, commissioning his apostles, undertaking to build his church on a rock, which the gates of hell should not prevail against; ascending up to heaven, sending down the wonderful and sanctifying Spirit, interceding for us, and reigning over all; who receiveth faithful souls to himself, and will raise our bodies, and judge the world. Can all this be believed and thought of, without admiring the manifold wisdom, the inconceivable love and mercy, the holiness and justice of God? This must be the daily study of believers.

Q. 11. How is this Name of God profaned?

A. When this wonderful work of man's redemption is not believed, but taken by infidels to be but a deceit: or, when it is heard but as a common history, and affecteth not the hearer with admiration, thankfulness, desire, and submission to Christ; when men live as if they had no great obligation to Christ, or no great need of him.

Q. 12. How is God's Name, as our Sanctifier, to be hallowed?

A. Therein he cometh near us, even into us, with illuminating, quickening, comforting grace, renewing us to his nature, will, and image, marking us for his own, and maintaining the cause of Christ against his

---

[3] Ps 14:1, 2; 50:21, and 78:19; Titus 1:16.

enemies; and therefore must, in this, be specially notified, honoured, obediently observed, and thankfully and joyfully admired.

Q. 13. But how can they honour God's Spirit and grace, who have it not; or they that have so little as not well to discern it?

A. The least prevailing sincere holiness hath a special excellency, turning the soul from the world to God, and may be perceived in holy desires after him, and sincere endeavours to obey him; and the beauty of holiness in others may be perceived by them that have little or none themselves, if they be not grown to malignant enmity. You may see, by the common desire of mankind to be esteemed wise and good, and their impatience of being thought and called foolish, ungodly, or bad men, that even corrupted nature hath a radicated testimony in itself for goodness and against evil.

Q. 14. Who be they that profane this Name of God?

A. Those that see no great need of the Spirit of holiness, or have no desire after it, but think that nature and art may serve the turn without it. Those that think that there is no great difference between man and man, but what their bodily temperature and their education maketh, and that it is but fanatic delusion, or hypocrisy, to pretend to the Spirit. Those that hate or deride the name of spirituality and holiness, and those that resist the Holy Ghost.

Q. 15. How is God known and honoured in his providence?

A. By his providence he so governeth all the world, and particularly all the affairs of men, as shows us his omnipotence, his omniscience, and his goodness and love, ordering them all to his holy end, even the pleasing of his good-will in their perfection.[4]

Q. 16. How can we see this while the world lieth in madness, unbelief, and wickedness, and the worst are greatest, and contention, and confusion, and bloody wars, do make the earth a kind of hell, and the wise, holy, and just, are despised, hated, and destroyed?

A. (1) Wisdom, and holiness, and justice, are conspicuous and honourable by the odiousness of their contraries, which, though they fight against them, and seem to prevail, do but exercise them to their

---

[4] Mal 2:2.

increase and greater glory: and all the faithful are secured and purified, and prepared for felicity, by the love and providence of God.

(2) And as the heavens are not all stars, but spangled with stars, nor the stars all suns, nor beasts and vermin men, nor the earth and stones are gold and diamonds, nor is the darkness light, the winter summer, or sickness health, or death life; and yet the wonderful variety and vicissitude contributeth to the perfection of the universe, as the variety of parts to the perfection of the body; so God maketh use even of men's sin and folly, and of all the mad confusions and cruelties of the world, to that perfect order and harmony, which he that accomplisheth them doth well know, though we perceive it not, because we neither see the whole, nor the end, but only the little particles and the beginnings of God's unsearchable works.

(3) And this dark and wicked world is but a little spot of God's vast creation, and seemeth to be the lowest next to hell, while the lucid, glorious, heavenly regions are incomprehensibly great, and no doubt possessed by inhabitants suitable to so glorious a place: and as it is not either the gallows or the prison that is a dishonour to the kingly government, so neither is hell, or the sins on earth, a dishonour to the government of God.

(4) And as every man is nearest to himself, it is the duty of us all carefully to record all the mercies and special providences of God to ourselves, that we may know his government and him, and use the remembrance of them to his glory.

Q. 17. How is the heavenly glory as a Name of God to us that see it not?

A. We see vast lucid bodies and regions above us; and, by the help of things seen, we may conceive of things unseen, and by divine revelation we may certainly know them. We have in the gospel, as it were, a map of heaven, in its description, and a title to it in the promises, and a notifying earnest and foretaste in our souls, so far as we are sanctified believers.

Q. 18. How must we hallow this Name of God?

A. (1) Firmly believing the heavenly glory, not only as it shall be our own inheritance, but as it is now the most glorious and perfect part of God's creation, where myriads of angels and glorious spirits, in perfect happiness, love, and joy, are glorifying their most glorious Creator; and as the saints with Christ, their most glorious Head, shall for ever make up that glorious society, and the universe itself be seen by us in that glorious perfection, in which the perfection of the Creator will appear.

(2) And in the constant delightful contemplation of this supernal glorious world, by heavenly affections and conversation, keeping our minds above while our bodies are here below, and looking beyond this prison of flesh, with desire and hope. As heaven is the state and place where God shineth to the understanding creature in the greatest glory, and where he is best known, so it is this heavenly glory, seen to us by faith, which is the most glorious of all the names or notices of God to be hallowed by us.

Q. 19. What is the profaning of this Name of God?

A. The minding only of earthly and fleshly things, and not, believing, considering, or admiring the heavenly glory: not loving and praising God for it, nor desiring and seeking to enjoy it.

Q. 20. So much of God's works which make him known. Next, tell us what you mean by the words which you call his Name?

A. (1) All the sacred Scripture, as it maketh known God to us, by history, precepts, promises, or penal threats; with all God's instituted means of worship. (2) More especially the descriptions of God by his attributes. (3) And, more especially, his proper name, God, Jehovah, &c.[5]

Q. 21. I will not ask you what his attributes are, because you have told us that before; but how is this Name of God to be hallowed?

A. When the soul is affected with that admiration, reverence, love, trust, and submission to God, which the meaning of these names bespeaks: and when the manner of our using them expresseth such affections, especially in public praises with the churches.[6]

Q. 22. How is this Name of God profaned?

A. When it is used lightly, falsely, irreverently, without the aforesaid holy regard and affections.

Q. 23. What is that which you call 'God's Name imprinted on man's mind?'

---

[5] Exod 3:15, and 6:3; Ps 83:18; Acts 9:15.

[6] Exod 34:5-7, and 33:19; Acts 21:13; 1 Tim 6:1; Titus 2:5; Rom 2:21; Ps 22:22; Heb 2:12; Neh 9:5; Ps 50:23, and 66:2; Mich. 4:5; Rev 11:15.

A. God made man very good at first, and that was in his own image; and so much of this is either left by the interposition of grace in lapsed nature, or by common grace restored to it, as that all men, till utterly debauched, would fain be accounted good, pious, virtuous, and just, and hate the imputation of wickedness, dishonesty, and badness; and on the regenerate the divine nature is so renewed, as that their inclination is towards God, and "holiness to the Lord" is written on all their faculties; and the Spirit of God moveth on the soul, to actuate all his graces, and to plead for God and our Redeemer, and bring him to our remembrance, to our affections, and to subject us wholly to his will and love. And thus, as the law was written in stone, as to the letter, which is written only on tender, fleshy hearts, as to the spirit and holy effect and disposition; so the Name of God, which is in the Bible in the letter, is, by the same Spirit, imprinted on believers' hearts, that is, they have the knowledge, faith, fear, and love of God.[7]

Q. 24. How must we hallow this inward Name of God?

A. (1) By reverencing and loving God, that is, God's image and operations in us; not only God as glorified in heaven, but God, as dwelling by grace in holy souls, must be remembered and reverenced by us. (2) By living as in habitual communion and conversation with that God who dwelleth in us, and who hath made us his habitation by the Spirit. (3) And by readily obeying the moving operations of the Spirit of God.

And to contemn or resist these inward ideas, inclinations, and motions, is to profane the Name of God.

Q. 25. But what is all this to the sanctifying of God himself?

A. The signs are but for him that is signified. It is God himself that is to be admired, loved, and honoured, as notified to us by these signs or Name, otherwise we make idols of them. In a word, God must be esteemed, reverenced, loved, trusted, and delighted in, transcendently as God, with affections proper to himself; and this is to sanctify him, by advancing him in our heart, in his prerogative above all creatures; and all creatures must be used respectively to this holy end, and especially those ordinances and names which are especially separated to

---

[7] Ps 29:2, and 48:10.

this use: and nothing must be used as common and unclean, especially in his worship and religious acts.[8]

---

[8] Acts 1:15, and 4:12; Rev 3:4, and 11:13; Joel 2:23; Deut 28:58; Exod 33:19, and 34:5–7; 1 Kgs 5:3, 5; Lev 10:3; Num 20:12, 13.

26

"Thy Kingdom Come"

Q. 1. Why is this made the second petition?

A. To tell us, that it must be the second thing in our desires. We are to begin at that which is highest, most excellent, and ultimate in our intentions, and that is, God's glory shining in all his works, and seen, admired, honoured, and praised by man, which is the hallowing of his Name, and the holy exalting him in our thoughts, affections, words, and actions, above all creatures. And we are next to desire that in which God's glory most eminently shineth, and that is his kingdom of grace and glory.

Q. 2. What is here meant by the kingdom of God?

A. It is not that kingdom which he hath over angels, and the innumerable glorious spirits of the heavenly regions, for these are much unknown to us, and we know not that there is any rebellion among them which needeth a restoration. But man, by sin, is fallen into rebellion, and under the condemnation due to rebels:[1] and by Christ, the reconciling Mediator, they are to be restored to their subjection to God, and so to his protection, blessing, and reward. And because they are sinners, corrupt and guilty, they cannot be subjects as under the primitive law of innocency: and therefore God hath delivered them to the Mediator, or his Vicegerent, to be governed under a law of healing grace,

---

[1] Col 1:13; Matt 12:28, and 21:31, 43; Mark 1:45; 4:26, 30; 12:34; 10:14, 15, 23, and 15:43.

and so brought on to perfect glory. So that the kingdom of God now is his reign over fallen man by Christ the Mediator, begun on earth by recovering grace, and perfected in heavenly glory.[2]

Q. 3. But the Scriptures sometimes speak of the kingdom of God as come already when Christ came, or when he rose and ascended to his glory, and sometimes as if it were yet to come at the great resurrection day.

A. In the first case, the meaning is, that the King of the church is come, and hath established his law of grace, and commissioned his officers, and sent forth his Spirit, and so the kingdom of healing grace is come: but in the second case, the meaning is, that all that glorious perfection which this grace doth tend to, which will be the glory of the church, the glory of Christ therein, and the glorification of God's love, is yet to come.

Q. 4. What is it, then, which we here desire?

A. That God will enlarge and carry on the kingdom of grace in the world, and bear down all that rebels, and hindereth it, and particularly in ourselves, and that he would hasten the kingdom of glory.

Q. 5. Who is it, then, that is the King of this kingdom?

A. God, as the absolute supreme, and Jesus Christ, the Son of God and man, as the supreme Vicegerent and Administrator.[3]

Q. 6. Who are the subjects of this kingdom?

A. There are three sorts of subjects. (1) Subjects only as to obligation,[4] and so those without the church are rebellious, obliged subjects. (2) Subjects by mere profession, and so all baptised, professing Christians, though hypocrites, are the church visible, and his professed subjects. (3) Subjects by sincere heart consent, and so all such are his subjects as make up the church mystical, and shall be saved. So that the kingdom of God is a word which is sometimes of a larger signification than the church, and sometimes, in a narrower sense, is the same. Christ is Head over all things to the church. (Eph. 1:23.)

Q. 7. What are the acts of Christ's kingly government?

---

[2] Luke 7:28; 8:1, 10; 10:9; 11:20; 13:18, 20, 28, 29; 16:16; 17:21, and 18:3, 17, 29.

[3] Rev 1:9; Luke 9:27; 14:15; 22:16, 18, and 23:51.

[4] Acts 14:22; Gal 5:21; Eph 5:5; 2 Thess 5; Rev 12:10; Matt 16:28; 2 Tim 4:1; 1 Thess 2:12.

A. Law-making, judging according to that law, and executing that judgment.[5]

Q. 8. What laws hath Christ made, and what doth he rule by?

A. (1) He taketh the law of nature now as his own, as far as it belongeth to sinful mankind. And, (2) He expoundeth the darker passages of that law. And, (3) He maketh new laws, proper to the church since his incarnation.

Q. 9. Are there any new laws of nature since the fall?

A. There are new obligations and duties arising from our changed state: it was no duty to the innocent to repent of sin, and seek out for recovery, and beg forgiveness, but nature bindeth sinners not yet under the final sentence to all this.

Q. 10. What new laws hath Christ made?

A. Some proper to church officers, and some common to all.

Q. 11. What are his laws about church officers?

A. First, He chose himself the first chief officers, and he gave them their commission,[6] describing their work and office, and he authorised them to gather and form particular churches, and their fixed officers or pastors, and necessary orders, and gave them the extraordinary conduct and seal of his Spirit, that their determinations might be the infallible significations of his will, and his recorded law to his universal church to the end of the world, his Spirit being the Perfecter of his laws and government.

Q. 12. How shall we be sure that his apostles, by the Spirit, were authorised to give laws to all future generations?

A. (1) Because he gave them such commission, to teach men all that he commanded.[7] (2) And promised them his Spirit to lead them into all truth, and bring all things to their remembrance, and to tell them what to say and do. And, (3) Because he performed this promise, in sending them that extraordinary measure of the Spirit. And, (4) They spake as

---

[5] Heb 7:12; Isa 2:3; 8:16, 20; 13:4, 21, and 2:4; Mic. 4:2; Rom 3:27, and 8:2, 4; Gal 6:2; Isa 2:7; Jer 31:33; Heb 8:10, 10:16.

[6] Matt 28:19; Eph 4:6–9, 16; Acts 14:23, and 15.

[7] Acts 10:42, and 13:47; Matt 28:19, 21; John 14:16, 17, 26; 15:26, 27, and 16:7, 13–15; Rev 2:7, 11, 16, 17, 29, and 3:6, 13, 22; 1 Pet 1:11.

from Christ, and in his name, and as by his Spirit. And, (5) They sealed all by the manifestation of that Spirit, in its holy and miraculous, manifold operation.[8]

Q. 13. Have not bishops and councils the same power now?

A. No: to be the instruments of divine legislation, and make laws which God will call his laws, is a special, prophetical power and office, such as Moses had in making the Jewish laws, which none had that came after him. But when prophetical revelation hath made the law, the following officers have nothing to do, but (1) To preserve that law. (2) And to expound it and apply it, and guide the people by it, and themselves obey it. (3) And to determine undetermined, mutable circumstances. As the Jewish priests and Levites were not to make another law, but to preserve, expound, and rule by Moses's law, so the ordinary ministers, bishops, or councils are to do as to the laws of God, sufficiently made by Christ, and the Spirit in his apostles.[9]

Q. 14. What are the new laws which he hath made for all?

A. The covenant of grace in the last edition is his law,[10] by which he obligeth men to repent and believe in him as incarnate, crucified, and ascended, and interceding and reigning in heaven, and as one that will judge the world at the resurrection: as one that pardoneth sin by his sacrifice and merit, and sanctifieth believers by his Spirit, and to believe in God as thus reconciled by him, and in the Holy Ghost as thus given by him. And he promiseth pardon, grace, and glory, to all true believers, and threateneth damnation to impenitent unbelievers. And he commandeth all believers to devote themselves thus to God the Father, the Son, and the Holy Ghost, by a solemn vow in baptism, and live in the communion of saints, in his church and holy worship, and the frequent celebration of the memorial of his death in the sacrament of his body and blood, especially on the first day of the week, which he hath separated to that holy commemoration and communion by his

---

[8]   Acts 2:4; Gal 1, and 2; Mark 13:11; Luke 12:12; Isa 33:22.

[9]   Jas 4:12; Acts 1:5, 8; 2:4, 33, and 15:28; 1 Cor 2:13; 2 Pet 1:21; 1 Cor 7:25; Acts 1:2; 1 Cor 14:37; Col 2:22; Matt 15:9.

[10]   John 1:9–11, and 3:16; Matt 28:19, 20; 1 Cor 15:3–5, and 11:28; Acts 13:47, and 10:42; John 14:21.

resurrection, and the sending of his Spirit, and by his apostles. And he hath commanded all his disciples to live in unity, love, and beneficence, taking up the cross, and following him in holiness and patience, in hope of everlasting life.[11]

Q. 15. But some say that Christ was only a teacher, and not a awgiver.

A. His name is King of kings, and Lord of lords, and all power in heaven and earth is given him, and all things put into his hands; the government is laid on his shoulders, and the Father (without him) judgeth no man, but hath committed all judgment to the Son. For this end he died, rose, and revived, that he might be Lord of the dead and of the living; he is at God's right hand, above all principalities and powers, and every name, being head over all things to the church.[12]

Q. 16. May not this signify only his kingdom as he is God, or that which he shall have hereafter only at the resurrection?

A. (1) It expressly speaketh of his power as God, and man the Redeemer. (2) And he made his law in this life, though the chief and glorious part of his judgment and execution be hereafter. How else should men here keep his law, and hereafter be judged according to it?

He that denieth Christ to be the Lawgiver, denieth him to be King; and he that denieth him to be King, denieth him to be Christ, and is no Christian.

Q. 17. Hath Christ any vicegerent, or universal governor, under him on earth?

A. No: it is his prerogative to be the universal Governor: for no mortal man is capable of it; as no one monarch is capable of the civil government of all the earth, nor was ever so mad as to pretend to it; much less is any one capable of being an universal church teacher, priest, and governor over all the earth; when he cannot so much as know it, or send to all, or have access into the contending kingdoms of the world: to pretend to this is mad usurpation.[13]

---

[11] John 13:34; Rev 1; Matt 28:18; John 13:2; 17:3, and 5:22; Isa 9:6; Rom 14:9; Col 1; Heb 1, and 7.

[12] Eph 1:23; Luke 17:9, 10, and 19:15, &c.; Rev 22:14; 1 John 2:4; 3:24,and 5:3.

[13] 1 Cor 12:5, 18, 20, 27–29, and 3:4–6, 11, 22, 23; Matt 23:7, 8, 10, 11; Eph 4:5, 7, 8, 11–16, and 5:23, 24; Matt 18:1, 4; Mark 9:34; Luke 9:46, and 22:24–26; 1 Pet 5:2–4.

Q. 18. But had not Peter monarchical government of all the church on earth in his time?

A. No: he was governor of none of the eleven apostles, nor of Paul; nor ever exercised any such government: no, nor it seems, so much as presided at their meeting. (Acts 15)

Q. 19. But is not a general council the universal governor?

A. No: (1) Else the church would be no church, when there is no general council, for want of its unifying government. And (2) There, indeed, never was a general council of all the christian world: but they were called by the Roman emperors, and were called general as to that empire (as the subscriptions yet show). (3) And there never can be an universal council: it were madness and wickedness to attempt it: to send for the aged bishops from all nations of the christian world, (when none is empowered to determine whither or when,) even from the countries of Turks, and other infidels, or princes in war with one another, that will not permit them: and what room shall hold them, and what one language can they all speak? And how few will live to return home with the decrees? And will not the country where they meet, by nearness, have more voices than all the rest? And what is all this to do? To condemn Christ, as not having made laws sufficient for the universal part of government, but leave such a burden on incapable men: and to tell the church that christian religion is a mutable, growing thing, and can never be known to attain its ripeness, but, by new laws, must be made still bigger, and another thing.

Q. 20. But the bishops of the world may meet by their delegates?

A. Those delegates must come from the same countries and distance: and how shall the whole world know that they are truly chosen? And that all the choosers have trusted them with their judgments, consciences, and salvation, and will stand to what they do?

Q. 21. But if the universal church be divided into patriarchates, and chief seats, those can govern the whole church when there is no general council: even by their communicatory letters?

A. (1) And who shall divide the world into those chief seats, and determine which shall be chief in all the kingdoms of infidels, and christian kings, in the world? and which shall be chief when they differ among themselves? How many patriarchs shall there be, and where? There were never twelve pretenders to succeed the twelve apostles:

the Roman empire had three first, and five after, within itself: but that was by human institution, and over one empire, and that is now down; and those five seats have many hundred years been separated, and condemning one another: so far are they from being one unifying aristocracy to govern all the world: and if they were so, then Europe is schismatical, that now differs from the major vote of those patriarchs.

Q. 22. But did not the apostles, as one college, govern the whole church?

A. (1) I proved to you before, that the Holy Ghost was given the apostles to perfect universal legislation, as Christ's agent and advocate, and that in this they have no successors. (2) And it was easy for them to exercise acts of judicial determination over such as were among them, and near them when the church was small. (3) And yet we read not that ever they did this in a general council, or by the authority of a major vote. For that meeting in Acts 15 was no general council, and the elders and brethren joined with them that belonged to Jerusalem: and they were all by the same Spirit of the same mind, and none dissenters. Every single apostle had the spirit of infallibility for his proper work: and they had an indefinite charge of the whole church, and in their several circuits exercised it. Paul could by the Spirit deliver a law of Christ to the world, without taking it from the other apostles. (Gal. 2) The apostles were foundation-stones, but Christ only was the head corner-stone. They never set up a judicial government of all the churches under themselves as a constitutive, unifying aristocracy, by whose major vote all must be governed. When they had finished the work of universal legislation, and settled doctrine and order, for which they stayed together at Jerusalem, they dispersed themselves over the world; and we never find that they judicially governed the churches, either in synods or by letters, by a major vote, but settled guides in every church as God by Moses, did priests and Levites, that had no legislative power.[14]

Q. 23. But hath not Christ his subordinate, official governors?

A. Yes: magistrates by the sword, and pastors by the word and keys. These are rulers in their several circuits, as all the judges and justices, and schoolmasters of England are under the king: but he that should say that all these judges and justices are one sovereign aristocracy, to make

---

[14] Eph 2:20; 1 Cor 3:11; 1:11, 12, and 3:21, 22; Gal 2:9; 2 Cor 11:5, and 12:11.

laws and judge by them by vote, (as one person political, though many natural,) would give them part of the supreme power, and not only the official: all the pastors in the world guide all the churches in the world by parts, and in their several province and not as one politic person.

Q. 24. But how is the universal church visible, if it have no visible, unifying head and government under Christ?

A. It is visible, (1) In that the members and their profession are visible. (2) And Christ's laws are visible, by which he ruleth them. (3) And their particular pastors are visible in their places. (4) And Christ was visible on earth, and is now visible in his court in heaven, and will visibly judge the world ere long: and God hath made the church no farther visible, nor can man do it.

Q. 25. But should not the whole church be one?

A. It is one: it is one body of Christ, having one God, and one Head, or Lord, one faith, one baptism, one Spirit, one hope of glory.[15]

Q. 26. But should they not do all that they do in unity and concord?

A. Yes, as far as they are capable. Not by feigning a new, universal, legislative power in man, or making an universal head under Christ, but by agreeing all in the faith and laws that Christ hath left us: and synods may well be used to maintain such union as far as capacity reacheth, and the case requireth. But an universal synod, and a partial or national, a governing synod, and a synod for concord of governors, differ as much as doth a monarch, or governing senate, over all the world, and a diet, or an assembly of Christian princes, met for mutual help and concord, in the conjunction of their strength and councils.

Q. 27. What is the pastoral power of the church keys?

A. It is the power of making Christians by the[16] preaching of the gospel, and receiving them so made into communion of Christ and his church, by baptism, and feeding and guiding them by the same word, and communicating the sacrament of Christ's body and blood in his name, declaring pardon and life to the penitent, and the contrary to the impenitent, and applying this to the particular persons of their

---

[15] Eph 4:1, 3, 6, 7, 14–16; 1 Cor 12.

[16] Matt 28:19, 20; 1 Thess 5:12, 13; Heb 13:17, 24; Titus 3:10, 11, and 1:13; 1 Pet 5:1–5; 1 Tim 3:5; Isa 22:22; Luke 11:52; Rev 3:7, and 1:18; Matt 16:19.

own charge on just occasion, and so being the stated judges who shall by them be received to church communion, or be rejected, and this as a presage of Christ's future judgment.

Q. 28. But have not pastors or bishops, a power of constraint by the sword, that is, by corporeal punishments, or mulcts?

A. No: that is proper to magistrates, parents, and masters, in their several places. Christ hath forbidden it to pastors, (Luke 22,) and appointed them another kind of work.[17]

Q. 29. But if bishops judge that civil magistrates are bound to destroy or punish heretics, schismatics, or sinners, are not such magistrates thereby bound to do it?

A. They are bound to do their duty whoever is their monitor: but if prelates bid them sin, they sin by obeying them. Nor may a magistrate punish a man merely because bishops judge him punishable, without trying the cause themselves.

Q. 30. But if it be not of divine institution that all the church on earth should have one governing, unifying head, (monarchical or aristo-cratical,) is it not meet as suited to human prudence?

A. Christ is the builder of his own church or house, and hath not left it to the wit or will of man[18] to make him a vicegerent, or an unifying head or ruler of his whole church, that is, to set up an usurper against him under his own name, which is naturally incapable of the office.

Q. 31. But sure unity is so excellent that we may conceive God delighteth in all that promoteth it?

A. Yes: and therefore he would not leave the terms of unity to the device of men, in which they will never be of a mind; nor would he have usurpers divide his church, by imposing impossible terms of unity. Must God needs make one civil monarch, or senate, to be the unifying governor of all the earth, as one kingdom, because he is a lover of unity? The world is politically unified by one God and Sovereign Redeemer, as this kingdom is by one king, and not by one civil, human, supreme ruler, personal or collective: men so mad as to dream of one unifying,

---

[17] Luke 22:24–26; 1 Pet 5:3, 4; 2 Tim 2:24; Titus 1:7.

[18] Heb 3:2, 5, 6.

church-governing monarch, or aristocracy, are the unfittest of all men to pretend to such government.[19]

Q. 32. At least, should we not extend this unifying government as far as we can, even to Europe, if not to all the world?

A. (1) Try first one unifying, civil government (monarchical or aristocratical) for Europe, and call princes schismatics (as these men do us) for refusing to obey it, and try the success. (2) And who shall make this European church sovereign? and by what authority; and limit his kingdom? (3) And what it all this to do? To make better laws than Christ's? When were any so mad as to say, that all Europe must have one sovereign person, or college of physicans, schoolmasters, philosophers, or lawyers, to avoid schism among them? (4) Is not agreement by voluntary consent a better way to keep civil and ecclesiastical unity in Europe, than to have one ruling king, senate, or synod, over all? Councils are for voluntary concord, and not the sovereign rectors of their brethren.

Q. 33. But are not national churches necessary?

A. No doubt but Christ would have nations discipled, baptised, and obey him: and kings to govern them as Christian nations, and all men should endeavour that whole nations may be Christians, and the kingdoms of the world be voluntarily the kingdoms of Christ. But no man can be a Christian against his will: nor hath Christ ordained that each kingdom shall have one sacerdotal head, monarchical or aristocratical. But princes, pastors, and people, must promote love, unity, and concord in their several places.

Q. 34. So much for God's public kingdom on earth: but is there not also a kingdom of God in every Christian's soul?

A. One man's soul is not fitly called a kingdom; but Christ, as King, doth govern every faithful soul.

Q. 35. What is the government of each believer?

A. It is Christ's ruling us by the laws which he hath made for all his church, proclaimed, and explained, and applied by his ministers, and imprinted on the heart by his Holy Spirit, and judging accordingly.

Q. 36. What is the kingdom of glory?

---

[19] John 17:22–24; Eph 4:3–5, 7, 8, 16.

A. It hath two degrees: (1) The glorious reign of our glorified Redeemer over this world, and over the heavenly city of God before its perfection; which began at the time of Christ's ascension, (his resurrection being the proem,) and endeth at the resurrection. (2) The perfect kingdom of glory, when all the elect shall be perfected with Christ, and his work of redemption finished, which begins at the resurrection, and shall never end.

Q. 37. What will be the state of that glorious kingdom?

A. It containeth the full collection of all God's elect, who shall be perfected in soul and body, and employed in the perfect obedience, love, and praise of God, in perfect love and communion with each other, and all the blessed angels, and their glorified Redeemer; and this is in the sight of his glory, and the glory of God, and in the continual, joyful sense of his love and essential, infinite perfection. All imperfection, sin, temptation, and suffering, being for ever ceased.

Q. 38. But some think this kingdom will be begun on earth a thousand years before the general resurrection; and some think that after the resurrection it will be on earth.[20]

A. This very prayer puts us in hope that there are yet better things on earth to be expected than the Church hath yet enjoyed. For when Christ bids us pray that "his Name may be hallowed, his kingdom come, and his will done on earth, as it is done in heaven," we may well hope that some such thing will be granted; for he hath promised to give us whatever we ask, according to his will, in the name of Christ: and he hath not bid us pray in vain.

But whether there shall be a resurrection of the martyrs a thousand years before the general resurrection, or whether there shall be only a reformation by a holy magistracy and ministry, and how far Christ will manifest himself on earth, I confess are questions too hard for me to determine: he that is truly devoted to Christ, shall have his part in his kingdom, though much be now unknown to him, of the time, place, and manner.[21]

---

[20] Rev 20:2; Pet. 12:13.

[21] Matt 6:20, 21; 5:12, and 19:21; Eph 1:3; 2 Tim 4:18; Heb 11:16, and 12:22, 23; 1 Cor 15:49; Phil 3:20; Col 1:6; 1 Pet 1:4; Heb 10:34.

And as to the glory after the general resurrection, certainly it will be heavenly, for we shall be with Christ, and like to the angels. And the new Jerusalem, being the universality of the blessed now with Christ, may well be said to come down from heaven, in that he will bring all the blessed with him, and, in the air with them, will judge the world: but whether only a new generation shall inhabit the new earth, and the glorified rule them as angels now do; or whether heaven and earth shall be laid common together, or earth made as glorious as heaven, I know not.

But the perfect knowledge of God's kingdom is proper to them that enjoy it: therefore even we who know it but imperfectly, must daily pray that it may come, that we may perfectly know it when we are perfected therein.

27

"Thy Will Be Done on Earth, As it Is in Heaven"

Q. 1. Why is this made the third petition?

A. Because it must be the third in our desires. I told you this prayer in perfect method beginneth at that which must be the first in our intention; and that is, God's interest as above our own, which is consistent, and expressed in these three gradations. (1) The highest notion of it is, the hallowing and glorifying of his name, and resplendent perfections. (2) The second is, that in which this is chiefliest notified to man, which it his kingdom. (3) The third is the effect of this kingdom in the fulfilling his will.

Q. 2. What will of God is it that is here meant?

A. His governing and beneficent will, expressed in his laws and promises, concerning man's duty, and God's rewards and gifts.[1]

Q. 3. Is not the will of his absolute dominion expressed in the course of natural motion, here included?

A. It may be included as the supposed matter of our approbation and praise: and as God's will is taken for the effects and signs of his will, we may and must desire that he will continue the course of nature, sun, and moon, and stars, earth, winds, and water, &c., till the time of their dissolution, and mankind on earth: for these are supposed as the subject, or accidents, of government. But the thing specially meant is God's

---

[1] John 4:34, and 6:39, 40.

governing will, that is, that his laws may be obeyed, and his promises all performed.[2]

Q. 4. But will not God's will be always done, whether we pray or not?

A. (1) All shall be done which God hath undertaken or decreed to do himself, and not laid the event on the will of man: his absolute will of events is still fulfilled. But man doth not always do God's will; that is, he doth not keep God's laws, or do the duty which God commandeth him, and therefore doth not obtain the rewards or gifts which were but conditionally promised. (2) And even some things, decreed absolutely by God, must be prayed for by man: for he decreeth the means as well as the end: and prayer is a means which his commands and promises oblige us to.

Q. 5. Why is it added, "as it is done in heaven?"

A. To mind us, (1) Of the perfect, holy obedience of the glorified. (2) And that we must make that our pattern, and the end of our desires. (3) And to keep up our hopes and desires of that glorious perfection; and strive to do God's will understandingly, sincerely, fully, readily, delightfully, without unwillingness, unweariedly, concordantly, without division, in perfect love to God, his work, and one another; for so his will is done in heaven. And these holy heavenly desires are the earnest of our heavenly possession.

Q. 6. What is it that we pray against in this petition?

A. Against all sin, as a transgression of his law, and against all distrust of his promises, and discontentedness with his disposals; and so against every will that is contrary to the will of God.

Q. 7. What will is it that is contrary to the will of God?

A. (1) The will of Satan, who hateth God and holiness, and man, and willeth sin, confusion, calamity, and who is obeyed by all the ungodly world.

(2) The will of all blind, unbelieving, wicked men, especially tyrants, who fill the world with sin, and blood, and misery, that they may have their wills without control or bounds.

---

[2] Acts 21:14; Matt 7:21; 12:50; 18:14, and 21:31.

(3) Especially our own sinful self-willedness, and rebellious and disobedient dispositions.[3]

Q. 8. What mean you by our self-willedness?

A. Man was made by the creating will of God, to obey the governing will of God, and rest and rejoice in the disposing, rewarding, and beneficent will of God, and his essential love and goodness: by sin he is fallen from God's will to himself and his own will, and would fain have all events in the power and disposal of his own will, and fain be ruled by his own will, and have no restraints, and would rest in himself, and the fulfilling of his will: yea, he would have all persons and things in the world to depend on his will, fulfil and please it, and ascribe unto it; and so would be the idol of himself, and of the world; and all the wickedness, and stir, and cruelty of the world is but that every selfish man may have his will.

Q. 9. What then is the full meaning of this petition?

A. That earth, which is grown so like to hell by doing the will of Satan, of tyrants, and of self-willed, fleshly, wicked men, may be made liker unto heaven, by a full compliance of the will of man with the will of God, depending submissively on his disposing will, obeying his commanding will, fearing his punishing will, trusting, rejoicing, and resting in his rewarding and beneficent will, and renouncing all that is against it.[4]

Q. 10. But if it be God's will to punish, pain, and kill us, how can we will this when it is evil to us; and we cannot will evil?

A. As God himself doth antecedently or primarily will that which is good without any evil to his subjects, and but consequently will their punishment on supposition of their wilful sin, and this but as the work of his holiness and justice for good; so he would have us to will first and absolutely, next his own glory and kingdom, our own holiness and happiness, and not our misery; but to submit to his just punishments, with a will that loveth (not the hurt, but) the final good effect, and the wisdom, holiness, and justice of our chastiser. Which well consisteth with begging mercy, pardon, and deliverance.[5]

---

[3] John 1:13; 5:36, and 6:38; Luke 22:42; Acts 13:22; Heb 13:21.

[4] Luke 12:47; John 7:17; Acts 22:14; Rom 2:18; Col 1:9.

[5] Matt 26:42.

Q. 11. But is not heaven too high a pattern for our desires?

A. No: though we have much duty on earth which belongs not to them in heaven; and they have much which belongeth not to us, yet we must desire to obey God fully in our duty, as they do in theirs; and desiring and seeking heavenly perfection is our sincerity on earth.[6]

Q. 12. What sin doth this clause specially condemn?

A. (1) Unbelief of the heavenly perfection. (2) Fleshly lusts and wills, and a worldly mind. (3) The ungodliness of them that would not have God have all our heart, and love, and service, but think it is too much preciseness, or more ado than needs, and give him but the leavings of the flesh.

---

[6] Ps 4:80.

28

"Give Us this Day Our Daily Bread"

Q. 1. Why is this the fourth petition?

A. I told you that the Lord's prayer hath two parts: the first is for our end, according to the order of intention, beginning at the top, and descending: the second part is about the means, according to the order of execution, beginning at the bottom, and ascending to the top. Now this is the first petition of the second part, because our substance and being is supposed to all accidents; and if God continue not our humanity, we cannot be capable of his blessings.[1]

Q. 2. What is meant by bread?

A. All things necessary to sustain our natures, in a fitness for our duty and our comforts.[2]

Q. 3. It seems, then, that we pray that we may not want, or be sick, or die, when God hath foretold us the contrary events?

A. We justly show that our nature is against death, and sickness, and wants, as being natural evils: and God giveth us a discerning judgment to know natural good from evil, and an appetite to desire it accordingly: but because natural good and evil are to be estimated, as they tend to spiritual and everlasting good or evil, God giveth us reason and faith to order our desires accordingly: and because our knowledge of this is

---

[1] Luke 12:23.

[2] Jer 45:5; 1 Tim 4:8; 2 Pet 1:3.

imperfect, (when and how far natural good or evil conduceth to spiritual and eternal) it is still supposed that we make not ourselves but God the Judge; and so desire life, health, and food, and natural supplies, with submission to his will, for time and measure, they being but means to higher things.

Q. 4. Why ask we for no more than bread?

A. To show that corporeal things are not our treasure, nor to be desired for any thing but their proper use; and to renounce all covetous desires of superfluity, or provision, for our inordinate, fleshly lusts.[3]

Q. 5. Some say that by bread is meant Jesus Christ, because there is no petition that mentioneth him?

A. Every part of the Lord's prayer includeth Christ: it is by him that God is our Father; by him that the holy name of God is hallowed: it is his kingdom that we pray may come; it is his law or will which we pray may be done: it is he that purchased our right to the creature, and redeemed nature: it is by him that we must have the forgiveness of sin, and by his grace that we are delivered from temptations, and all evil, &c.

Q. 6. Why ask we bread of God, as the Giver?

A. To signify that we are and have nothing but by his gift, and must live in continual dependence on his will, and begging, receiving, and thanksgiving are our work.[4]

Q. 7. But do we not get it by our labour, and the gift of men?

A. Our labours are vain without God's blessing, and men are but God's messengers to carry us his gifts.[5]

Q. 8. What need we labour, if God give us all?

A. God giveth his blessings to meet receivers, and in the use of his appointed means: he that will not both beg and labour as God requireth him, is unmeet to receive his gifts.[6]

Q. 9. Why do we ask bread from day to day?

A. To show that we are not the keepers of ourselves, or our stock of provisions, but, as children, live upon our Father's daily allowance,

---

[3] 2 Cor 9:10; 1 Tim 6:8.

[4] Matt 6:25–27, &c.; Ps 136:25.

[5] Ps 127:1; Matt 4:3, 4.

[6] 2 Cor 9:10; Prov 12:11, and 28:19; Ps 8:13; Prov 31:27.

and continually look to him for all, and daily renew our thanks for all, and study the daily improvement of his maintenance in our duties.[7]

Q. 10. But when a man hath riches for many years, what need he ask daily for what he hath?

A. He hath no assurance of his life or wealth an hour, nor of the blessing of it, but by God's gift.[8]

Q. 11. Why say we "give us" rather than "give me?"

A. To exercise our common love to one another, and renounce that narrow selfishness which confineth men's regard and desires to themselves; and to show that we come not to God merely in a single capacity, but as members of the world, as men, and members of Christ's body or church, as Christians; and that in the communion of saints, as we show our charity to one another, so we have a part in the prayers of all.

Q. 12. May we then pray against poverty, and sickness, and hurt?

A. Yes, as aforesaid, so far as they are hurtful to our natures, and thereby to our souls, and the ends of life.[9]

Q. 13. Doth not naming bread before forgiveness and grace, show that we must first and most desire it?

A. We before expressed our highest desire of God's glory, kingdom, and will; and as to our own interests, all the three last petitions go together, and are inseparable; but the first is the lowest, though it be first in place. Nature sustained is the first, but it will be but the subject of sin and misery without pardon and holiness: I told you that the three last petitions go according to the order of execution, from the lowest to the highest step. God's kingdom and righteousness must be first sought in order of estimation and intention, by all that will attain them.

Q. 14. But if God give us more than bread, even plenty for our delight, as well as necessaries, may we not use it accordingly?

A. Things are necessary to our well-being, that are not necessary to our being. We may ask and thankfully use all that, by strengthening and comforting nature, tendeth to fit the spirit for the joyful service of

---

[7] Matt 6:24, &c.; Luke 12:19–21.

[8] 1 Cor12.

[9] Prov 30:8.

God, and to be helpful to others. But we must neither ask nor use any thing for the service of our lusts, or tempting, unprofitable pleasure. Q. 15. What if God deny us necessaries, and a Christian should be put to beg, or be famished, how then doth God make good his word, that he will give us whatever we ask through Christ, and that other things shall be added, if we seek first his kingdom and righteousness, and that godliness hath the promise of this life and that to come?[10]

A. Remember, as aforesaid, (1) That the things of this life are promised and given, not as our happiness, but as means to better. (2) And that we are promised no more than we are fit to receive and use. (3) And that God is the highest Judge, both how far outward things would help or hinder us; and how far we are fit to receive them. Therefore, if he deny them, he certainly knoweth that either we are unmeet for them, or they for us.[11]

Q. 16. When should a man say, he hath enough?

A. When having God's grace and favour, he hath so much of corporeal things, as will best further his holiness and salvation, and as it pleaseth the will of God that he should have.

Q. 17. May not a man desire God to bless his labours, and to be rich?

A. A man is bound to labour in a lawful calling that is able, and to desire and beg God's blessing on it: but he must not desire riches, or plenty for itself, or for fleshly lusts; nor be over importunate with God to make him his steward for others.[12]

Q. 18. What if God give us riches, or more than we need ourselves?

A. We must believe that he maketh us his stewards, to do all the good with it that we can to all, but specially to the household of faith. But to spend no more in sinful lust and pleasure than if we were poor.[13]

Q. 19. What doth daily bread oblige us to?

A. Daily service, and daily love, and thankfulness to God, and to mind the end for which it is given, to be always ready, at the end of a day, to give up our account, and end our journey.

---

[10] Matt 6:19, 20, 33; John 5:40.

[11] 1 Sam 2:29–31; Jas 4:3; Phil 4:10, 11; Heb 13:5.

[12] Prov 10:22; Ps 129:8; Deut 28:8, 9, &c., and 33:11.

[13] 1 Pet 4:10; Luke 12:21, 24.

Q. 20. What is the sin and danger of the love of riches?

A. The love of money, or riches, is but the fruit of the love of the flesh, whose lust would never want provision, but it is the root of a thousand farther evils. As it shows a wretched soul, that doth not truly believe and trust God for this life, much less for a better, but is worldly, and sensual, and idolatrous, so it leadeth a man from God, holiness, heaven, yea and from common honesty, to all iniquity: a worldling, and lover of riches, is false to his own soul, to God, and never to be much trusted.[14]

---

[14] Luke 18:23, 24; Mark 10:24; 1 Tim 6:10; 1 John 2:15.

29

"And Forgive us our Trespasses, as We Forgive them that Trespass against Us." (Or, as we Forgive our Debtors.)

Q. 1. Why is this made the fifth petition, or the second of the first part?

A. Because it is for the second thing we personally need. Our lives and natural being supposed, we next need deliverance from the guilt and punishment which we have contracted. Else to be men, will be worse to us than to be toads or serpents.[1]

Q. 2. What doth this petition imply?

A. (1) That we are all sinners, and have deserved punishment, and are already fallen under some degree of it.[2]

(2) That God hath given us a Saviour who died for our sins and is our Ransom and Advocate with the Father.

And, (3) That God is a gracious, pardoning God, and dealeth not with us on the terms of rigorous justice according to the law of innocency, but hath brought us under the Redeemer's covenant of grace, which giveth pardon to all penitent believers: so that sin is both pardonable, and conditionally pardoned to us all.[3]

---

[1] Ps 32:1–3.

[2] Rom 3, throughout.

[3] 1 John 2:1; John 3:16; Ps 130:4; Acts 5:31; 13:38, and 26:18.

Q. 3. What, then, are the presupposed things which we pray not for?

A. (1) We pray not that God may be good and love itself, or a merciful God, for this is presupposed. (2) We pray not that he would send a Saviour into the world, to fulfil all righteousness, and die for sin, and that his merit and sacrifice may procure a conditional, universal pardon and gift of life, viz., to all that will repent and believe, for all this is done already.[4]

Q. 4. Is it to the Father only, or also to the Son, that we pray for pardon?

A. To the Father primarily, and to the Son as glorified, for now the Father without him judgeth no man, but hath committed all judgment to the Son. (John 5:22.) But when Christ made this prayer, he was not yet glorified, nor in full possession of his power.

Q. 5. What sin is it whose forgiveness we pray for?

A. All sin, upon the conditions of pardon made by Christ; that is, for the pardon of all sin to true penitent believers. Therefore we pray not for any pardon of the final non-performance of the condition, that is, to finally impenitent unbelievers.[5]

Q. 6. Sin cannot hurt God; what need, then, is there of forgiveness?

A. It can wrong him by breaking his laws, and rejecting his moral government, though it hurt him not: and he will right himself.

Q. 7. What is forgiving sin?

A. It is by tender mercy, on the account of Christ's merits, satisfaction, and intercession, to forgive the guilt of sin, as it maketh us the due subjects of punishment, and to forgive the punishment of sin, as due by that guilt and the law of God, so as not to inflict it on us.[6]

Q. 8. What punishment doth God forgive?

A. Not all: for the first sentence of corporeal punishment and death is inflicted. But he forgiveth the everlasting punishment to all true believers, and so much of the temporal, both corporeal and spiritual, as his grace doth fit us to receive the pardon of: and so he turneth temporal, correcting punishments to our good.[7]

---

[4] Luke 23:34; Matt 9:6, and 12:31, 32.

[5] Luke 15:3, 5.

[6] Col 2:18; Jas 5:15; Matt 18:27, 32; Luke 7:43, 43; Rom 1:21, 23; 1 Cor 15:22.

[7] Ps 103:2; 1 John 1:9.

Q. 9. Doth he not pardon all sin at once, at our conversion?

A. Yes, all that is past, for no other is sin. But not by a perfect pardon.

Q. 10. Why must we pray for pardon, then, every day?

A. (1) Because the pardon of old sins is but begun, and not fully perfect till all the punishment be ceased: and that is not till all sin and unholiness, and all the evil effects of sin, be ceased. No, nor till the day of resurrection and judgment have overcome the last enemy, death, and finally justified us.[8]

(2) Because we daily renew our sins by omission and commission, and though the foundation of our pardon be laid in our regeneration, that it may be actual and full for following sins, we must have renewed repentance, faith, and prayer.

Q. 11. God is not changeable, to forgive to-day what he forgave not yesterday, what, then, is his forgiving sin?

A. The unchangeable God changeth the case of man. And, (1) By his law of grace, forgiveth penitent believers who were unpardoned in their impenitence and unbelief. And, (2) By his executive providence he taketh off and preventeth punishments both of sense and loss, and so forgiveth.

Q. 12. How can we pray for pardon to others, when we know not whether they be penitent believers, capable of pardon?

A. (1) We pray as members of Christ's body for ourselves, and all that are his members, that is, penitent believers.

(2) For others, we pray that God would give them faith, repentance, and forgiveness. As Christ prayed, "Father, forgive them, for they know not what they do;" that is, qualify them for pardon, and then pardon them; or give them repentance and forgiveness.

Q. 13. Why say we, "As we forgive them that trespass against us?"

A. To signify that we have this necessary qualification for forgiveness; God will not forgive us fully till we can forgive others; and to signify our obligation to forgive; and as an argument to God to forgive us, when he hath given us hearts to forgive others. But not as the measure

---

[8] 1 Cor 11:30–32; Matt 18:27; Ps 85:2–4, &c.; Luke 6:37; Jas 5:15.

of God's forgiving us, for he forgiveth us more freely and fully than we can forgive others.[9]

Q. 14. Are we bound absolutely to forgive all men?

A. No; but as they are capable of it. (1) We have no power to forgive wrongs against God. (2) Nor against our superiors, or other men, or the commonwealth, or church, further than God authoriseth any man by office. (3) A magistrate must forgive sins, as to corporeal punishment, no further than God alloweth him, and as will stand with the true design of government, and the common good. And a pastor no further than will stand with the good of the church; and a father no further than will stand with the good of the family: and so of others. (4) An enemy that remaineth such, and is wicked, must be forgiven by private men, so far as that we must desire and endeavour their good, and seek no revenge; but not so far as to be trusted as a familiar, or bosom friend. (5) A friend that offended, and returneth to his fidelity, must be forgiven and trusted as a friend, according to the evidence of his repentance and sincerity, and no further.

The rest about forgiveness is opened in the exposition of that article in the creed, "The forgiveness of sins." Still remembering that all forgiveness is by God's mercy, through Christ's merits, sacrifice, and intercession.

---

[9] Matt 6:14, 15, and 18:35; Mark 11:25, 26.

30

"And Lead us Not into Temptation, but Deliver us from Evil"

Q. 1. Why is this made the sixth petition?

A. Because it is the next in order to the attainment of our ultimate end. Our natures being maintained, and our sin and punishment forgiven, we next need deliverance from all evils that we are in danger of for the time to come, and then we are saved.

Q. 2. What is meant by temptation?

A. Any such trial as may overcome us or hurt us, whether by Satan, or by the strong allurements of the world and flesh, or by persecutions or other heavy sufferings, which may draw us to sin, or make us miserable.[1]

Q. 3. Doth God lead any into temptation?

A. (1) God placeth us in this world in the midst of trials, making it our duty to resist and overcome. (2) God permitteth the devil, by his suggestions, and by the world and flesh, to tempt us. (3) God trieth us himself by manifold afflictions, and by permitting the temptations of persecutors and oppressors.[2]

Q. 4. Why will God do and permit all this?

---

[1] 2 Pet 2:9; Rev 3:10; Matt 26:41; Luke 8:18.

[2] 1 Pet 1:6; Matt 4; Gen 22:1.

A. It is a question unmeet for man to put. It is but to ask him why he would make a rank of reasonable creatures below confirmed angels? And why he would make man with free-will? And why he would not give us the prize without the race, and the crown without the warfare and victory? And you may next ask why he did not make every star a sun, and every man an angel, and every beast and vermin a man, and every stone a diamond.[3]

Q. 5. Doth God tempt a man to sin?

A. No: sin is none of God's end or desire. Satan tempts men to sin, and God tempteth men to try them whether they will sin, or be faithful to him, to exercise their grace and victory.[4]

Q. 6. Is it not all that we need that God lead us not into temptation?

A. The meaning is, that God, who overruleth all things, will neither himself try us beyond the strength which he will give as, nor permit Satan, men, or flesh, to overtempt us unto sin.

Q. 7. But are we not sure that this life will be a life of trial and temptation, and that we must pass through many tribulations?

A. Yes: but we pray that they may not be too strong and prevalent to overcome us, when we should overcome.[5]

Q. 8. What be the temptations of Satan which we pray against?

A. They are of so many sorts that I must not here be so large as to number them. You may see a great number with the remedies, named in my Christian Directory; but, in general, they are such by which he deceives the understanding; perverteth the will, and corrupteth our practice; and this is about our state of soul, or about our particular actions, to draw us to sins of commission, or of omission, against God, ourselves, or others. The particulars are innumerable.[6]

Q. 9. What is the evil that we pray to be delivered from?

A. The evil of sin and misery, and from Satan, ourselves, and men, and all hurtful creatures, as the causes.

---

[3] Jas 1:2, 12; 1 Cor 10:13.

[4] Jas 1:13–15.

[5] 1 Cor 10:13; Heb 2:18.

[6] 1 Thess 3:5; Eph 6:11.

Q. 10. What is the reason of the connexion of the two parts of this petition, "Lead us not into temptation, but deliver us from evil?"

A. Temptation is the means of sin, and sin the cause of misery. And
they that would be delivered from sin, must pray and labour to be delivered from temptation; and they that would be delivered from misery,
must be delivered from sin.[7]

Q. 11. May not a tempted man be delivered from sin?

A. Yes, when the temptation is not chosen by him, and cannot be
avoided, and when it is not too strong for him, grace assisting him.

Q. 12. What duty doth this petition oblige us to, and what sin doth
it reprehend?

A. (1) It binds us to a continual, humble sense of our own corrupt
dispositions, apt to yield to temptations, and of our danger, and of the
evil of sin; and it condemneth the unhumbled that know not, or fear
not, their pravity, or danger.

(2) It binds us all to fly from temptations, as far as lawfully we can;
and condemneth them that rush fearlessly on them, yea, that tempt
themselves and others. The best man is not safe that will not avoid such
temptations as are suited to his corrupt nature, when he may. While
the bait is still near unto his senses, he is in continual danger.[8]

(3) It binds us to feel the need of grace and God's deliverance, and
not to trust our corrupted nature, and insufficient strength.

Q. 13. How doth God deliver us from evil?

A. (1) By keeping us from over-strong temptation. (2) By his assisting grace. (3) By restraining Satan and wicked men, and all things that
would hurt us, and, by his merciful providence, directing, preserving,
and delivering us from sin and misery.

---

[7] Prov 4:14, 15; 1 Thess 5:22; Prov 7:23; 2 Tim 3:7, and 6:9; 1 Cor 7:35; Matt 5:29–31.

[8] Matt 18:6–9, and 16:22–24; 1 Cor 8:9; Rom 14:13; Rev 2:14.

31

"For Thine is the Kingdom, the Power, and the Glory, for ever.—Amen"

Q. 1. What is the meaning of this conclusion, and its scope?

A. It is a form of praise to God, and helps to our belief of the hearing of our prayers.

Q. 2. Why is it put last?

A. Because the praise of God is the highest step next heaven.[1]

Q. 3. What is the meaning of kingdom, power, and glory here?

A. By kingdom is meant that it belongeth only to God to rule all the creatures, dispose of all things; and by power is meant that, by his infinite perfection and sufficiency, he can do it; and therefore can give us all that we want, and deliver us from all that we fear. And by glory is meant that all things shall be ordered so as the glory of all his own perfections shall finally and everlastingly shine forth in all, and his glory be the end of all for ever.[2]

Q. 4. What is the reason of the order of these three here?

A. I told you that the last part ascendeth from the lowest to the highest step. God's actual government is the cause of our deliverances and welfare. God's power and perfection is it that manageth that government.

---

[1] Ps 119:164; 71:6, 8, and 78:13.

[2] Ps 103, 19, and 145:12; Dan 4:3, 34; Matt 16:28; Ps 145:11, 13; Heb 1:8; Luke 2:14; Matt 16:27, and 24:30; Acts 12:23.

God's glory shining in the perfected form of the universe, and especially in heaven, is the ultimate end of all.

Q. 5. But it seems there is no confession of sin, or thanksgiving, in this form of prayer?

A. It is the symbol or directory to the will's desire: and when we know what we should desire, it is implied that we know what we want, and what we should bewail, and what we should be thankful for: and praise includeth our thanksgiving.[3]

Q. 6. Why say we, "for ever?"

A. For our comfort and God's honour, expressing the everlastingness of his kingdom, power, and glory.

Q. 7. Why say we "Amen?"

A. To express both our desire, and our faith and hope, that God will hear the desires which his Spirit giveth us through the mediation of Jesus Christ.

---

[3] Ps 145:4, 10; 148; 66:2, 8; 147:1, 7, and 106:2, 47; Phil 4:20; Jude 25: Rev 5:13, and 7:12; Rom 11:36, and 16:27.

PART IV

32

Of the Ten Commandments in General

Q. 1. Are the ten commandments a law to Christians, or are they abrogated with the rest of Moses's law?

A. The ten commandments are considerable in three states: (1) As part of the primitive law of nature. (2) As the law given by Moses, for the peculiar government of the Jews' commonwealth. (3) As the law of Jesus Christ.[1]

(1) The law of nature is not abrogate, though the terms of life and death are not the same as under the law of innocency.[2]

(2) The law of Moses to the Jews as such, never bound all other nations, nor now bindeth us, but is dead and done away. (2 Cor. 3:7, 9, 10, 11; Rom. 2:12, and 14:15; 3:19, and 7:1-3; Heb. 7:12; 1 Cor. 9:21.) But seeing it was God that was the Author of that law, and by it expressly told the Jews what the law of nature is, we are all bound still to take those two tables to be God's own transcript of his law of nature, and so are, by consequence, bound by them still. If God give a law to some one man, as that which belongs to the nature of all men, though it bind us not as a law to that man, it binds as God's exposition of the law of nature when notified to us.

(3) As the law of Christ, it binds all Christians.

---

[1] Exod 20, and 34:28; Deut 5.

[2] Luke 1:6.

Q. 2. How are the ten commandments the law of Christ?

A. (1) Nature itself, and lapsed mankind, is delivered up to Christ as Redeemer, to be used in the government of his kingdom. And so the law of nature is become his law.[3]

(2) It was Christ, as God Redeemer, that gave the law of Moses, and as it is a transcript of the common law of nature, he doth not revoke it, but suppose it.

(3) Christ hath repeated and owned the matter of it in the gospel, and made it his command to his disciples.

Q. 3. Is there nothing in the ten commandments proper to the Israelites?

A. Yes: (1) The preface, "hear, O Israel;" and "that brought thee out of the land of Egypt, out of the house of bondage." (2) The stating the seventh day for the Sabbath, and the strict ceremonial rest commanded as part of the sanctifying of it.

Q. 4. How doth Christ and his Apostles contract all the law into that of love?

A. God, who as absolute Lord, owneth, moveth, and disposeth of all,[4] doth, as sovereign Ruler, give us laws, and execute them, and, as Lord and Benefactor, giveth us all, and is the most amiable object and end of all: so that as to love and give is more than to command, so to be loved is more than as a commander to be obeyed: but ever includeth it, though it be eminently, in its nature, above it. So that, (1) Objectively, love to God, ourselves, and others, in that measure that it is exercised wisely, is obedience eminently, and somewhat higher. (2) And love, as the principle in man, is the most powerful cause of obedience, supposing the reverence of authority and the fear of punishment, but is somewhat more excellent than they. A parent's love to a child makes him more constant and full in all that he can do for him,[5] than the commands of a king alone will do. In that measure that you love. God, you will heartily and delightfully do all your duty to him; and so far as

---

[3] Matt 5:18, 19, and 24:40; Mark 10:19, and 12:29, 30; John 14:21. 1 Cor 7:19, and 14:37; 1 John 51:4; 3:24, and 5:3; John 15:12.

[4] Mark 12:30, 33; Rom 13:9, 10; 1 Cor 13; Titus 3:4; Rom 5:5, and 8:39; 1 John 4:16; John 14:23.

[5] 2 Tim 1:7; 1 John 4:17, 18; Gal 5:14.

you love parents or neighbours, you will gladly promote their honour, safety, chastity, estates, rights, and all that, is theirs, and hate all that is against their good. And as parents will feed their children, though no fear of punishment should move them; so we shall be above the great necessity of the fear of punishment, so far as God and goodness is our delight.[6]

Q. 5. How should one know the meaning and extent of the commandments?

A. The words do plainly signify the sense: and according to the reasonable use of words, God's laws being perfect, must be thus expounded.[7]

(1) The commanding of duty includeth the forbidding of the contrary.

(2) Under general commands and prohibitions, the kinds and particulars are included which the general word extendeth to.

(3) When one particular sin is forbidden, or duty commanded, all the branches of it, and all of the same kind and reason are forbidden or commanded.

(4) Where the end is commanded or forbidden, it is implied that so are the true means as such.

(5) Every commandment extendeth to the whole man, to our bodies and all the members, and to the soul and all its faculties respectively.

(6) Commands bind us not to be always doing the thing commanded. Duties be not at all times duty: but prohibitions bind us at all times from every sin, when it is indeed a sin.

(7) Every command implieth some reward or benefit to the obedient, and every sin of omission or commission is supposed to deserve punishment, though it be not named.[8]

(8) Every command supposeth the thing commanded to be no natural impossibility, (as to see spirits, or to dive into the heart of the earth, to know that which is not intelligible, &c.) But it doth not suppose us to be morally or holily disposed to keep it, or to be able to change our corrupt natures without God's grace.

---

[6]   Ps 1:2, 3, and 119.

[7]   Matt 8:12; Phil 2:14, and 3:8; 1 Cor 14:26.

[8]   Mal 3:14.

(9) So every command supposeth us to have that natural freedom of will which is a self-determining power, not necessitated or forced to sin by any: but not to have a will that is free from vicious inclinations: nor from under God's disposing power.[9]

(10) The breach of the same laws may have several sorts of punishment: by parents, by masters, by magistrates, by the church; on body, on name, on soul, in this life, by God; and, finally, heavier punishment in the life to come.

(11) The sins here forbidden, are not unpardonable, but by Christ's merits, sacrifice and intercession, are forgiven to all true penitent, converted believers.

---

[9]   Rom 8:6–8; Jer 13:23.

33

Of the Preface to the Decalogue

Q. 1. What are the parts of the Decalogue?

A. (1) The constitution of the kingdom of God over men described. And, (2) The administration, or governing laws of his kingdom.

Q. 2. What words express the constitution of God's kingdom?

A. "I am the Lord thy God, which brought thee out of the land of Egypt, out of the house of bondage."

Q. 3. What is the constitution here expressed?

A. (1) God, the Sovereign. (2) Man, the subject. (3) The work of God, which was the next foundation or reason of the mutual relation between God and man, as here intended.[1]

Q. 4. What is included in the first part, of God's sovereignty?

A. (1) That there is a God, and but one God in this special sense. (2) That the God of Israel is this one true God, who maketh these laws. (3) That we must all obey him.

Q. 5. What is God, and what doth that word here mean?

A. This was largely opened in the beginning. Briefly to be God is to be a Spirit, infinite in being, in vital power, knowledge, and goodness, of whom, as the efficient cause, and through whom as the Governor, and to whom as the end, are all things else; related to us as our Creator, and

---

[1] Mal 2:10; Matt 19:17; Mark 12:32; Jer 7:23; John 20:17.

as our absolute Owner, our supreme Ruler, and our greatest Benefactor, Friend, and Father.

Q. 6. What words mention man as the subject of the kingdom?

A. "Hear, O Israel," and "Thy God that brought thee," &c.

Q. 7. What relations are here included?

A. That we, being God's creatures and redeemed ones, are, (1) His own. (2) His subjects, to be ruled by him. (3) His poor beneficiaries, that have all from him, and owe him all our love.

Q. 8. What do the words signify "that brought thee out of the land of Egypt?"

A. That besides the right of creation, God hath a second right to us as our Redeemer. The deliverance from Egypt was that typical one that founded the relation between him and the commonwealth of Israel. But as the Decalogue is the law of Christ, the meaning is, 'I am the Lord thy God, who redeemed thee from sin and misery by Jesus Christ.'[2] So that this signifieth the nearest right and reason of this relation between God and man. He giveth us his law now, not only as our Creator, but as our Redeemer, and as such we must be his willing subjects, and obey him.

Q. 9. Are all men subjects of God's kingdom?

A. (1) All are subjects as to right and obligation.

(2) All that profess subjection as professed consenters.

(3) And all true hearty consenters are his sincere subjects, that shall be saved.

God the Creator and Redeemer hath the right of sovereignty over all the world, whether they consent or not. But they shall not have the blessing of faithful subjects without their own true consent, nor of visible church members without professed consent. But antecedent mercies he giveth to all.

Q. 10. Why is this description of God's sovereignty, and man's subjection, and the ground of it, set before the commandments?

A. Because, (1) Faith must go before obedience.[3] He that will come to God and obey him, must believe that God is God, and that he is the rewarder of them that diligently seek him. (Heb. 11:6.) And he that will

---

[2] Matt 28:19; Rom 14:9; John 5:22, and 17:2, 3.

[3] John 17:3, and 14:1, 2; Gal 3:16; Josh 24:18; John 20:28.

obey him as our Redeemer, must believe that we are redeemed by Jesus Christ, and that he is our Lord and King. (2) And relations go before the duties of relation: and our consent foundeth the mutual relation. The nature and form of obedience is, to obey another's commanding will, because he is our rightful Governor. No man can obey him formally whom he taketh not for his Ruler. And subjection, or consent to be governed, is virtually all obedience.

Q. 11. But what, if men never hear of the Redeemer, may they not obey God's law of nature?

A. They may know that they are sinners, and that the sin of an immortal soul deserveth endless punishment: and they may find, by experience, that God useth them not as they deserve, but giveth many mercies to those that deserve nothing but misery; and that he obligeth them to use some means in hope for their recovery, and so that he governeth them by a law (or on terms) of mercy: and being under the first edition of the law of grace, though they know not the second, they ought to keep that law which they are under, and they shall be judged by it.

Q. 12. How, then, doth the christian church, as Christ's kingdom, differ from the world without, if they be any of his kingdom too?

A. As all the world was under that common law of grace which was made for them to Adam and Noah, and yet Abraham and his seed were only chosen out of all the world as a peculiar, holy nation to God, and were under a law and covenant of peculiarity, which belonged only unto them; so, though Christ hath not revoked those common mercies given to all by the first edition of the law of grace, nor left the world ungoverned and lawless, yet he hath given to Christians a more excellent covenant of peculiarity than he gave the natural seed of Abraham, and hath elected them out of the world to himself, as a "chosen generation, a royal priesthood, an holy nation, a peculiar people, to show forth the praises of him that hath called them out of darkness into his marvellous light." (1 Pet. 2:9.)

Q. 13. It seems, then, we must take great heed that we make not Christ's kingdom either less or greater than it is?

A. To make it greater than it is, by equalling those without the church, or church hypocrites with the sincere, doth dishonour God's holiness, and the wonderful design of Christ in man's redemption, and the grace of the Spirit, and the church of God, and obscureth the doctrine of

election, and God's peculiar love, and tendeth to the discomfort of the
faithful, and even to infidelity.

And to make Christ's kingdom less than it is, by denying the first
edition of the law of grace made to all, and the common mercies given
to all, antecedently to their rejection of them, doth obscure and wrong
the glory of God's love to man, and deny his common grace and law,
and feigneth the world either to be under no law of God, or else to be
all bound to be perfectly innocent at the time when they are guilty,[4]
and either not bound at all to hope and seek for salvation, or else to
seek it on the condition of being innocent, when they know that it is
impossible, they being already guilty: and it maketh the world, like
the devils, almost shut up in despair; and it leaveth them as guiltless
of all sin against grace, and the law of grace, as if they had none such:
and it contradicteth the judgment of Abraham, the father of the faithful, who saw Christ's day; for he thought that even the wicked city of
Sodom had fifty persons so righteous as that God should have spared
the rest for their sakes, to say nothing of Job, Nineveh, &c. In a word,
the ungrounded extenuating the grace of Christ, and the love of God,
hardeneth infidels, and tempteth Christians to perplexing thoughts of
the gospel, and of the infinite goodness of God, and maketh it more difficult than indeed it is, to see his amiableness, and consequently to glorify and love him, as the essential love, whose goodness is equal to his
greatness. It is Satan, as angel of light and righteousness, who, pretending the defence of God's special love to his elect, denieth his common
mercies to mankind, to dishonour God's love, and strengthen our own
temptations against the joyful love of God.

Q. 14. Is government and subjection all that is here included?

A. No: God's kingdom is a paternal kingdom, ruling children by love,
that he may make them happy. "I am the Lord thy God," signifieth 'I am
thy greatest Benefactor, thy Father,' who gave thee all the good thou
hast, and will give to my obedient children grace and glory, and all that
they can reasonably desire, and will protect them from all their enemies, and supply their wants, and deliver them from evil, and will be

---

[4] Ps 145:9.

for ever their sun and shield, their reward and joy, and better to them, than man in flesh can now conceive, even love itself.[5]

---

[5] 2 Cor 6:16, 18; John 20:28.

34

Of the First Commandment

Q. 1. What are the words of the first commandment?

A. "Thou shalt have no other gods before me." Exod. 20:3.[1]

Q. 2. What is the meaning of this commandment?

A. It implieth a command that we do all that is due to God; which is due to God from reasonable creatures, made by him, and freely redeemed by him from sin and misery. And it forbiddeth us to think there is any other God, or to give to any other that which properly belongs to him.[2]

Q. 3. Doth not the Scripture call idols and magistrates gods?

A. Yes; but only in an equivocal, improper sense: idols are called gods, as so reputed falsely by idolaters; and magistrates only as men's governors under God.[3]

Q. 4. What are the duties which we owe to God alone?

A. (1) That our understandings know, believe, and esteem him as God. (2) That our wills love him, and cleave to him as God. (3) That we practically obey and serve him as God.

---

[1] Deut 5:7, and 10:21.

[2] Deut 26:17; Dan 6:16; Isa 16:19.

[3] Gal 4:8; 1 Cor 8:5; John 10:34, 35; 17:3, and 14:1, 2; Deut 10:12, and 30:16, 20; Mich. 6:8.

Q. 5. When doth the understanding know, believe, and esteem him as God?

A. No creature can know God with an adequate, comprehensive knowledge: but we must in our measure know, believe and esteem him to be the only infinite, eternal, self-sufficient Spirit, vital Power, Understanding, and Will, or most perfect Life, Light, and Love; Father, Son, and Holy Ghost, of whom, and through whom, and to whom, are all things; our absolute Owner, Ruler, and Father, reconciled by Christ; our Maker, our Redeemer, and Sanctifier.

Q. 6. When doth man's will love and cleave to him as God?

A. When the understanding believing him to be best, even infinitely good in himself, and best to all the world, and best to us, we love him as such; though not yet in due perfection, yet sincerely above all other things.[4]

Q. 7. How can we love God above all, when we never saw him, and can have no idea or formal conception of him in our minds?

A. Though he be invisible, and we have no corporeal idea of him, nor no adequate or just formal conception of him, yet he is the most noble object of our understanding and love, as the sun is of our sight, though we comprehend it not. We are not without such an idea or conception of God, as is better than all other knowledge, and is the beginning of eternal life, and is true in its kind, though very imperfect.[5]

Q. How can you know him that is no object of sense?

A. He is the object of our understanding; we know in ourselves what it is to know and to will, though these acts are not the objects of sense, (unless you will call the very acts of knowing and willing, an eminent, internal sensation of themselves.) And by this we know what it is to have the power of understanding and willing: and so what it is to be an invisible substance with such power. And as we have this true idea or conception of a soul, so have we more easily of him, who is more than a soul to the whole world.[6]

Q. 9. How doth the true love of God work here in the flesh?

---

[4] Ps 73:25; 119:68, and 114:9; Matt 22:37.

[5] Matt 19:17; John 17:3.

[6] 1 Cor 13:12, and 2:3, 8, 18; John 1:18.

A. As we here know God, so we love him: as we know him not in the manner as we do things sensible, so we love him not in that sort of sensible appetite, as we do things sensible immediately. But as we know him as revealed in the glass of his works, natural and gracious, and in his word, so we love him as known by such revelation.[7]

Q. 10. Do not all men love God, who believe that there is a God, when nature teacheth men to love goodness as such, and all that believe that there is a God, believe that he is the best of beings?

A. Wicked men know not truly the goodness of God, and so what God is indeed. To know this proposition, 'God is most good,' is but to know words and a logical, general notion: as if a man should know and say that light is good, who never had sight; or sweetness is good, who never tasted it. Every wicked man is predominantly a lover of fleshly pleasure, and therefore no lover, but a hater, of all the parts and acts of divine government and holiness, which are contrary to it, and would deprive him of it. So that there is somewhat of God that a wicked man doth love, that is, his being, his work of creation, and bounty to the world, and to him in those natural good things which he can value: but he loveth not, but hateth God as the holy governor of the world and him, and the enemy of his forbidden pleasure and desires.[8]

Q. 11. What be the certain signs, then, of true love to God?

A. (1) A true love to his government, and laws, and holy word; and that as it is his, and holy; and this so effectual, as that we unfeignedly desire to obey that word as the rule of our faith, and life, and hope; and desire to fulfil his commanding will.

(2) A true love to the actions which God commandeth (though flesh will have some degree of backwardness).

(3) A true love to those that are likest God in wisdom, holiness, and doing good; and such a love to them as is above the love of worldly riches, honour, and pleasure; so that it will enable us to do them good, though by our suffering or loss in a lower matter, when God calls us to it. For if we see our brother have need, and shut up the bowels of compassion,

---

[7] Exod 20:6; Prov 8:17, 21; John 14:15, 23.

[8] 1 Cor 8:3; Rom 8:28; Jas 1:12, and 2:5; 1 John 3:16, 17; 4:20, and 5:3, and 14:23; Jude 21.

so that we cannot find in our hearts to relieve his necessities by the loss of our unnecessary superfluities, how dwelleth the love of God in us?

(4) True love to God doth love itself. It is a great sign of it, when we so much love to love God as that we are gladder when we feel it in us, than for any worldly vanity; and when we take the mutual love of God and the soul to be so good and joyful a state as that we truly desire it as our felicity, and best in heaven to be perfectly loved of God, and perfectly to love him, joyfully express it in his everlasting praises. To long to love God as the best condition for us, is a sign that we truly love him.[9]

Q. 12. But must not all the affections be set on God as well as love?

A. All the rest are but several ways of loving or willing good, and of nilling, or hating and avoiding, evil.

(1) It is love that desireth after God, and his grace and glory. (2) It is love that hopeth for him. (3) It is love that rejoiceth in him, and is pleased when we and others please him, and when his love is poured out on the sons of men, and truth, peace, and holiness prosper in the world. (4) It is love that maketh us sorrowful, that we can please him no more, nor more enjoy him; and that maketh us grieved that we can no more know him, love him, and delight in him, and that we have so much sin within us to displease him, and hinder our communion of love with him. (5) And love will make us fearful of displeasing him, and losing the said communion of love. (6) And it will make us more angry with ourselves, when we have most by sin displeased God, and angry with others that offend him.[10]

Q. 13. What is the practical duty properly due from us to God?

A. To obey him in doing all that he commandeth us, either in his holy worship, or for ourselves, or for our neighbour; and this by an absolute, universal obedience, in sincere desire and endeavour, as to a Sovereign of greatest authority, and a Father of greatest love, whose laws and works are all most wise, and just, and good.[11]

---

[9] Luke 11:42; John 5:42, and 15:10; 1 John 2:5, and 3:17; Ps 42:1-4, &c.

[10] Deut 5:29; 11:13; 13:3; 26:16, and 30:2, 6, 10; Josh 22:5; 1 Sam 12:24; Matt 6:21, and 22:37.

[11] John 14:15, 23; 1 John 5:3.

Q. 14. What if our governors command or forbid us any thing, must we not take our obeying them to be obeying God, seeing they are his officers whom we see, but see not him?

A. Yes: when they command us by the authority given them of God: but God's universal laws are before and above their laws; and their power is all limited by God; they have no authority but what he giveth them; and he giveth them none against his laws: and therefore if they command any thing which God forbiddeth, or forbid what God commandeth, you must obey God in not obeying them. But this must never be made a pretence for disobedience to their true authority.[12]

Q. 15. What is the thing forbidden in the first commandment?

A. (1) To think that to be God which is not God, as the heathens do by the sun. (2) To ascribe any part of that to creatures which is essential and proper to God; and so to make them half gods.

Q. 16. How are men guilty of that?

A. (1) When they think that any creature hath that infiniteness, eternity, or self-sufficiency, that power, knowledge, or goodness, which is proper to God alone. Or that any creature hath that causality which is proper to God, in making and maintaining, or governing the world, or being the ultimate end. Or that any creature is to be more honoured, loved or obeyed, than God, or with any of that which is proper to God.[13]

(2) When the will doth actually love and honour the creature, with any of that love and honour which is due to God as God, and therefore to God alone.

(3) When in their practice men labour to please, serve, or obey any creature against God, before God, or equal with God, or with any service proper to God alone. All this is idolatry.

Q. 17. Which is the greatest and commonest idol of the world?

A. Carnal self: by sin man is fallen from God to his carnal self, to which he giveth that which is God's proper due.

Q. 18. How doth this selfishness appear and work as idolatry?[14]

---

[12] Rom 13:2, 3; Acts 4:19, 24, and 5:29, 32; Dan 3 and 6.

[13] Isa 2:22, and 13:8; Acts 12:22, 23; Mic. 2:9.

[14] Rev 16:9; 1 Chr. 16:28, 29; 1 Cor 10:31; Gal 1:10.

A. (1) In that such men love their carnal self, and pleasure, and prosperity, and the riches that are the provision for the flesh, better than God: I mean not only more sensibly, but with a preferring, choosing love; and that which as best is most loved, is made a man's god. The images of heathens were not so much their idols as themselves; for none of them loved their images better than themselves; nor than a worldling loveth his wealth, power and honour.[15]

(2) In that such are their own chief ultimate end, and prefer the prosperity of carnal self before the glorifying of God in perfect love and praise in the heavenly society for ever. And so did idolaters, by their images, or other idols.

(3) In that such had rather their own will were done than God's; and had rather God's will were brought to theirs than theirs to God's. Their wills are their rule and end; yea, they would have God and man, and all the world, fulfil their wills; even when they are against the will of God: self-will is the great idol of the world: all the stir and striving, and war, and work of such, is but to serve it.[16]

(4) Selfish men do measure good and evil chiefly by carnal self-interest: they take those for the best men that are most for them herein; and those for the worst that are against their interest in the world: and their love and hatred is placed accordingly. Let a man be never so wise and good, they hate him if he be against their interest.[17]

(5) And as holy men live to God in the care and endeavour of their lives, so do selfish men to their carnal selves: their study, labour, and time is thus employed, even to ruin the best that are but against their carnal interest: and if they be princes or great men in the world, the lives and estates of thousands of the innocent, seem not to them too dear a sacrifice by bloody and unlawful wars or persecutions, to offer to this grand idol self.

(6) And when it cometh to a parting choice, as the faithful will rather let go liberty, honour, estate, and life, than forsake God and the heavenly

---

[15] Rom 12:3, and 14:7; Matt 16:24; 18:4, and 23:12; Mark 12:33; Phil 2:4, 21.

[16] Tit 1:7; 2 Pet 2:10.

[17] 1 Kgs 22:8; 2 Chron. 18:7.

glory: so selfish men will let go their innocency, their Saviour, their God and all, rather than part with the interest of carnal self.[18]

(7) And in point of honour, they are more ambitious to be well thought and spoken of, and praised themselves, both living and dead, than to have God, and truth, and goodness honoured: and they can more easily bear one that dishonoureth God, and truth, and holiness, yea, and common righteousness and honesty, than one that (though justly) dishonoureth them.

So that all the world may easily see that carnal self, and specially self-will, is the greatest idol in the world.[19]

Q. 19. But is not that a man's idol which he trusteth most? and all men are so conscious of their own insufficiency, that they cannot trust themselves for their own preservation?

A. I say not that any selfish man[20] is a perfect idolater, and giveth all God's properties to himself. He must know whether ho will or not, that he is not infinite, eternal, almighty, omniscient, self-sufficient; he knoweth he must suffer, and die. But self hath more given it that is due only to God, than any other idol hath. And though such men know their own insufficiency, yet they have so little trust in God, that they trust their own wits and the choice of their own wills, before the wisdom and choice of God; and had far rather be at their own wills and choice if they could: and indeed had rather that all things in the world were at their will and choice, than at the will and choice of God. And therefore they like not his laws and government, but make their wit, will, and lust, the governors of themselves, and as many others as they can.

Q. 20. Is there not much selfishness in all? By this you will make all men, even the best, to be idolaters. But a man cannot be saved that liveth in idolatry.

A. It is not every subdued degree of any fault that denominateth the man, but that which is predominant in him: every man hath some unbelief, some backwardness to God and goodness, some hypocrisy, pride, &c., and yet every man is not to be called an infidel, an enemy to

---

[18] Luke 14:26, 33.

[19] 2 Tim 3:2, 3; Prov 21:4; Ps 10:2, 4.

[20] Mark 10:24; 1 Tim 6:17; Ps 20:7, and 118:8; Prov 3:5.

God and goodness, an hypocrite, &c. So every man hath some idolatry and some atheism remaining, and yet is not an idolater or atheist. If a man could not be saved till he were perfectly healed of every degree of these heinous sins, no man could be saved. But God's interest is predominant in holy souls.

Q. 21. Doth not Paul say of all, save Timothy, that all seek their own, and not the things that are Jesus Christ's?

A. He meaneth not that they predominantly do so, except those among them who were hypocrites: but that all did[21] too much seek their own, and too little the things that are Jesus Christ's, and were not so self-denying as Timothy, who, as it were, naturally cared for the good of the church: as Demas forsook Paul in his suffering, and went after his own worldly business; but yet did not forsake Christ and prefer the world before him (for ought we find of him).

Q. 22. You make this first commandment to be the sum of all.

A. It is the summary of all, and our obedience to it is virtually (but not actually) our obedience to all the rest. This is it which Christ calleth the first and greatest command, "Then shalt love the Lord thy God with all thy heart, and soul, and might." This is the foundation of all the rest of the commandments, and the root of all: the rest are but branches from it. When we are obliged to love God and obey him, we have a general obligation to keep all his commandments. But as this general command doth not put the special, particular commands in existence, so neither doth it oblige us to obey them till they exist; and then as the genus and species constitute every defined being; so the general and special obligation concur to make up every duty. He that sincerely obeyeth this first command, is a true subject of God, and in a state of salvation, and will sincerely obey all particular commands in the main course of his life, when they are revealed to him.[22]

---

[21] Jer 45:4, 5; Mich. 6:8.

[22] Hos 9:1, 2; 4:6, and 12:2.

35

Of the Second Commandment

Q. 1. What are the words of the second commandment?

A. "Thou shalt not make to thyself any graven image, or any likeness of any thing that is in heaven above, or that is in the earth beneath, or that is in the water under the earth: thou shalt not bow down thyself to them nor serve them. For I, the Lord thy God, am a jealous God, visiting the iniquity of the fathers upon the children unto the third and fourth generation of them that hate me, and showing mercy to thousands of them that love me, and keep my commandments."

Q. 2. How prove you against the papists, that this is not part of the first commandment?

A. (1) By the matter, which is different from it.

(2) And by the Scripture, which saith there were ten, and without this there are but nine. (3) And by historical tradition, which we can prove that the papists falsify.

Q. 3. What is the true meaning of the second commandment, and wherein doth it differ from the first?

A. The first commandment bindeth us to give God his own, or his due as God, both in heart and life, and to give it to no other. The second commandeth men to keep so wide a difference between God and heathen idols, as not to worship him as the heathens do their idols, nor yet to seem by their bodily action to worship an idol, though they despise it in their thoughts, and pretend to keep their hearts to God. Corporeal, and outward, and seeming idolatry is here forbidden. For though a man renounce in heart all other gods, yet if he be seen to bow down before an image, (1) He seemeth to the beholder to mean as idolaters do, while he symboliseth with them. And as lying and perjury with the tongue is sin, though a man's inward thoughts do own the truth, so bowing as worshippers do before an image, is idolatry, though the mind renounce all idols. And God is the God of the body as well as of the soul: and God would not have others encouraged to idolatry by so scandalous an example. (2) And if it be the true God that such profess to worship, it is interpretative blasphemy; as if they told men that God is like to that creature whose image they make, So that scandal, and bodily idolatry, and blasphemy, are the things directly forbidden in this command-ment, as the real choosing and worshipping a false god is in the first.[1]

Q. 4. By this, it seems that scandal is a heinous sin?

A. Scandal is enticing, tempting, or encouraging others to sin, by doing or saying that which is like to be abused by them to such an effect: or laying a stumbling-block in the way of blind or careless souls. If they will make our necessary duty the occasion of sin, we may not therefore omit our duty, if indeed it be an indispensable duty at that time: but if it be no duty, yea, or if it be only a duty in other senses and circum-stances, it is a heinous sin to give such scandal to another, much more to multitudes or public societies.

Q. 5. Wherein lieth the evil of it?

A. (1) It is a countenancing and furthering sin.

(2) It is uncharitableness and cruelty to men's souls.

(3) And therefore it is the devil's work.[2]

Q. 6. But if our rulers command us to do a thing indifferent, which others will turn to an occasion of sin and damnation, must we disobey our lawful governors, to prevent men's sin and fall?

A. If the thing in its own nature tended to so great and necessary good as would weigh down the contrary evil to the scandalized, we must do our duty to help them some other way. But supposing it either indif-ferent or of so small benefit as will not preponderate against the sin and danger of the scandalized, we are soul-murderers if we do not forbear

---

[1]   Deut 4:16, 17; 7:5, and 16:22; Lev 26:1, 2; Dan 3; Isa 40:18, 25, and 46:5.

[2]   Matt 18:6–9, &c. and 13:41; 1 Cor 8:13; Lev 19:14, Ezek 14:3, 4, 7; Rom 16:13; Rev 2:14.

it. For, (1) God hath given no rulers power to destruction of souls, but to edification; no power to command us that which is so contrary to the indispensable duty of love or charity. If an apothecary, or physician, or king, command his servant to sell arsenic to all that will buy it, without exception, the servant may not lawfully sell it to such as he knoweth mean to poison themselves or others by it. If the commander be a sober man, the servant ought to suppose that he intended such exceptions, though he expressed them not. But if he expressed the contrary, he commanded contrary to God's command, without authority, and is not to be obeyed. (2) But God himself dispenseth with his own commands about rituals, or smaller matters, when greater good or hurt stands on the other side. The disciples did justly pluck and rub the ears of corn, and the priests in the temple break the rest of the Sabbath, and an ox or an ass was to be watered or pulled out of a pit on that day. If the king or priest had made a law to the contrary, it had been null: if God's laws bind not in such cases, man's cannot. God bids us preach and pray, &c., and yet to quench a fire, or save men's lives, we may or must at that time forbear preaching, or sacraments, or other public worship.[3]

Q. 7. But what if as many will be scandalized, or tempted to sin, on the other side, if I do it not?

A. No duty being a duty at all times, much less a thing indifferent, though commanded, every Christian must prudently use the scales, and by all the helps of wise men that he can get, must discern which way is like to do most good or hurt, considering the persons, for number, for quality, and probability of the effect. God binds us to charity and mercy, and no man can disoblige us from that. And he that sincerely desireth to do the greatest good, and avoid the greatest hurt, and useth the best means he can to know it, shall be accepted of God, though men condemn him.[4]

Q. 8. But is nothing here forbidden but symbolizing with idolaters, in seeming to mean as they by doing as they?

A. That is it that is directly forbidden. But by consequence it is implied that all doctrines are forbidden that falsely represent God, and

---

[3] Rom 14:15, 17, 20; 2 Cor 10:8, and 13:10.

[4] 1 Cor 10:33; 6:12, 13; 9:22, and 14:26.

all worship or acts pretended to be religious, which are unsuitable to God's holy nature, attributes, will, or word, as being profanation, and an offering to God that which is unclean.[5]

Q. 9. What is the command which is here implied?

A. That we keep our souls chaste from all outward and seeming idolatry; and that we worship him who is the infinite, almighty, holy Spirit, with reverence, holiness, in spirit and truth, according to his blessed, perfect nature, and his holy will and word.[6]

Q. 10. Hath God given us a law for all things in his worship?

A. The law of nature is God's law, and obligeth man to that devotion to God and worship of him which is called natural: and the sacred Scripture prescribeth both that and also all those positive means or ordinances of God's worship, which are made necessary to the universal church on earth: and as for the mere accidents of worship, which are not proper parts, as time, place, words, methods, gesture, vesture, &c., God's laws give us general precepts, only telling us how to order them, leaving it to human prudence, and church guides, to order them according to those general rules.

Q. 11. Is all use of images unlawful?

A. God did so much hate idolatry, and the neighbourhood of idolaters made it so dangerous to the Israelites, that he did not only forbid the worshipping of images, but all such making or using of them as might become a snare or temptation to any. So that though it be lawful to make images for civil uses, and, when they are made, to fetch holy thoughts or meditations from them, as from all other creatures or things in the world; yet, in any case when they become a snare or danger, being not necessary things, they become a sin to those that so use them as a snare to others or themselves.[7]

Q. 12. Is it lawful to make any picture of God?

A. No; for pictures are the signs of corporeal things, and it is blasphemy to think God like a bodily substance: but it is lawful to make such

---

[5] Ps 50:21–23,

[6] 1 John 5:21; 2 Cor 6:16; 1 Cor 8:10, 11, and 10:19, 29, 27, 28; Rev 2:14, 20; Isa 2:18.

[7] Exod 34:13–15; Num 33:52; Deut 7:5; 2 Kgs 18:4, and 23:14, 24.

pictures, (as of a glorious light,) from which occasion may be taken of good thoughts concerning God.[8]

Q. 13. Is it lawful to make the picture of Christ as man, or as crucified?

A. The doing it as such is not forbidden, nor the right we of it when done: but the abuse, that is, the worshipping of it, or of Christ by it, is forbidden, and the making or using such, when it tendeth to such abuse, and hath more of snare than profit.

Q. 14. Why is God's jealousy here mentioned?

A. To make us know that God doth so strictly require the great duty of worshipping him as the true God, and hate the sin of idolatry, or giving his glory to another, or blaspheming him, as if he were like to painted things, that he would have us accordingly affected.

Q. 15. Why doth God threaten to visit the iniquities of the fathers on the children, in this command, rather than in the rest?

A. God hath blessings and curses for societies, as well as for individual persons; and societies are constituted and known by the symbols of public profession. And as God's public worship is the symbol of his church which he will bless, so idolatrous worship is the symbol of the societies which he will curse and punish; and it was especially needful that the Israelites should know this, who could never else have been excused from the guilt of murdering man, woman, and child, of all the nations which they conquered, had not God taken it on himself as judging them to death for their idolatry and other crimes, and making the Israelites his executioners.[9]

Q. 16. But doth not God disclaim punishing the children for the father's sins, and say the soul that sinneth shall die?

A. Yes; when the children are either wholly innocent of that sin, or else are pardoned through Christ upon their true repentance, and hating and renouncing their father's sins; but not else.

Q. 17. Are any children guilty of their parents' sins?

A. Yes; all children are guilty of the sins which their parents committed before their birth, while they were in their loins. Not with the

---

[8] Exod 25:18-20; 1 Sam 4:4; Ps 18:1; Ezek 10:2.

[9] Jer 10:25; Deut 2:34; 3:6; 4:20; 7:2, 23, 24; 12:2, 3, and 20:17, 20, Num 33:50-52.

same degree and sort of guilt as the parents are, but yet with so much as exposeth them to just penalties.

Q. 18. How prove you that?

A. (1) By the nature of the case; for though we were not personally existent in them when they sinned, we were seminally existent in them, which is more than causally or virtually; and it was that semen which was guilty in them, that was after made a person, and so that person must have the same guilt. (2) From the whole history of the Scripture, which tells of the children of Cain, the old world, Sodom, Shem, the Canaanites, Saul, David (as an adulterer), Achan, Gehazi, and others punished for their parents' sins, and the Jews cast off and cursed on that account to this day. (3) And our common, original sin from Adam proveth it.

Q. 19. But our original sin from Adam had another cause; God decreeing that Adam should stand or fall for all his posterity?

A. We must not add to God's word, much less blaspheme him, as if it were God himself that, by a decree or covenant, made all the world sinners, save Adam and Eve. If Adam had not sinned, it would not have saved all or any of his posterity unless they also had continued innocent themselves. Nor did God make any promise to continue and keep innocent all Adam's posterity, in case he sinned not. We sinned in Adam, because we were seminally in him, and so are our children in us; and who can bring a clean thing out of an unclean, if it were essentially in it?

Q. 20. If we are guilty of all nearer parents' sin, will not our guilt increase to the end of the world, and the last man have the greatest guilt?[10]

A. (1) No; because all guilt from Adam, and from our nearer parents too, is pardoned by Christ, when we were baptised as sincere believers, or their seed. But it is true that we are so far more guilty as to have the more need of a Saviour's grace. (2) And guilt is considerable, either as more obligations to the same punishment, or as obligation to more or greater punishment. It is true that impenitent persons, who are the seed of a line of wicked ancestors, have more obligations to the same

---

[10] On this I have written a peculiar Treatise of Original Sin.

punishment, but not obligation to greater punishment; because as great as they were capable of was due before.

Q. 21. But many say that for nearer parents' sins no punishments but temporal are due?

A. (1) If any at all are due, it proveth an answerable guilt. (2) To say that Adam's sin deserveth our spiritual and eternal punishment, and all other parents' sin only temporal, is to speak without and against Scripture, and the nature of the case. The case of the seed of the old world, the Sodomites, the Canaanites, and the present heathens, speaks much more. (3) It is clear that nearer parents' sin is a cause that many of their posterity are more sinful, in lust, pride, fornication, heresy, and ignorance, than others: and sin, as well as grace, hath a tendency to perpetuity, if not cured and remitted.

Q. 22. Why doth God name only the third and fourth generation?

A. To show us, that though he will punish the sins of his enemies on their posterity who imitate their parents, yet he sets such bounds to the execution of his justice, as that sinners shall not want encouragement to repent and hope for mercy.

Q. 23. Who be they that be called here haters of God?

A. All that have a predominant hatred to his servants, his service, and his holy laws. But the next specially meaneth those societies of infidels, heathens, and malignants, who are the professed enemies of his church and worship. As I said before, the outward symbols of idolatry were the professing signs by which his church's enemies were openly noted in the world; as baptism and the Lord's supper were the badges of his church and servants.[11]

Q. 24. What is the meaning and extent of the promise of mercy to thousands of them that love him and keep his commandments?

A. (1) As to the subject, it must be noted, that such a belief in God as causeth men to love him and keep his commandments, is the qualification of them that have the promise of God's saving mercy: faith working by love and obedience.

(2) The words signify God's wonderful mercy, and his delight to do good to those that are qualified to receive it.

---

[11] Deut 32:41; Ps 81:15; Rom 1:30; Luke 19:27.

(3) And they signify, that God will not only love and bless a godly offspring for their own sake, but also for the sake of their godly ancestors; and while they succeed them in true piety, God will increase his blessings on them.

(4) And though those forfeit all, that prove ungodly when they come to age, yet the infant seed of the faithful, while such, are in covenant with God, on the account of their relation to those godly parents who dedicate themselves and theirs to him.

Q. 25. How doth God perform this promise, when many godly parents have wicked and miserable children?

A. This promise doth not say that God will keep all the children of the faithful from sinning against him, and casting away his mercy and salvation. But if men be sincerely godly, and dedicate themselves and their children to God, and enter them into his covenant, and perform their own part promised by them, God will accept them into his family, and pardon their original sin, and give them the necessary helps for their personal faith and obedience when they come to the use of reason.[12] And if the children keep their covenant according to their capacity, and do not violate it, and reject his grace, God will accept and save them, as actual, obedient believers.

Q. 26. Will he not do so also by the children of unbelievers?

A. If such at age see their parents' sin, and forsake it, and devote themselves to God, he will accept them. But as infidels and wicked hypocrites have no promise of God's acceptance of them and theirs, so such do not dedicate themselves and their children to God; he that will devote his child to God, must do it, as it were a part of himself; and cannot do it sincerely if he first devote not himself to God.

Q. 27. But may not others do it for his children?

A. In infancy they are considered in the covenant of grace but as infants, that is, appurtenances to another. As the infidels' infants they have neither capacity nor promise; but if any other adopt them, and take them truly as their own, I am in hope that God accepteth such so devoted to him.

---

[12] Prov 20:7; Ps 37:28, 29; Matt 19:13, 14; Acts 2:39; 1 Cor 7:14; Isa 14:25, and 65:25, Matt 2:15; Rom 4:16, and 9:8.

36

Of the Third Commandment

Q. 1. What are the words of the third commandment?

A. Thou shalt not take the name of the Lord thy God in vain, for the Lord will not hold him guiltless that taketh his name in vain.

Q. 2. What is it that is specially here forbidden?

A. Profaneness; that is, the unholy using of God's holy name, and holy things; especially by perjury, or any other entitling him to false-hood, or to any of the sins of men, as if he were the author or approver of them.

Q. 3. What is meant by the name of God?

A. Those words, or other signs, by which he is described, denominated, or otherwise notified to man; which I opened so fully on the first petition of the Lord's Prayer, that to avoid repetition I must refer you thereto.

Q. 4. What is meant by taking the name of God in vain?

A. Using it profanely, and specially falsely. It is contrary to the hallowing of God's name, which is mentioned in the Lord's Prayer.

In the Scripture, (1) The creature is called vanity, as being but a shadow, and untrusty thing; and to use God's name and holy things in a common manner, as we use the creature's, is to profane his name, and take it vainly.

(2) And falsehood and lies are usually called vanity; for vanity is that shadowyness which seemeth something and is nothing, and so deceiveth men. A lie is that which deceiveth him that trusteth it: so

idols are called vanity and lies, for their falsehood and deceit; and all men are said to be liars, that is, untrusty and deceitful.

Q. 5. What is an oath?

A. I have said heretofore as others, that it is but an appeal to God as the Witness of the truth, and the Avenger of a lie; but, on further thoughts, I find that the common nature of an oath is to pawn some greater thing in attesting of the truth of our words; or to take some grievous thing on ourselves as a penalty if we lie; or to make some certain truth a pledge of the truth of what we say. And to swear by our faith, or truth, or honesty, by the temple, the altar, the fire, the sun, is as much as to say, 'If this be not true, then I have no faith, truth, honesty; there is no temple, altar, fire, sun:' or 'Let me be taken for one that denieth that I have any faith, that there is any sun, fire,' &c.: or, 'It as true as that this is fire, sun,' &c. So to swear by God is to say, 'It is as true as that there is a God,' or 'as God liveth,' &c.; or, 'If I lie, take me for one that denieth God to be God;' and consequently it is an appeal to him as the Avenger; so, 'By the life of Pharaoh' was 'As true as Pharaoh liveth,' or 'Else take me for one that denieth the life of Pharaoh.' So that there is somewhat of an imprecation, or self-reproach, as the penalty of a lie, in every oath, but more dreadfully of divine revenge when we swear by God, and of idolatry when men swear by an idol, as if it were a God.

Q. 6. Which be the chief ways of taking God's name in vain?

A. (1) Fathering on him false doctrine, revelations, or laws; saying as false prophets, 'God sent me,' and 'Thus saith the Lord,' when it is false; saying, 'This doctrine, or this prophecy, God's Spirit revealed to me,' when it is not so. Therefore all Christians must be very fearful of false revelations and prophecies, and see that they believe not every spirit, nor pretend to revelations; and to take heed of taking the suggestions of Satan, or their crazed, melancholy fancies, for the revelations of God.

(2) So also gathering false doctrines out of Scripture by false expositions, and fathering these on God. And therefore all men should, in dark and doubtful cases, rather suspend their judgments till they have overcome their doubts by solid evidence, than rashly to conclude, and confidently and fiercely dispute for error. It is a great profanation to father lies on God, who is the hater of them, when lying is the devil's work and character.

(3) The same I may say of a rash and false interpretation of God's providences.

(4) And also of fathering false laws on God, and saying that he either commandeth or forbiddeth what he doth not; to make sins and duties which God never made, and say he made them, is to father falsehood on him, and corrupt his government.

(5) Another way is by false worship. (1) If men say that God commanded such worship, which he commanded not, it is the sin last mentioned. (2) If they worship him with their own inventions without his command, (particular or general,) they profane his name, by offering him that which is unholy, common, and unclean.

(6) Another way is by false pretending that God gave them that authority which he never gave them; like counterfeiting a commission from the king. If princes should pretend that God gave them authority to oppose his truth, to persecute godliness, unjustly to silence faithful ministers of Christ, to raise unnecessary wars, to oppress the innocent; this were a heinous taking of God's name in vain. If priests shall pretend that God gave them authority to make themselves pastors of the flocks that are unwilling of them, without a just call, or to make laws for any that are not rightfully their subjects, and to impose their dictates, words, and forms, and unnecessary inventions, as conditions of ministration or communion, without true right, and to make themselves the rule of other men's words and actions by usurpation; this is all taking God's name in vain. And so it is, if they preach false doctrine in his name, and if they pronounce false excommunications and absolutions, and justify the wicked, and condemn, reproach, and slander the just, and brand unjustly the servants of Christ as hypocrites, schismatics, or heretics, and this as by ministerial power from Christ: especially if they silence Christ's ministers, impose wolves or incompetent men, scatter the flocks, and suppress serious godliness, and all this in the name of Christ. Much more if any pretend, as the pope or his pretended general councils, to be Christ's vicar general, or head, or supreme, unifying governor over all the church on earth, and to make laws for the whole church: or if they corrupt God's worship with imposed superstitions, falsehood, or profanations, and say God hath authorised them to do this; it is heinous profaning God's name by a lie; such doing brought

up the proverb, *In nomine Domini incipit omne malum:* when all their abuses began with, "In the name of God, Amen."

And they that make new church forms which God made not, either papal, universal aristocracy, patriarchial, and such like, and either pretend that God made them, or gave them, or such other power to make them, must prove what they say, lest they profane God's name by falsehood.

But the highest profanation is, when they pretend that God hath made them absolute governors, and set them so far above his own laws, and judgment, and himself, as that whatever they say is the word of God, or the sense of the Scripture, though never so falsely, must be taken for such by all; and whatever they command or forbid, they must be obeyed, though God's word command or forbid the contrary: and that God hath given power (to popes or councils) to forbid men the worship which God commandeth; yea, to interdict whole kingdoms, and excommunicate and depose kings; and that from these, as a supreme power, no man must appeal to the Scripture, or to God and his final judgment. This is, by profane lying, to use God's name to the destroying of souls, the church, and the laws and government of God himself.[1]

(7) Another way of taking God's name in vain is, by heresies; that is, embodying in separated parties or churches, against the church and truth of God, for the propagating of some dangerous false doctrine which they father on God, and so militate in his name against his church. If men, as aforesaid, do but promote false doctrine in the church without separation, it is bad; but to gather an army against the truth and church, and feign Christ to be the leader of it, is worse.[2]

(8) Another way is by perjury, appealing to God, or abusing his name, as the witness and owner of a lie.

(9) Another way is by false vows made to God himself. When men either vow to God to do that which he abhorreth, or hath forbidden; or when they vow that which is good, with a false, deceitful heart, and, as Ananias and Sapphira, with false reserves; or when they vow and pay

---

[1] Jer 14:14; 23:32, and 37:14; Mark 13:22; 2 Cor 11:13; 2 Pet 2:1; Jer 27:15, and 29:9, 10, 31; 1 John 4:1, 2.

[2] Acts 20:30; Rom 16:16, 17; Eph 4:14.

not, but wilfully break the vows which they have made. The breach of covenants between princes, or between them and subjects, or between husband and wife, confirmed by appeal to God, is a dreadful sin; but the violation of the great baptismal vow in which we are all solemnly devoted and obliged to God, is one of the most heinous sins in the world. When it is not about a lesser duty, but even our oath of allegiance to God, by solemn vow taking him for our God, our Saviour, and Sanctifier, and giving up ourselves to him accordingly, renouncing the contrary, and laying on this covenant all our hopes of grace and glory, pardon and salvation, what can be more heinous than to be false to such a vow and covenant?[3]

(10) And hypocrisy itself is a heinous taking God's name in vain. When we offer God the dead carcass of religious acts without the life and soul, find present him with ceremony, self-exalting pomp, mere heartless words, an artificial image of religion, that hath not the spiritual nature, life, or serious desire of the heart; that is, seeking to mock God, or making him like an idol that seeth not the heart, and knows not what is offered him, Alas! how much of the preaching, hearing, praying, and sacraments of many is a taking God's name in vain, as if he did accept a lie.

(11) Another way of this profanation is making God's name and acts of religion an engagement to wickedness: as when men bind themselves to treason, murder, or any sin, by taking the sacrament. As many, alas! (which I unwillingly name) have done in a blind zeal for the Roman usurpation, being told, that it pleaseth God and Saint Peter, and meriteth salvation to destroy the enemies of the church, that is, of the pope and his clergy. And those that bound themselves with an oath to kill Paul, thought God accepted the oath and deed. And the general council at Lateran, under Innocent III., which bound temporal lords to take an oath to exterminate such as they called hereties, fathered the work on God by that oath. And the pope and council of Trent, which hath brought in on all the clergy a new oath to many new and sinful things, by that oath make God the approver of all. And the Mahometans that give liberty of religion, yet think it pleaseth God and meriteth heaven,

---

[3] Jer 4:2; 5:2; 7:9, and 23:10; Mal 3:5; Ps 15:4; Zech. 5:3, 4; Hos 4:2, and 10:4.

to kill the enemies of Mahomet. And Christ saith, "They that kill you, shall think they do God good service." And is it not profaning the name of God, to make him the author of the murder of his servants?

(12) Another way of taking God's name profanely, and pleading it for vanity and lies, is by making God the determining first cause of all the acts of men in the world, as specified by their objects and circumstances; that is, of all the lies, and all the other sins that are done in the world: as if God had given no such free-will to men or devils, by which they can lie, murder, hate God, or commit any sin, till God move their wills, tongues, and hands to do it, by an unavoidable, predetermining efficacy. This is so much to profane and take in vain God's name, as that it maketh him the chief cause of all the devil's works.

(13) Another way of vain abuse, and profanation of God's name, is by blasphemy, and contempt, and scorn of God, or of the word or ways of God: and, alas! who would think that this should be so common among men, when even the devils believe and tremble! I hope posterity will account it so odious as hardly to believe that ever there were men, and so many men, even in England, who used to deride the name, word, providence, and worship of God, and make serious regard of God and religion the common scorn; and familiarly to wish, by way of imprecation, as a by-word, 'God damn me,' and to swear by the name, the wounds, and blood of God.

(14) Lastly, another way of taking God's name in vain, is by an unholy, irreverent tossing of it in common talk, in jest, and on every ludicrous occasion. Plays and play books use it; it is made an ordinary accident to all common and profane discourse; beggars profanely beg by it; children cry by it; 'O God,' and 'O Lord,' is become an interjection.

Q. 7. Why do we take ordinary, light swearing, specially by God, or by sacred things, to be a sure sign of a wicked man?

A. Because it showeth a predominant habit of profaneness; that the man liveth without the reverence of God's holiness, majesty, knowledge, and presence, and is hardened into a senselessness or contempt of God, and of his dreadful judgment, as if he derided God, or dared him; or as if he did believe that there is no God that heareth him. To live in the fear of God, and subjection to his government, is the property of every godly man.

Q. 8. What is meant by the words, "The Lord will not hold him guiltless?"

A. God will not leave him unpunished, nor account this as a small offence: he himself will be revenged for this sin.

Q. 9. Why is this threatening annexed more to this commandment than to others?

A. Because this sin is, (1) An immediate injury to God, while it expressly fathereth lies and other sin on him; it doth, as we may say, engage him to vindicate himself. When rulers or usurpers pretend that God authoriseth them to do mischief, and fight against himself; when persecutors and corrupters of religion pretend God's interest and will for all, that it is for order, unity, government, and obedience for the church, that they corrupt, destroy, silence, and tyrannise; they invite God to cast the lie and cruelty back on them, which they would father upon him, and to turn their canons, prisons, and inquisitions, and other devilish plagues of the world, upon the author, in disowning them himself.

(2) And they that by perjury, hypocrisy, false doctrine, and the rest of the forementioned sins, do appeal to God, and make him openly the author of all, do thereby, as it were, summon God to revenge. As they said to Paul, "Hast thou appealed to Cæsar? To Cæsar shalt thou go:" so it may be said to the perjured, the hypocrite, the usurper, the false judge, &c., 'Hast thou appealed to God, and do you father on him your lies, cruelties, tyrannies, and usurpations, and false doctrines? To God shall you go, who will undertake the cause which you cast upon him, and will judge the secrets of men's hearts, as he did Ananias and Sapphira's.' If men sin under the laws of men, God requireth magistrates to judge them: but if they appeal to God, or, by falsehood, escape the judgment of man, they more immediately cast themselves on the justice of God; and it is a fearful thing to fall into his hands who is a consuming fire: God is the avenger especially on such.[4]

Q. 10. Is it meant of God's vengeance in this life, or in the next?

A. In both: usually profanation of God's name and holy things, especially by perjury, and by fathering cruelty and wickedness on God, is more notably punished by him in this life. Though such may seem to

---

[4] Deut 32:43; 1 Thess 4:6; Rom 12:19; Heb 10:30, and 12:29; Isa 35:4; 47:3; 61:2; 63:4, and 1:24; Luke 18:7, 8.

prosper for awhile, God usually overtaketh them here, and their sins do find them out: but if they escape such bodily punishment here, they are usually more dreadfully forsaken of grace than other men, and heap up wrath against the day of wrath.

I will only add, in the conclusion, that even true Christians should take great care lest their very thoughts of God, and their prayers and speaking of him, should be customary and dead, and like their thoughts and talk of common things, and in some degree of taking of God's name in vain.

37

Of the Fourth Commandment

Q. 1. What are the words of the fourth commandment?

A. Remember the Sabbath day, to keep it holy: six days shalt thou labour, and do all thy work: but the seventh day is the Sabbath of the Lord thy God; to it thou shalt not do any work, thou, nor thy son, nor thy daughter, thy man-servant, nor thy maid-servant, nor thy cattle, nor the stranger that is within thy gates: for in six days the Lord made heaven and earth, the sea, and all that in them is, and rested the seventh day: where fore the Lord blessed the Sabbath day, and hallowed it.[1]

Q. 2. Why doth Deut. 5 repeat it in so different words?

A. Because the words are but for the sense, and they being kept in the ark as written in stone, and safe from alteration, Moses, in Deut. 5., gave them the sense, and added some of his own explication; and nothing is altered to obscure the sense,[2]

Q. 3. Which day is it which was called the Sabbath in this commandment?

A. The seventh, commonly called, from the heathen custom, Saturday.

Q. 4. Why was that day made the Sabbath?

A. God having made the world in six days' space, seeing all good, and very good, rested in his own complacency; and appointed the seventh

---

[1] Exod 20:10, 11, and 31:17; Heb 4:4.

[2] Gen 2:2, 3.

day every week to be separated as holy, to worship and praise him the Great Creator, as his glorious perfections shine forth in his works.

Q. 5. What is meant by God's resting from his work?

A. Not that he had been at any labour or weariness therein; but, (1) That he finished the creation. (2) That he was pleased in it as good. (3) And that he would have it be a day of holy, pleasant rest to man.

Q. 6. What is meant by keeping holy the Sabbath day?

A. Separating it to the holy worship and praise of the Creator, and resting to that end from unnecessary, bodily labour.

Q. 7. What doth the word "remember" signify?

A. (1) First, it is an awakening *caveat*, to bid us take special care that we break not this commandment. (2) And then that we must prepare, before it comes, to avoid the things that would hinder us in the duty, and to be fit for its performance.

Q. 8. Why is "remember" put before this more than before the rest of the commandments?

A. Because, (1) Being but of positive institution, and not naturally known to man, as other duties are, they had need of a positive excitation and remembrance. And (2) It is of great importance to the constant and acceptable worship, and the avoiding of impediments, to keep close to the due time which God hath appointed for it: and to violate it, tendeth to atheistical ungodliness.

Q. 9. Why is it called "The Sabbath of the Lord thy God?"

A. Because, (1) God did institute and separate it. (2) And it is separated to the honour and worship of God.

Q. 10. When and how did God institute and separate it?

A. Fundamentally by his own resting from the work of creation: but immediately by his declaring to Adam his will for the sanctifying of that day, which is expressed Gen. 2:3.

Q. 11. Some think that the Sabbath was not instituted till man had sinned, and Christ was promised, and so God rested in Christ?

A. When the text adjoineth it close to the creation, and giveth that only as the reason of it (that God ended his works which he had made, and rested from them), this is human, corrupting presumption.

Q. 12. But some think the Sabbath was first instituted in the Wilderness, when they were forbid to gather manna?

A. It is not there mentioned as newly instituted, and it is mentioned Gen. 2:2, 3, and then instituted with the reason of it: "And God blessed the seventh day, and sanctified it, because in it he rested from all his works which God created and made." And the same reason is repeated in the fourth commandment.

Q. 13. Is this commandment of the law of nature as are the rest?

A. It was more of the law of nature to Adam than to us; his nature knowing otherwise than ours, both when God ended his works, and how beautiful they were before the curse. It is now of the law of nature (that is, known by natural light without other revelation). (1) That God should be worshipped. (2) That societies should assemble to do it together. (3) That some set time should be separated, statedly to that use. (4) That it should be done with the whole heart, without worldly diversions or distractions.

But I know nothing in nature alone from whence a man can prove that, (1) It must be either just one day in seven. (2) Or, just what day of the seven it must be. (3) Nor just what degree of rest is necessary. Though reason may discern that one day in seven is a very convenient proportion.

Q. 14. Are the words "Six days shalt thou labour," &c., a command, or only a license?

A. They are not only a license, but a command to man,[3] to live in an ordinary calling, or lawful course of labour, according to each one's ability and place, and diligently to exercise it, and not spend time in idleness: and the ordinary time is here assigned thereto.

Q. 15. Then how can it be lawful to spend any of the week days in religious exercises, any more than to spend any part of the Sabbath day in labour?

A. All labours are to be done as the service of God, and as a means to holy and everlasting ends; and therefore it is implied still that God be sought, and remembered, and honoured in all; as our eating and drinking is our duty, but to be done to the glory of God, and therefore with the seeking of his blessing, and returning him our thanks.[4]

---

[3] 1 Thess 4:11; 2 Thess 3:10–12; Prov 18:9; Matt 25:26; Rom 12:11.

[4] Prov 31:27; Ezek 16:41; 1 Tim 5:13; Matt 20:6.

Q. 16. But is it lawful, then, to separate whole days either weekly, or monthly, or yearly, to religious exercises, when God hath commanded us to labour on them?

A. As God's command of resting on the Sabbath is but the stating of the ordinary times; supposing an exception of extraordinary cases; (as in time of war, of fire, of dispersing plagues, of hot persecution, &c.; as circumcision was omitted in the wilderness forty years;) so this command to labour six days doth state our ordinary time, but with supposed exception of extraordinary occasions for days of humiliation and thanksgiving. And all God's commands, suppose that when two duties meet together, and cannot both be then done, the greater must ever be preferred: and therefore saving the life of a man, or a beast, yea, feeding and watering beasts, labouring in temple service, &c., were to be preferred before the rest of the Sabbath: and so when our necessity or profit make religious exercises more to our good, and so a greater duty, (as lectures, fasts, &c.,) we must prefer them to our ordinary labour. For as the Sabbath was made for man, and not man for the Sabbath, so were the other days.[5]

Q. 17. May not rich men, that have no need, forbear the six days' labour?

A. No; if they are able. It is part of God's service, and riches are his gift: and to whom he giveth much, from them he expecteth not less, but more. Shall servants work less because they have more wages? It is not only for their own supplies that God commandeth men to labour, but also for the public good, and the benefit or relief of others, and the health of their bodies, and the suitable employment of their minds, and that none of their short, precious time be lost in sinful idleness.[6]

Q. 18. But it will seem sordid for lords, and knights, and ladies to labour?

A. It is swinish and sinful not to labour; but they must do it in works that are suitable to their places. As physicians, schoolmasters, and church ministers labour not in the same kind of employment as ploughmen and tradesmen do; so magistrates have their proper labour in government, and rich persons have families, children, and servants to oversee, their poor neighbours and tenants to visit, encourage, and

---

[5] Esth 9:26, 28, 31.

[6] See Prov 31:27, &c.

relieve, and their equals so to converse with as tendeth to the greatest good; but none must live idly.[7]

Q. 19. Was rest on the Sabbath absolutely commanded?

A. It was always a duty to break it, when a greater duty came in which required it, as Christ hath told the pharisees, in the case of feeding man or beast, healing the sick, and doing such necessary good; for God preferreth morals before rituals; and his rule is, "I will have mercy, and not sacrifice."[8]

Q. 20. Why, then, was bodily rest commanded?

A. That body and mind might be free from diversion, weariness, and distraction, and fit with pleasure wholly to serve God in the religious duties of his worship.

Q. 21. Why doth God mention not only servants but beasts?

A. As he would not have servants enslaved and abused by such labour as should unfit them for Sabbath work and comfort, so he would have man exercise the clemency of his nature, even towards the brutes; and beasts cannot labour, but man will be put to some labour or diversion by it: and God would have the whole place where we dwell, and all that we have to do with, to bear an open signification of our obedience to his command, and our reverence to his sanctified day and worship.

Q. 22. Is this commandment now in force to Christians?

A. So much of it materially is in force as is of the law of nature, or of Christ by supernatural revelation, and no more. Therefore the seventh day (Sabbath) of corporal rest, is changed by Christ into the Lord's day, appointed for christian worship.

Q. 23. Was not all that was written in stone of perpetual obligation?

A. No; nor any as such; for as it was written on those stones it was the law of Moses for the Jews, and bound no other nations, and is done away by the dissolving of their republic, and by Christ.

Q. 24. How prove you all this?

A. (1) As Moses was ruler, or mediator, to none but the Jews, the words of the Decalogue are appropriate to them as redeemed from Egyptian bondage; so the tables were delivered to no other, and a law

---

[7] Ezek 16:49.

[8] Matt 12:5; Mark 2:27, 28; Luke 13:15.

cannot bind without any promulgation. All the world was not bound to send to the Jews for revelation, nor to be their proselytes.

(2) The Scripture expressly affirmeth the change, (2 Cor. 3:3, 7, 11,) "If the ministration of death written and engraven in stones was glorious, so that the children of Israel could not steadfastly behold the face of Moses for the glory of his countenance, which was to be (or is) done away," &c. "For if that which is done away was glorious, (or, by glory,) how much more that which remaineth is glorious (or, in glory)." Here it is evident that it is the law written on stone that is mentioned, and that it is not, as some say, the glory only of Moses' face, or the flaming mount, which is done away, for that was done away in a few days; but it is the law, which is called "glorious," that is said to be done away. The words can bear no other sense. It is too tedious to cite all. The texts following fully prove it;—Heb. 7:11, 12, 18, and 9:18, 19; Eph. 2:15; John 1:17; Luke 16:16; Rom. 2:12, 14–16, and 3:19–21, 27, 28, 31, and 4:13–16, and 5:13, 20, and 7:4–8, 16, and 9:4, 31, 32, and 10:5; Gal. 2:15, 16, 19, 21, and 3:2, 10–13, 19, 21, 24, and 4:21, and 5:3, 4, 14, 23, and 6:13; Phil. 3:6, 9; 1 Cor. 9:21.

(3) And the Sabbath itself is expressly said to be ceased with the rest; "Let no man judge you in meat or in drink, or in respect of an holy day (or feast), or of the new moon, or of the Sabbaths, which are a shadow of things to come; but the body is of Christ." (Col. 2:16.) It was the weekly Sabbath that was the chief of Sabbaths, and therefore included in the plural name, there being no exception of it.

(4) And to put all out of doubt, Christ (who commandeth not two weekly Sabbaths) hath appointed and sanctified the first day of the week, instead of the seventh day, Sabbath; not calling it the Sabbath, but the Lord's day.

Q. 25. How prove you that?

A. If you will search the Scripture, you shall see it proved by these degrees. (I) Christ commissioned his apostles to teach the churches all his doctrines, commands, and orders, and so to settle and guide them. (Luke 6:13, and 10:16; Matt. 10:40; 16:19; and 28:18–20; John 13:16, 20; 17:18; 20:21, and 21:15–17; Acts 1:2, 24, 25; 2:42; 10:5, and 26:17; 1 Cor. 4:1, 2; 11:23; 12:28, 29, and 15:3; Gal. 1:1, 11, 12; Eph. 2:20, and 4:11–16; 2 Pet. 3:2.)

(II) Christ promised his Spirit to them, to enable them to perform their commission, and lead them into all truth, and to bring them all to their remembrance, and to guide them as his church's guides, and so as the promulgators of his commands. For this see Jer. 3:15; Isa. 44:3; Joel 2:28, 29, &c., and Luke 24:49; John 15:26, 27; 16:7, 12–15, and 17:18; Matt. 28:20; Acts 1:4, 8.

(III) Christ performed this, and gave them the infallible Spirit accordingly to perform their commissioned work. See Heb. 10:23; Tit. 1:2; John 5:10, and 10:22; Acts 2, and 15:28; Heb. 2:4; 1 Pet. 1:12; Rom. 15:19, 20, &c.

(IV) Christ himself laid the foundation, by rising that day (as God did of the Sabbath by ceasing from his work). He appeared to his disciples congregate on that day; he sent down the Holy Ghost (his Agent, and the Perfecter of his work) on that day: the apostles settled that day as the stated time for constant church assemblies and communion; and all the churches in the world have constantly called it the Lord's day, and kept it as thus appointed, and used by the apostles, from their days till now with one consent. And because I must not here write a volume on this point, instead of a catechism; he that doubteth may see all this fully proved in my book, called "The Divine Appointment of the Lord's Day," and in Dr. Young's book, called "The Lord's Day Vindicated."

Q. 26. Is rest as necessary now as under Moses[9] law?

A. It was then commanded, both as a means to the holy work of the day, and also as a ceremony which was made a duty in itself, as a shadow of the christian rest. In the first respect, we are as much (or more) obliged to forbear labour, even so far as it hindereth holy work, as they were then; but not in the second respect.

Q. 27. When doth the Lord's day begin and end?

A. It is safest to judge of that according to the common estimation of your country, of the measure of all other days: remembering that it is not now as the Jewish Sabbath, to be kept as a ceremony, but as the season of holy works. As therefore you allow on other days a stated proportion of twenty-four hours for labour, and the rest for sleep or rest, do so by the Lord's day, and you need not be further scrupulous as to the time.

But remember, (1) That you avoid scandal. (2) That even the Sabbath (and so the Lord's day) was made for man, and Christ is the Lord of it, who will have the greatest works preferred.

---

[9] Exod 31:15, and 35:3; Num 15:32; Neh 13:16, 17; Jer 17:21, 22, 24, 27.

Q. 28. Doth not Paul tell us that all days are alike, and we must not judge one another for days? Why then should Christians make a difference, and not serve God equally every day?

A. Paul tells you that Christ hath taken away the Jewish ceremonial difference of days; for neglect of which none is to be judged: but it followeth not that Christ hath made no difference himself, and hath not stated a day for christian work in communion above the rest. One hour of the day doth not in itself now differ from another. And yet every wise master of a family will keep the order of stated hours, for dinner and for prayer. And so will a congregation for lectures, and other ordinary occasions. I told you in the beginning, that the light and law of nature tells us, that God's public worship should have a stated day; in which, as free from diversions and distractions, we should wholly apply ourselves thereto. And that all the Christians in the world assemble for the same work on the same day, hath much of laudable concord, harmony, and mutual help. And therefore it concerned him who only is the King and Lawgiver to the universal church, to make them a law for the determination of the day, which he hath done.

Q. 29. But is it not more spiritual to make every day a Sabbath?

A. It is most Christian-like to obey Christ our King. Thus the same men pretend to make every meal a sacrament, that they may break the law of Christ, who instituted the sacrament. Satan's way of drawing men from Christ's laws, is sometimes by pretending to do more and better. But to keep every day a Sabbath, is to keep none. It is not lawful to cast off our outward labour all the six days: nor can mind or body bear it to do nothing but religious worship. These men mean no more but to follow their earthly business with a spiritual mind, and at some seasons of the day to worship God solemnly: and this is but what every good Christian should do every day. But who knoweth not that the mind may, with far more advantage, attend God's instructions, and be raised to him in holy worship, when all worldly diverting businesses are laid by, and the whole man employed towards God alone?

If men will regard, (1) The experience of their own souls. (2) And of all others in the world, they might soon be resolved how mischievous a thing the neglect of the Lord's day is, and how necessary its holy observation. (1) That man never knew what it is to attend God's worship seriously, and therein to receive his special blessing, who hath not found the great advantage of our separation from all common business, to attend holy work only on the Lord's day. He that feeleth no miss, or loss of it, sure never knew what communion with God is. (2) And servants would be left remediless under such masters, as would both oppress them with labour, and restrain them from God's service. It is therefore the great mercy of the universal King to secure the liberties of the servants, and to bind all men to the means of their own felicity.

(3) And common reason will tell us, that a law, obliging all men to spend one day of seven in learning God's word, and offering him holy worship, must needs tend abundantly more to the increase of knowledge and holiness, than if all men were left to their own or to their rulers' wills herein.

(4) And common experience puts the matter of fact out of doubt, that where the Lord's day is most conscionably spent in holy exercises, there knowledge, piety, charity, and all virtue, do most notably prosper: and where the sanctifying of the Lord's day is neglected, ignorance, sensuality, and worldliness abound. O how many millions of souls hath grace converted, and comforted, and edified on the Lord's days! When men are obliged to hear, read, pray, and praise God, and to catechise their children and servants, as that which God requireth, is it not liker to be done, than if they be left to their own erroneous, backward, sluggish minds, or to the will of rulers perhaps worse than they?

Q. 30. How is it that the Lord's day must be spent and sanctified?

A. Not in diverting worldly thoughts, words, or deeds; much less in idleness, or vain pastimes; and, least of all, in such sinful pleasures as corrupt the mind, and unfit a man for holy work, such as gluttony, drunkenness, lasciviousnesss, stage plays, romances, gaming, &c. But the Lord's day is specially separated to God's public worship in church communion; and the rest to private and secret holy exercises. The primitive Christians spent most of the day together: and the public worship should not be only preferred, but also take up as much of the day as we can well spend therein.[10]

Q. 31. What are the parts of church service to be used on the Lord's day?

---

[10] Isa 58:13–14; Luke 4:16, 18; 6:1, 6, and 8:10; Acts 13:27, 42, 44; 15:21. 16:13, and 20:7; 1 Cor 14, and 16:1; Pss 1–3,&c.

A. (1) The reading of the sacred Scriptures, by the teachers, and expounding them to the people: their preaching the doctrine of the gospel, and their applying it to the case and consciences of the hearers. Their guiding them in the solemn exercise of God's praise, special worship, celebrating the sacraments, especially that of communion of the body and blood of Christ, and that with such conjunction of praises to God, as that it may be fitly called the eucharist, speaking and singing joyfully of God's perfections, and his mercies to man; but specially of the wonderful work of our redemption, and therein chiefly of the resurrection of Jesus Christ. For the day is to be spent as a day of thanksgiving, in joyful and praising commemoration of Christ's resurrection.

Q. 32. On days of thanksgiving men use to feast: may we labour on the Lord's day in providing feasts?

A. Needless cost and labour, and sensual excess, must be avoided, as unsuitable to spiritual work and rejoicing. But such provision as is suitable to a festival, for sober, holy persons, is no more to be scrupled, than the labour of going to the church, or the minister's preaching. And it is a laudable use for men to wear their best apparel on that day.

Q. 33. What are the private duties op the Lord's day?

A. Principally speaking and singing God's praises for our redemption in our families, and calling to mind what we were publicly taught, and catechising children and servants, and praying to God, and meditating on God's word, and works of nature, grace, and glory.[11]

Q. 34. Seeing the Lord's Day is for the commemoration of Christ's resurrection, must we cease the commemoration of the works of creation, for which the seventh day Sabbath was appointed?

A. No: the appointing of the Lord's day is accumulative, and not diminutive, as to what we were to do on the Sabbath. God did not cease to be our Creator and the God of nature, by becoming our Redeemer and the God of grace; we owe more praise to our Creator, and not less. The greater and the subsequent and more perfect work comprehendeth the lesser, antecedent, and imperfect. The Lord's Day is to be spent

---

[11] Ps 92; 95; 96, and 118:21–24; Col 3:16.

in praising God, both as our Creator and Redeemer; the creation itself being now delivered into the hands of Christ.[12]

Q. 35. But is it not then safest to keep two days; the seventh to honour the Creator, and the first to commemorate our redemption?

A. No; for when the world was made all very good, God delighted in man, and man in God, as his only rest. But upon the sin of man God is become a condemning judge, and displeased with man, and the earth is cursed; so that God is so far now from being man's rest, that he is his greatest terror, till he be reconciled by Christ. No man cometh to the Father but by the Son. So that now the work of Creation must be commemorated with the work of redemption, which restoreth it to its proper use.[13]

Q. 36. But what if a man cannot be satisfied that the seventh day is repealed, is it not safest for him to keep both?

A. God hath laid no such task on man, as to dedicate to religious duties two days in seven; and he that thinketh otherwise, it is his culpable error. But if he do it conscionably, without contentious opposing the truth, and dividing the church for it, good Christians will not despise him, but own him as a brother. Paul hath decided that case, Romans 14 and 15.

Q. 37. Why is mention here made of all within our gates?

A. To show that this commandment is not only directed to private persons, but to magistrates, and masters of families as such, who, though they cannot compel men to believe, they may restrain them from violating the rest of the Sabbath, and compel them to such external worship of God as all men are immediately obliged to; even all within the gates of their cities or houses.

Q. 38. What if one live where are no church meetings, or none that he can lawfully join with?

A. He must take it as his great loss and suffering, and with the more diligence improve his time in private.[14]

Q. 39. What preparation is necessary for the keeping holy that day?

---

[12] Jas 5:14; Rev 4:11, and 10:6; Col 1:16.

[13] Col 2:16.

[14] Rev 1:10.

A. (1) The chief part of our preparation is the habitual holiness of the soul, a love to God, and his word, and grace, and a sense of our necessities, and heart full of thankfulness to Christ, which relisheth sweetness in his Gospel, and in God's praise, and the communion of saints. (2) And the other part is our endeavour to prevent all distracting hinderances, and the greatest helps that we can in the most sensible means; and to meditate before of the great mercy of our redemption, of Christ's resurrection, the giving of the Holy Ghost, and the everlasting, heavenly rest which this prepareth for; and to pray for God's assistance and blessing.

38

Of the Fifth Commandment

Q. 1. What are the words of the fifth commandment?

A. "Honour thy father and thy mother, that thy days may be long in the land which the Lord thy God giveth thee."

Q. 2. Doth this commandment belong to the first table, or the second?

A. No man knoweth which of the two tables of stone it was written in by God: but if we may judge by the subject, it seemeth to be the hinge of both, or belong partly to each. As rulers are God's officers, and we obey God in them, it belongs to our duty to God; but as they are men, it belongs to the second.[1]

Q. 3. Why is father and mother named, rather than kings?

A. (1) Parents are our first governors, before kings. (2) Their government is deeplier founded, even in nature, and not only in contract. (3) Parents give us our very being, and we are more obliged to them than to any. (4) They have a natural love to us, and we to them; so that they are justly named first.

Q. 4. Is it only parents that are here meant?

A. No; all true governors are included. But so far as the Commandment is part of the law of nature, it bindeth us but to natural rulers

---

[1] Prov 1:8; 6:20; 13:1; 15:5; 20:20; 23:22, 25, and 30:17; Heb 12:9; Eph 6:1, 2; Mark 7:10, 11; Deut 21:18, 19, and 27:16; Lev 19:3, and 20:9; Exod 21:15, 17; Gen 9:23; Col 3:20, 22; Jer 35:8, 10.

antecedently to human contract and consent, and to those that rule us by contract, but consequently.[2]

Q. 5. What is the power of parents and rulers, which we must obey?

A. They are of various ranks and offices; and every one's power is special, in that which belongeth to his own place and office. But in general they have power first to command inferiors to obey God's laws: And, to command them such undetermined things in subordination to God's laws, which God hath left to their office to determine of; as corporations make by-laws, by virtue of the king's law.

Q. 6. What if parents or princes command what God forbids?

A. We must obey God, rather than men.[3]

Q. 7. Are we not then guilty of disobedience?

A. No, for God never gave them power to contradict his laws.

Q. 8. But who shall be judge when men's commands are contrary to God's? Must subjects and children judge?

A. While children are infants naturally uncapable of judging, we are ruled as brutes by our parents. But when we grow up to the use of reason, our obligation to govern ourselves is greater than to be governed by others.[4] God's government is the first in order of nature; and self-government is the next, though we are not capable of it till we come to some ripeness. A man is nearer to himself than his parents are, and his happiness or misery depends more on himself than on them. And indeed children's or men's obedience to others is but an act of self-government. It is a man's self-governing reason and will which causeth him to obey another; nor can a child perform any act of proper obedience differing from a brute, unless by a self-governing act. But parents' government is the next to self-government, and the government of husbands, princes, and masters, which are by contract, is next to that. Every subject, therefore, being first a subject of God, and next a self-governor, is to obey as a reasonable creature, and to understand

---

[2] Rom 13:1–3; Prov 5:13; Titus 3:1, 2; 1 Pet 2:13; 3:1, 5, and 5:5; 1 Tim 2:11; Heb 13:7, 17; 1 Cor 16:16.

[3] Acts 5:29.

[4] 1 Pet 1:14; 1 John 5:21; Jude 20, 21; Mark 13:9; Prov 25:28; 16:32, and 9:12; 2 Tim 2:15; 1 Tim 3:15; 4:7, 16, 16; 5:22, and 6:5

what is his duty and what not. And because all is our duty which God commandeth, but not all that man commandeth, God's power being absolute, and all men's limited; therefore we have nothing to do with the laws of God but to know them, and love them, and Obey them. But as to man's commands, we must know also, that they are not contrary to God's laws, and that they belong to the office of the commander.[5] If a parent or prince command you to blaspheme God, or worship idols, or deny Christ, or renounce heaven, or not to pray, &c. yon must obey God by disobeying him. And if a king command you not to obey your parents, or will choose for you your wife, your diet, your physic, the words you shall say to God in your secret prayers, &c., these are things which belong not to his office, no more than to a captain's, to become judge of the Common Pleas. Subjects, therefore, must judge what they must, or must not obey, as rulers must judge what they must, or must not command; or else they act not as men.

Q. 9. But what confusion will this cause, if every subject and child become judge whether their prince's or parents' commands be lawful? Will they not take all for unlawful which their folly or corrupt wills dislike, and so cast off all obedience?

A. It is not finding inconveniences in the miserable state of lapsed mankind that will cure them. Were there any avoiding error, sin, and confusion, by government, some would have found out the way before now. But while man is bad, he will do accordingly. In avoiding these evils, we must not run into far greater. Are they not greater, if men must not discern who is their lawful governor, but must fight for an usurper in power against his prince or parents, if commanded by him? And if every child and subject must renounce God, Christ, and heaven, that is commanded; and men become gods and antigods.[6]

Q. 10. But is there no remedy against both these confusions?

A. Yes, the remedies are these: (1) Rulers, that should have most reason, must give us the first remedy, by knowing God's laws, and taking care that they command and forbid nothing contrary to them, and not put on subjects a necessity of disobeying them.

---

[5] Dan 3, and 6:5

[6] Isa 9:6, 7; Job 34:17; Neh 5:14, 18.

(2) Children and subjects must be instructed also to know the laws of God, that they may not take that for his law which is not. It is not keeping them ignorant of God's laws, lest they pretend them against the laws of man, that is the way; no more than keeping them ignorant that there is a God, lest they obey him against man.

(3) They must be taught betime the difference between the capacity of children and of men at age, and of young unfurnished wits, and those that study and experience have ripened. And they must be taught the duty of self-suspicion, humility, and submission: and that as learning is necessary to knowing, so believing our teachers, with a human belief, is necessary to learning of them.[7] Who can learn, that will believe nothing which his teacher saith? But this is not taking him for infallible, nor resolving only to be ruled still by his knowledge, but in order to learn the same evidence of truth which our teachers themselves discern it by.[8]

(4) They must be taught to know, that if they mistake God's laws, and erroneously pretend them against their rulers, their error and abuse of the name of God is their sin, and will not excuse their disobedience; and therefore they must try well before they disobey.

(5) All the churches near them should agree publicly of all the necessary articles of divine faith and obedience, that the authority of their concord may he some awe to the minds of commanders and obeyers.

(6) Rulers are not to suspend the executive part of their government upon every conscientious error of the child or subject. If they will pretend God's law for intolerable sin or injury, they must nevertheless be restrained by punishment.

(7) But, lastly, the conscience of subjects' duty to God must be tenderly used and encouraged, and their mistakes through infirmity must be tolerated in all tolerable cases. Some differences and disorders in judgment and practice must be borne with by them that would not bring in greater.[9] Gentle reasoning, and loving usage, must cure as much of the rest as will be cured; and our concord must be placed in

---

[7] Eph 6:1–3.

[8] Eph 5:21; 1 Thess 5:12, 13; 1 Pet 5:5; 2 Pet 2:10.

[9] Rom 14:1, 2,&c.

the few plain and necessary things. The king hath more wit and clemency, than to hang all ignorant, erroneous, faulty subjects, or else he would have none left to govern. And if pastors have not more wit and clemency than to excommunicate all such, they would be no pastors, as having no flocks. But heinous is their sin that can tolerate multitudes of the ignorant and ungodly in their communion, who will but be for their power and wealth, and can tolerate none of the wise and conscionable if they do but differ from them in tolerable cases, or dislike them. Yet there goeth more to make a tolerable Christian and church member than a tolerable subject. And consent to the relation is necessary to both.

Q. 11. What duty doth the word honour contain and command?

A. (1) The first and chief of honouring them is to acknowledge their relation to God as his appointed officers, and the authority which God hath given them, that they may be obeyed reverently, and God in them.

(2) The next, is to take all their laws and commands, which God hath authorised them to make, to be the rule of our duty in subordination to God's laws, and so far to obey them for conscience' sake, believing it a sin to resist or disobey them.

(3) Another is to maintain them honourably, so far as we are able, and they need: though parents provide for children in youth, children must maintain parents if they need it, when they come to age: and so must people their princes and pastors, and pay tribute to whom it is due.[10]

(4) Also they ought to speak reverently to them, and honourably of them, and not use any unjust, dishonouring thoughts, words, or deeds, against them, specially which would disable them for government.

(5) Lastly, they ought to do their best to defend them against injuries.

Q. 12. But seeing parents are named, and not princes, must we defend our parents against our king, if he be their enemy?

A. If their cause be just, we must defend them by all lawful means; that is, by prayer to God, by argument, by petition to the king, and by helping their flight, or hiding them: and if a king would ravish or murder your mother or wife, you may hold his hands while they escape; as you may do if he would kill himself in drunkenness or passion. But

---

[10] Mal 1:6, 7; Matt 15:5, 6, and 21:30, 31; Eph 5:33, and 6:2; 1 Pet 2:17; 1 Tim 5:17; Rom 13:6, 7; Heb 12:9; 2 Sam 9:6; 1 King 1:31.

you may not, on such private accounts, raise a war against him, because war is a public action, and under the judgment of the public governor of the commonwealth, and not under the judgment of your parents, or any private person.[11]

Q. 13. But if the king command me one thing, and my parents another, which of them must I prefer in my obedience?

A. Each of them have their proper office, in which they must be preferred and obeyed: your mother must be obeyed before the king, in telling you when to suck or eat. Your parents must be obeyed before the king in matters proper to family government; as what daily food you shall eat, and what daily work for them you shall do, and what wife to choose, &c. But the king is to be obeyed before your parents in all matters belonging to national government.

Q. 14. But what if it be about religious acts, as what pastor I shall choose; what church I shall join with; how I shall spend the Lord's day, &c. Must I prefer the king, or my parents in my obedience?

A. While you are in your minority, and understand not the king's laws, you must obey your parents, and if they command you any thing contrary to the king's commands, they must be answerable for it as the case shall prove: some commands about your religion belong to your parents, and some to the king, and they are accordingly to be obeyed. It is not the king's, but your parents', to catechise you, to teach you to read and pray; to choose your schoolmaster or tutor: in these, therefore, your parents are first to be obeyed: and it is your parents' office to choose where you shall dwell, and, consequently, to what pastor you shall commit the conduct of your soul: and also how in the family, and in private, you shall spend the Lord's day. But the determination of all those public circumstances, which are needful to be imposed on all Christians in the land, belongs not to your parents, but to the supreme power.[12]

Q. 15. But what if the king and the bishops, or pastors, differ about matters of religion to be believed or done, which of them must I obey?

---

[11] 1 Sam 19:1, 4, 7, 11–13, 17; 20:16, 30, 42, and 14:44, 45.

[12] Deut 6:11, and 11:19.

A. If it be in things belonging to the king's determination, (as what translation shall be used in all the churches; when synods shall meet; who shall have the tithes, glebe, and temples; what national fasts or thanksgivings shall be kept, and such like,) you must obey the king. But if it be in things proper to the pastoral office, as who shall be judged capable of baptism, or of the Lord's supper and church communion; who shall be admonished, excommunicated, or absolved by the pastors; what text the minister shall preach on, and on what subject, in what method, and in what words; what he shall say to troubled consciences, or to the sick, or to others; what words he shall use in exhortation, prayer, or thanksgiving; all these being part of the pastor's work, you are to obey him in them all. But neither prince nor pastor have power against God.[13]

Q. 16. But what if the bishops or pastors be divided, which of them must we obey?

A. (1) Those that obey God's laws. (2) Those that impose the safest course, where the matter on one side is no sin, when on the other we fear it is. (3) All other things being equal, those that are most unanimous and concordant with the Universality of Christians, and the primitive church: and our own pastors rather than others. And the Godly and eminently wise, before the ignorant und ungodly.[14]

Q. 17. But what if the bishop or pastor who is over us, differ from most in the nation? And if the national bishops and ministry differ from most other foreign churches, as England from France, Spain, Italy, Germany, Muscovy, the Greeks, Armenians, Abyssinians?

A. (1) The things in which the difference is supposed, must not be thus confounded: either they are necessary points of faith or practice to all Christians in order to salvation. (2) Or else they are controverted opinions not so necessary. (3) Or else they are matters of local, occasional, mutable practice.

(1) As to the first, all true Christians are agreed in all things necessary to our common salvation: if any oppose these, and draw men from

---

[13] 2 Chron. 29:27. See all the examples of David, Solomon, Jehosaphat, Hezekiah, Josiah, and Nehemiah.

[14] Rom 16:16, 17; 1 Thess 5:12, 13; Heb 13:7, 17.

the church on that account, he is a heretic. In this case, God's law must be known to us, to which we must stick, whoever gainsay it.[15]

(2) In the second case, (of disputable, less necessary opinions,) we must suspend our judgments till evidence determine them: but judge them most probably to be in the right, who are in those matters discerned commonly to have greatest skill and sincerity. But the ignorant cannot subscribe to any of them in the dark.

(3) In the third case, (as what time and place we shall meet at; what subject we shall hear; what catechism questions we stall answer when we shall communicate, and with what individual persons, in what words the assembly shall pray and praise God, &c.,) we are to obey our own pastors, and not strangers: as every wife is to be governed by her own husband, and every child by his own parents, and every servant by his own master. I scarce think our papists (monarchical or aristocratical) would have art universal husband, parent, or master, or a council of husbands, parents, of masters of all the world, or all the kingdom; set up for such acts as these.

Q. 18. But is there no command to parents, princes, and pastors for their duty, as well as to children and subjects for theirs?

A. The commandments written on stone were necessarily brief, and the duty of rulers is here implied and included.

Q. 19. What is the duty of parents for their children?

A. (1) To take due care of their lives, health, and necessary maintenance.[16] (2) To teach them when they are capable to know God and his word, his doctrine, laws, promises, and penalties; to know themselves, their souls, their relation to God, their duty to him, their original pravity, and guilt, and danger. To know Jesus Christ, his person, life, doctrine, death, resurrection, ascension, glory, kingdom, intercession, and judgment. To know the Holy Ghost as sent by Christ, to indite and seal the Scripture, qualify the apostles and evangelists to deliver infallibly Christ's commands, and record them to all after ages, and accordingly settle the churches; to confirm their ministry by miracles, and to

---

[15] Gal 1:8, and 2. See the case of Paul and Peter.

[16] Deut 6:11; 11:19, and 32:46; Josh 4:6, 7, 22; Eph 6:3, 4; 1 Tim 3:12; Prov 22:6; 23:13, and 29:15.

sanctify all true Christians to the end of the world. To know the use of the ordinary ministry, and of the communion of saints. To know the covenant of grace, and the grace of pardon, adoption, and sanctification, which we must here receive, and the glory which we shall receive hereafter, at death, and at the general resurrection; and the great duties of faith and repentance, of obedience and love to God and man, and renouncing the lusts of the flesh, the world, and the devil, which must be done by all that will be glorified by and with Jesus Christ.[17]

This is the catechism which parents must teach their children.

Q. 20. Alas! it will be a hard and long work to teach children all this; or servants either, that are at age.

A. All this is but the plain meaning of the creed and ten commandments, which the church requireth all to learn; and no more than in their baptism the parents should, and the God-fathers do, solemnly promise to see them taught. It is these things for which God hath given them life, and time, and reason, and on which their present safety and comfort, and their everlasting life dependeth. And will you set them seven years apprentice to a trade, and set them seven and seven to schools and universities, and inns of court, where study must be their daily business: and will you think it too much to teach them the sense of the creeds, Lord's prayer, and ten commandments, needful to far greater and better ends?[18]

Q. 21. In what manner must parents teach their children?

A. (1) Very plainly, by familiar talk. (2) Gently and lovingly to win them, and not discourage them. (3) Beginning with the history and doctrine which they are most capable to receive. (4) Very frequently, that it be not neglected or forgotten. (Deut. 6 and 11) (5) Yet a little at a time, that they be not overwhelmed. (6) Praising them when they do well. (7) Doing all with such holy reverence that they may perceive it is the work of God, and not a common matter. (8) Teaching them by an answerable life.

Q. 22. What else, besides teaching, is the parents' duty?

---

[17] 1 Tim 3:16; 1 Cor 15:3–6; Heb 5:11, 12, and 6:1–3.

[18] 2 Tim 3:15.

A. (1) To use all just means to make religion pleasant to them, and win their hearts to love it; and therefore to tell them the Author, the excellency, the certainty, and profit of it here and hereafter. (2) To possess them with necessary fear of God, of death, of hell, and of sin. (3) To make a great difference between the good and the bad; rewarding good children, and correcting the bad, disobedient, and stubborn. (4) To choose safe and godly schoolmasters for them, if they teach them not all themselves. (5) To keep them out of ill company, and from temptations, especially to know their vices, and watch against all occasions of their sin. (6) To choose meet trades or callings for them, and faithful masters, ever preferring the welfare of their souls before their bodies. (7) To choose meet husbands or wives for them, if they are to be married.[19] (8) To settle them under a faithful pastor in the real communion of saints. And all this with constant, serious diligence, praying to God for his grace and blessing.

Oh! how happy were the church and world, if parents would faithfully do all this needful, certain duty, and not perfidiously and cruelly break the promise they made in baptism, and by negligence, worldliness, and ungodliness, betray the souls of their own children to sin and Satan. The happiness or misery of families, churches, cities, kingdoms, and of the world, lieth most eminently on parents' hands.

Q. 23. What is the duty of children to their parents in especial?

A. To honour their judgment and authority; to be thankful to them for their being, love, and education; to love them dearly; to learn of them willingly and diligently; to obey them faithfully; and to requite them as they are able; and what is included in the general duty of subjects opened before.[20]

Q. 24. What if the father be a papist and the mother a protestant, and one commandeth the child to read one book, and go to one church, and the other another, which must be obeyed?

A. Either the child is of age and understanding to try and judge which of them is contrary to God's law, or not. If he be, he must obey God first, and therefore not obey any thing that is contrary to his law;

---

[19] Deut 6:11, and 11:19, 20; Eph 6:3, 4; 2 Tim 3:15; 1 Thess 2:7.

[20] Eph 6:1, 2; Col 3:20, 21.

but if not, then he is one that will not put such questions, nor do what he doth out of conscience to God, but perform mere human obedience to man; and if his ignorance of God's law be through his own negligence, it will not excuse his sin if he mistake: but if it be from natural incapacity, he is ruled like a brute, and no doubt the father is the chief governor of the house, and will and must be obeyed before the mother, when obedience to God doth not forbid it, which this child understandeth not.

Q. 25. What, if children be rebellious in wickedness, as drunkenness, stealing, &c., must the parents cause them to be put to death, as Moses' law commanded, or what must they do with them?

A. Moses' law had some special severities, and was peculiar to that nation, and is abrogate. Whether the common good and safety require the death of such a son, or any, the Supreme Power is judge, and not the parents: nor is it meet, though some think otherwise, that parents have the power of putting to death their children; for the commonwealth, which is better than the family, is concerned in all the subjects' lives: and experience proveth it, that were this granted, whores, beggars, and raging, passionate persons would be common murderers of their children.

But if the magistrate would appoint one house of correction in every county for children that will not be ruled by parents, where they may be kept in labour till they are humbled and subdued, it would be an excellent work.

Q. 26. But what shall such sorrowful parents do?

A. First, use all means by wisdom, love, and patience, while there is hope; and, next, if they are past their correction, send them to the house of correction; and, lastly, disinherit them, or deny them all maintenance for their lust.

Q. 27. Is it a duty to disinherit an incorrigible, wicked son, or to deny such filial maintenance and portions?

A. Supposing it to be in the father's power, it is a duty to leave them no more than will maintain their lives in temperance; for all men are God's stewards, and must be accountable for all that he doth trust them with; and they ought not to give it to be the fuel of lust and sin, when they have reason to believe that it will be so used; that were to give God's mercies to the devil, to be turned against him. Nor are parents bound to give those children the necessary maintenance for their lives and health, or any thing at all, who, by obstinate rebellion, utterly forfeit it. Nature is not so strong a bond but that some sin may dissolve it, and forfeit life itself, and therefore forfeit fatherly maintenance. The rebellion and ingratitude of an incorrigible child is far more heinous than a neighbour's injuries. And though Moses' law, and its rigours, be ceased, the reason of it still remaineth, as directive to us, When thousands of good people want food, and we cannot give all, it is a sin to prefer an incorrigible, wicked son before them.[21]

Q. 28. But God may change them when the parents are dead?

A. It is supposed that the parents have tried to the utmost of their power; and parents cannot judge of what unlikelihoods God may bring to pass when they are dead. If God change them, God will provide for them. If parents have any hope, they may leave somewhat in trusty hands to give them when they see them changed. If not, such may work for themselves.

Q. 29. But what if a son be not deboist, but civil; but be of a corrupt understanding, inclined to ill opinions, and averse to serious piety, and like to use his estate to the hurt of the church or commonwealth, what shall parents do by such?

A. The public interest is to be preferred before a son's. If parents have good hopes that such a son may do more good than harm with his estate, they may trust him as far as reason requireth, rather than to trust a stranger. But if they have reason to believe that he will do more harm than good with it, they should settle it in trust to do all that good which he should do, and not leave it to do hurt, if it be in their power, allowing him necessary maintenance.

Q. 30. Should not parents leave all their estates to their children: or what proportion must they give them?

A. Nature makes children so near their parents, that no doubt they must be specially careful of their corporeal and spiritual welfare above others; and the Israelites, being tied to keep their possessions in their families and line, were under an extraordinary obligation in this matter. But, to all Christians, the interest of God and the common good is the

---

[21] Luke 15:16; Deut 21:18–21, and 18:11, 12; 2 Thess 3

chief, and to be preferred.[22] All they that sold their possessions, and laid down the money at the apostles' feet, did not scruple alienating them from their heirs. In this case, children are to be considered, (1) As mere receivers of their own due. (2) Or, as their parents' trustees for doing good. If they be like to prove faithful, their parents should rather trust them than others with their estates to do them good when they are gone. But if not, they should secure a due proportion for good works.

And however all men should in their life do all the good that regularly they can do; for who can expect that his son should do that good with his estate which he had not a heart to do himself? And who would not rather secure a reward to himself than to his son?

Q. 31. Do you disallow of the common course, which is to give all that men can get to their children, save some small droppings now and then to the poor?

A. I take it to be the effect of that selfishness which is the grand enemy to the love of God and man. A carnal, selfish man doth live to his flesh and carnal self, for which he gathers all that he can get: and when he must needs die, and can no longer enjoy it, he takes his children to be as parts of himself, and what they have he thinks he almost hath himself; and so out of mere self-love, doth love them and enrich them. But a holy person thinks all is God's, and that it is best used which is best improved to his will and kingdom.

But, alas! what have selfish, carnal worldings to account for when the best they can say of the use of God's talents is, that they pampered the flesh with as much as it craved, and the rest they gave their children to make them rich, that their flesh also might be pampered, and their lust might want no fuel or provision, nor their souls want temptation? Hundreds or thousands given to daughters, and lands purchased for their sons, and now and then a farthing or a penny given to the poor. And though the hypocrites take on them to believe Christ, that it is harder for a rich man to enter into the kingdom of God than for a camel to go through a needle's eye, yet they live as if nothing were the desire

---

[22] Acts 4 and 5:1–3; 1 Cor 4:2; 1 Pet 4:10; Ps 17:14; Job 21:11; Luke 19:8.

and business of their lives, but to make their own and their children's salvation by riches thus next to impossible.[23]

Q. 32. Is it well, as is usual, to give the eldest son all the inheritance?[24]

A. Nature and Scripture tell us of some pre-eminence of the eldest: this birth-right Jacob thought worth the buying of Esau: Christ is called the first-born of every creature, because the first-born have the pre-eminence of rule, wealth, and honour: and the heavenly society are called "The general assembly of the first-born whose names are enrolled in heaven." (Heb. 12.) Because they are in honour and power above others. But yet, (1) The younger also are sons, and must have their part: and it pleased God to leave on record how oft he hath preferred the younger: even an Abel before Cain, a Seth before his seniors; a Shem before Japhet and Ham; Isaac before Ishmael; Jacob before Esau; David and Solomon before their elder brethren.

(2) But to the faithful, though nature be not disregarded, yet grace teacheth us what to prefer. And Christ and his members are dearer to us than our sons or natural members.[25] In cases where we must deny ourselves for Christ and the public good, we may also deny our natural kindred: for they are not nearer to us than ourselves. And if an eldest son be wicked or unprofitable, a believing parent should give him the less, and more to a younger (yea, to a stranger) that will do more service to God and his country; and not prefer a fleshly difference and privilege before a spiritual, and his Master's service.

Q. 33. What is the duty of husbands to their wives?

A. To love them as themselves, and live with them in conjugal chastity, as guides and helpers, and provide for them and the family; to endeavour to cure their infirmities and passions, and patiently bear what is not cured; to preserve their honour and authority over inferiors, and help them in the education of their children, and comfort them in all their sufferings.[26]

Q. 34. What is the duty of wives to their husbands?

---

[23] Ps 49:9–15.

[24] Gen 25:31.

[25] Matt 19:21; Mark 10:21; Luke 12:33, and 18:22.

[26] Eph 5:25; Col 3:19; 1 Pet 3:7.

A. To live with them in true love and conjugal chastity and fidelity; to help them in the education of children, and governing servants, and in worldly affairs; to learn of them and obey them: to provoke them to duties of piety and charity, and to bear with their infirmities, and comfort and help them in their sufferings: and both must live as the heirs of heaven, in preparation for the life to come.[27]

Q. 35. What is the duty of masters to their servants?

A. To employ them suitably, not unmercifully, in profitable labour, and not in sin or vanity: to allow them their due wages, and maintenance, keeping them neither in hurtful want, nor in idleness, or sinful fulness: to teach them their duty to God and man, and see that they join in public and family worship, and live not in any wilful sin: and as fellow Christians (if they are such) to further their comfortable passage to heaven.[28]

Q. 36. But what if we have slaves that are no Christians?

A. You must use them as men that are capable of Christianity, and do your best, with pity, to cure their ignorance, and unbelief, and sin, and to make them Christians, preferring their souls before your worldly commodity.

Q. 37. Is it lawful to buy and use men as slaves?

A. It is a great mercy accidentally for those of Guinea, Brazil, and other lands, to be brought among Christians, though it be as slaves: but it is a sin in those that sell and buy them as beasts, merely for commodity, and use them accordingly: but to buy them in compassion to their souls, as well as for their service, and then to sell them only to such as will use them charitably like men, and to employ them as aforesaid, preferring their salvation, is a lawful thing, especially such as sell themselves, or are sold as malefactors.

Q. 38. What is the duty of servants to their masters?

A. To honour and obey them, and faithfully serve them, as part of their service of Christ, expecting their chief reward from him: to be trusty to them in word and deed, not lying, nor stealing, or taking any thing of theirs without their consent, nor wronging them by idleness,

---

[27] Eph 5:22, 24; Col 3:18; Titus 2:4, 5; 1 Pet 3:1-3.

[28] Eph 6:9; Col 4:1.

negligence, or fraud. Learning of them thankfully, and sincerely, and obediently, joining with them in public and family worship of God.[29]

Q. 39. Doth God require family teaching, and daily worship?

A. Yes, both by the law of nature and Scripture. All christian societies must be sanctified to God: christian families are christian societies: they have, as families, constant dependence on God, constant need of his protection, help, and blessing, and constant work to do for him, and therefore constant use of prayer to him: and as nature and necessity will teach us to eat and drink every day, though Scripture tell us not how oft, nor at what hour, so will they tell us that we must daily ask it of God. And stated times are a hedge to duty, to avoid omissions and interruptions: and Scripture commandeth parents to teach and persuade their children constantly, lying down and rising up, &c.[30] (Deut. 6 and 11.) And to bring them up in the nurture and admonition of the Lord: Cornelius, Crispus, and others converted, brought in their households with them to Christ. Daniel prayed openly daily in his house. The fourth commandment requireth of masters that all in their house do sanctify the Sabbath. Reason and experience tell us, that it is the keeping up religion and virtue in families, by the constant instruction, care, and worship of God, by the governors, that is the chief means of the hopes and welfare of the world, and the omission of it the great cause of all public corruption and confusion.[31]

Q. 40. What must children, wives, servants, and subjects do that have bad parents, husbands, masters, and magistrates?

A. Nature bindeth children in minority so to their parents, and wives to their husbands (except in case of lawful divorce) that they must live in patient bearing with what they cannot amend: and so must such servants and subjects as by law or contract may not remove, nor have legal remedy. But those that are free may remove under better masters and princes when they can.

Q. 41. But whole nations cannot remove from enemies and destroyers?

---

[29] 1 Pet 2:18; Titus 2:9; 1 Tim 1:1, 2; Eph 6:5–7; Col 3:22.

[30] Acts 10:2, 3; 1 Cor 1:16; Gen 18:10; 2 Sam 6:11, 20; Exod 12:3, 4.

[31] Acts 2:46; 5:42, and 12:12; Prov 3:33.

A. It is God, and not I, that must answer such cases. Only I say: (1) That there is no power but of God.

(2) That governing power is nothing but right and obligation to rule the people in order to the common good.[32]

(3) That destroying the common good is not ruling, nor any act of power given by God.

(4) That all man's power is limited by God, and subordinate to his universal government and laws, and he hath given none authority against himself or his laws.

(5) That so far as God's laws have not determined of the species and degrees of power, they must be known by the human contracts or consent which found them.

(6) Nations have by nature a right to self-preservation against destroying enemies and murderers.

(7) And when they only seek to save themselves against such, they resist not governing authority.

(8) But particular persons must patiently bear even wrongful destruction by governors: and whole nations tolerable injuries, rather than by rebellions and wars to seek their own preservation or right, to the hurt of the commonwealth.[33]

(9) They are the great enemies of government who are for perjury, by which mutual trust is overthrown.

---

[32] Rom 13:2–7; 2 Cor 10:8, and 13:10; 1 Pet 3:11–14,

[33] Matt 17:25, 26 and 22:19, 20.

— CHAPTER

39

Of the Sixth Commandment

Q. 1. What are the words of the sixth commandment?

A. Thou shalt do no murder.

Q. 2. What is murder?

A. Killing unjustly a reasonable creature. And all that culpably tends to it bringeth an answerable degree of guilt.

Q. 3. Why is this command the first that forbiddeth private wrongs?

A. Because a man's life is more precious than the accidents of his life; death deprived him of all further time of repentance and earthly mercies, and depriveth all others of the benefit which they might receive by him. They rob God and the king of a subject. Therefore God, who is the Giver of life, is a dreadful Avenger of the sin of murder; Cain was cast out with terror for this sin; for it was the devil's first service, who was a murderer from the beginning. Therefore God made of old the law against eating blood, lest men should be hardened to cruelty, and to teach them his hatred of blood-guiltiness.[1] And it was the murder of the prophets, and of Christ himself, and his apostles, that brought that dreadful destruction on the Jews, when wrath came upon them to the uttermost.[2]

---

[1] Deut 19:10, 13; 1 Kgs 2:31; 2 Kgs 21:16, and 22:4; Prov 6:17, and 28:17; Gen 4:10, 11; 9:4–6; 37:26, and 42:22; Hos 4:2.

[2] Matt 23:31, and 27:4, 25; Luke 11:50; Rev 16:6; Acts 22:20.

Q. 4. If God hate murder, why did he command the Israelites to kill all the Canaanites, men, women, and children?

A. Justice done by God, or his authority, on capital malefactors, is not murder. You may as well ask why God will damn so many in hell, which is worse than death. The curse was fallen on Ham's posterity. They were nations of idolaters, and murderers of their own children, offering them to idols, and so drowned in all wickedness that God justly made the Israelites his executioners, to take away their forfeited lands and lives.[3]

Q. 5. When is killing murder, or unlawful?

A. When it is done without authority from God, who is the Lord of life.

Q. 6. To whom doth God give such authority to kill men?

A. To the supreme rulers of commonwealths, and their magistrates, to whom they communicate it.[4]

Q. 7. May they kill whom they will?

A. No, none but those whose crimes are so great as to deserve death by the law of God in nature, and the just laws of the land; even such whose crimes make their death the due interest of the republic, and needful to its good and safety.

Q. 8. What if a prince think that the death of an innocent man is accidentally necessary to the safety of himself or the commonwealth, through other men's fault, may he not kill him?[5]

A. No; he is a murderer if he kill the innocent, or any whose fault deserveth not death; should God permit killing on such pretences, no men's lives would be safe. In factions there be other ways of remedy; and such wicked means do but hasten and increase the evil which men would so prevent.[6]

Q. 9. May not parents have power to kill bad children?

A. No; I have given you the reason under the fifth commandment.

---

[3] Deut 27:16; 18:9, 12, and 29:17; 2 Kgs 16:3; Lev 18:26, 27.

[4] Gen 26:11; Exod 19:12, and 21:12, 15–17; Deut 17:6, 7; 21:22, and 24:16; Josh 1:18.

[5] John 18:14.

[6] 1 Sam 14:43–45.

Q. 10. May not a man kill another in the necessary defence of his own life?

A. In some cases he may, and in some not; he may, in case it be his equal or inferior, as to public usefulness, and he have no other means, being assaulted by him to save his life from him. But he may not, (1) If by flight, or other just means, he can save his own life. (2) Nor if it be his king, or father, or any public person, whose death would be a greater loss to the commonwealth than his own.[7]

Q. 11. How prove you that?

A. Because the light of nature tells us, that seeing good and evil are the objects of our willing and nilling; therefore the greatest good should still be preferred, and the greatest evil be most avoided; and that the good or hurt of the commonwealth is far greater than of a single, private person.

Q. 12. But doth not nature teach every creature to preserve its life, and rather than die to kill another?

A. The nature of man is to be rational, and above brutish nature, and to choose by reason, though against sensitive inclination.[8] Why else must martyrs choose to die rather than to sin? and soldiers choose their own death before their captain's, or their king's, in which God and reason justify them?

Q. 13. But by this rule an army should kill their general, rather than to be killed or betrayed to death by him; because all their lives are better than one man's.

A. If they be but some part of an army, and the general's life be more useful to the rest, and to their king and country, and the public good, than all theirs, they should rather die, as the Theban legion did. But if the general be a traitor to his king and country, and would destroy all, or part, of the army to the public loss and danger, it is no murder if they kill him when they have no other way to save their lives.

Q. 14. How many sorts of murder are there, and which are the worst?

A. (I) One of the worst is persecution: killing men because they are good, or because they will not break God's laws. And lower degrees of

---

[7] So David to Saul.

[8] 1 Chron. 11:19; 1 John 3:16; Rev 12:11.

persecution by banishment, imprisonment, mulcts, participate of guilt against this command.[9]

(II) A second sort of heinous murder is by massacres, and unlawful wars, in which multitudes are murdered, and that studiously, and with greatest industry, and countries ruined and undone. The multitude of heinous crimes that are contained in an unlawful war are hardly known, but by sad experience.

(III) Another sort of heinous murder is, when parents kill their own children, or children their parents.

(IV) Another is, when princes destroy their own subjects, whom by office they are bound to protect: or subjects their princes, whom they are bound to obey, and defend, and honour.

(V) Another sort of heinous murder is, when it is committed on pretence of justice, by perjured witnesses, false accusers, or false judges, or magistrates:[10] as Naboth was murdered by Jezebel and Ahab, and Christ by the Jews, upon false accusations of blasphemy and treason. For in this case the murder is fathered on God, and on justice, which must abhor it, and the best things which should preserve the peace of the innocent are used to the worst ends, even to destroy them. And a man hath no defence for himself, as he may have against murderers, or open enemies; and he is destroyed by those that are bound to defend him. And the most devilish, wicked, perjured men, are made the masters of men's lives, and may conquer subjects by perverting law.

(VI) One of the most heinous crimes is, soul-murder, which is done by all that draw or drive men into sin, or from their duty to God and the care of their salvation, either by seducing, false opinions, opposing necessary truth and duty, or by scorns, or threats. But none here sin so grievously as wicked rulers, and wicked teachers and pastors of the churches. Others kill souls by one and one, but these by hundreds and thousands. And therefore it is the devil's main endeavour, through the world, to get rulers and teachers on his side, and turn the word and sword against him that did ordain them. All the idolatrous world that know not Christ are kept under the power of the devil, principally by

---

[9] Prov 29:10; Rev 6:10, 12; 18:24, and 19:2; Matt 23:35

[10] 1 Kgs 21:19.

wicked rulers and teachers. And so is the infidel and Mahometan world. When the Turks had once conquered the eastern empire, how quickly did those famous churches and large nations forsake Christ, and turn to the grossest of deceivers! Oh, how many millions of souls have been since hereby destroyed! And what wicked, deceitful, and contentious teachers have done to the murdering of souls, alas! the whole christian world is witness. Some by heresy, and some by proud tyranny, and some by malignant opposition to the serious practice of that holy law of God which they preach; and some by ignorance, and some by slothful, treacherous negligence, and some by church divisions, by their snares, or contentiousness. Such as Paul speaks of Phil. 1:15, 16, and 2:3. And some, in envy, malign and hinder the preaching of the Gospel, by such as they distaste. (1 Thes. 2:16.)

(VII) But of all soul-murder, it is one of the greatest which is done by wicked parents on their own children, who breed them up in ignorance, wickedness, and profane neglect, if not hatred and scorn, of serious holiness,[11] and teach them malignant principles, or hinder them from the necessary means of their salvation: that by example teach them to swear and lie, and be drunken or profane. For parents to be the cruel damners of their own children, and this when in false hypocrisy they vowed them in baptism to God, and promised their godly education, is odious cruelty and perfidiousness.

(VIII) And it is yet a more heinous sin to be a murderer of one's own soul, as every ungodly and impenitent sinner is: for nature teacheth all men to love themselves, and to be unwilling of their own destruction. And no wonder that such are unmerciful to the souls of wives, children, and servants, who will damn themselves, and that for nothing; and that, after all the importunities of God and man to hinder them.[12] Q. 15. When may a man be accounted a soul-self-murderer, seeing every man hath some sin?

A. Every sin, (as every sickness to the body,) is an enemy to life, though it destroy it not: and as wounding a man, yea, or injurious hurting him, or desiring his hurt, is some breach of this command, as Christ

---

[11] Deut 12:31; Ps. 104:37, 38.

[12] Prov 13:18; 29:1; 6:32, and 21:15.

tells us, (Matt. 5,) so every sin is as hurtful to the soul. But those are the mortal, murdering sins, which are inconsistent with the predominant habitual love of God and holiness, and are not only from the imperfection of this divine nature and image, but from the absence of it: such as are the sins of the unbelievers and impenitent.

Q. 16. But he shall not be hanged for killing another that doth it against his will: and no man is willing to damn himself?

A. But a man will himself be a dead man if he kill himself unwillingly: and all wicked men do willingly murder their own souls. They be not willing to burn in hell, but they are willingly ungodly, worldly, sensual: and unholiness is the death or misery of the soul, and the departing of the heart or love from God, and choosing the world and fleshly pleasure before his grace and glory, is the true soul-murdering.[13] When God maketh poison destructive to man's nature, and forbids us taking it, and tells a man that it will kill him; if this man will yet take the poison because it is sweet, or will not believe that it is deadly, it is not his being unwilling to die that will save him. When God hath told men that unholiness and a fleshly mind is death, he destroyeth his soul that yet will choose it.[14]

And it is a heinous aggravation that poor sinners have so little for the salvation which they sell. The devil can give them nothing that is to be put into the balance against the least hope or possibility of the life to come; and for a man to sell his own soul and all his hopes of heaven, for a base lust, or a transitory shadow, as profane Esau sold his birthright for a morsel, is self-murder of a most odious kind.

Q. 17. But you make also our friends that love us to be murderers of us, if they draw us to sin, or neglect their duty?

A: As the love of his own flesh doth not hinder, but further the drunkard's, fornicator's, and idle person's murder of his own soul; so your friend's carnal love to you may be so far from hindering, that it may further your destruction. They that draw each other to fornication,

---

[13] Rom 2:5, 6, 8; 1 Cor 6:9, 10; Eph 5:5–7.

[14] Heb 12:14, 16; Mark 8:36.

to gaming, to time-wasting plays, to gluttony and drunkenness, may do it in love. If they give you poison in love, it will kill you.[15]

And if parents that are bound to feed their children do famish them, do you think they do not murder them by omission? So may they; and so may ministers murder the souls that they are by nature or office entrusted to instruct and diligently govern.

Q. 18. Are there any other ways of murder?

A. So many that it is hard to number them. As by rash anger, hatred, malice, by drunkenness disposing to it. By magistrates not punishing murderers: by not defending the lives of others when we ought, and abundance more, which you may read in Bishop Downam's tables on the commandments.

Q. 19. Must I defend my parents or children against the magistrate, or any one that would kill them by his commission?

A. Not against justice, no doubt; what you must do against subjects who pretend an illegal commission to rob or kill yourself, parents, or children, or destroy cities and countries, is partly touched on under the fifth commandment, and partly matter unmeet for a catechism, or private, unlearned men's unnecessary discourse.

Q. 20. Are there more ways of self-murder?

A. Among others, excess of meat and idleness, destroy men's health, and murder millions.

---

[15] Gal 4:17, 18.

40

Of the Seventh Commandment

Q. 1. What are the words of the seventh commandment?

A. Thou shalt not commit adultery.

Q. 2. What is the sin here forbidden?

A. All unlawful, carnal copulation, and every evil inclination, or action, or omission which tendeth thereto, or partaketh of any degree of unchastity or pollution.

Q. 3. Is all lust or inclination to generation a sin?

A. No: for (1) Some is natural to man, and that not as corrupt; but as God said, "increase and multiply," before the fall, so no doubt he inclined nature thereto.[1] (2) And the regular propagation of mankind is one of the noblest, natural works that man is instrumental in; a man being a more excellent thing than a house or any work of art. (3) And God hath put some such inclination into nature, in great wisdom and mercy to the world: for if nature had not some considerable appetite to generation, and also strong desire of posterity, men would hardly be drawn to be at so much care, cost, and labour, to propagate mankind; but especially women would not so commonly submit to all their sickness, pain, danger, and after-trouble which now they undergo. But if a few self-denying persons did propagate mankind only as an act of obedience to God, the multitude of the ungodly would not do it.

---

[1] Heb 13:4; Gen 1:22, 28; 9:7; 22:17, and 26:4, 24.

Q. 4. If it be so, why is any carnal act of generation forbidden? especially when it is an act of love, and doth nobody any harm?

A. God hath in great wisdom and mercy to man made his laws for
restraining men from inordinate lust and copulation.

(1) The noblest things are basest when corrupted. Devils are worse
than men, because they were higher and better before. A wicked man is
incomparably worse and more miserable than a beast or a toad, because
he is a nobler nature depraved. And so human generation is worse than
that of swine or dogs, when it is vicious.

(2) Promiscuous, unregulated generation, tends to the utter ruin
and vitiating of mankind, by the overthrow of the just education of
children, on which the welfare of mankind doth eminently depend.
Alas, all care and order is little enough, and too little to keep corrupted
nature from utter bestiality and malignity, much more to make youth
wise and virtuous, without which it had been better never to have been
born! When fathers know their own children, and when mothers have
the love, and encouragement, and household advantage of order, which
is necessary, some good may be done. But lawless exercise of lust will
frustrate all. (1) Women themselves will be slaves, or their advantage
mutable and uncertain; for such lust will serve its turn of them but
for novelty, and will be still for change; and when a younger or a fairer
comes, the mother is cast off and hated.[2] And then the next will hate
her children, or at least not love them as a necessary education doth
require. And when the father hath forsaken the mother, it is like he will
forsake the children with her. And when women's lusts are lawless as
well as men's, men being uncertain what children are their own, will
be regardless both of their souls and bodies; so that confusion would
destroy religion and civility, and make the world worse than most of the
American savages are, who are taught by nature to set bounds to lust.

And besides all this, the very lust itself thus increased by lawless liberty would so corrupt men's minds, and fantasies, sad affections, into
a sordid, beastly sensuality, that it would utterly indispose them to
all spiritual and heavenly, yea, and manly, employments of heart and

---

[2] Acts 15:20, 29; Rom 1:29, 30; 1 Cor 5:11; 6:13, 18; 7:2, and 10:8; Gal 5:19; Eph 5:9, 4;
Col 3:5; 1 Thess 4:3; Rev 2:14, 20; Matt 15:19; Heb 12:16.

life; men would grow sottish and stupid, unfit to consider of heavenly things, and incapable of holy pleasures.

Q. 5. But if these evil consequents be all, then a man that can moderately use fornication, so as shall avoid these evils, sinneth not?

A. Sin is the breach of God's law; these mischiefs that would follow lawless lust show you that God made this law for the welfare of mankind. But God's own wisdom and will is the original reason of his law, and must satisfy all the world. But were there none but this fore-mentioned, to avoid the world's confusion and ruin, it was needful that God set a law to lust; and when this is done for the common good, it is not left to man to break God's law, whenever he thinks he can avoid the consequents, and secure the end of the law. For if men he left to such liberty, as to judge when they may keep God's law, and when they may break it, lust will always find a reason to excuse it, and the law will be in vain. The world needed a regulating law, and God's law must not be broken.

Q. 6. Which are the most heinous sorts of filthiness.?

A. Some of them are scarce to be named among Christians. (1) Sodomy. (2) Copulation with brutes. (3) Incest; sinning thus with near kindred. (4) Rapes, or forcing women. But the commonest sorts, are adultery, fornication, self-pollution, and the filthiness of the thoughts and affections, and the words and actions which partake of the pollution.[3]

Q. 7. Why is adultery so great a sin?

A. Besides the aforesaid evils that are common to it and fornication, it is a perfidious violation of the marriage covenant, and destroys the conjugal love of husband and wife, and confoundeth progeny, and, as is aforesaid, corrupteth family order and human education.[4]

Q. 8. Why may not a man have many wives now, as the Jews had?

A. As Christ saith of putting away, from the beginning it was not so, but it was permitted for the hardness of their hearts; that their seed might be multiplied, in which they placed their chief prosperity. And (that we may not think worse of them than they were) as God hath taught the very brutes to use copulation no oftener than is necessary to generation, so it is probable, by many passages of Scripture, that it

---

[3] Gen 18; 1 Cor 5; Lev 18.

[4] Matt 5:32, and 19:6; Mal 2:13.

was so ordinarily then with men; and, consequently, that they that had many wives, used them not so often as now too many do one; and did not multiply wives so much for lust as for progeny.[5]

Q. 9. But is no oftener use of husband and wife lawful than for generation?

A. Yes, in case of necessitating lust; but such a measure of lust is to be accounted inordinate, either as sin, or a disease; and not to be causelessly indulged, though this remedy be allowed it.[6]

Q. 10. But why may not many wives be permitted now, as well as then?

A. (1) No man can either dispense with God's laws, or forgive sin against them, but God himself. If he forbear men in sin, that doth not justify it. (2) If a few men and many women were cast upon a wilderness, or sent to plant it by procreation, the case were liker the Israelites, where the men were ofter killed by wars and God's judgments than the women: but with us there is no pretence for the like polygamy, but it would confound and disquiet families.

If one should make a difficult case of it, whether a prince that hath a barren wife may not take another for the safety of a kingdom, when it is in notorious danger of falling into the hands of a destroyer (as Adam's own sons and daughters lawfully married each other, because there were no others in the world) this would be no excuse, where no such public notorious necessity can be pleaded.

Q. 11. Why must marriage be a public act?

A. Because else adultery and unlawful separations cannot be known nor punished, but confusion will come in.

Q. 12. But is it not adultery that is committed against secret marriage, which was never published or legally solemnized?

A. Yes: secret consent makes a marriage before God, though not before the world: and the violation of it is adultery before God.

Q. 13. May not a man put away his wife, or depart from her if she seek his death, or if she prove utterly intolerable?

A. While he is governor, he hath divers other remedies first to be tried: a Bedlam must be used as a Bedlam: and, no doubt, but if he have

---

[5]   Gen 29:30, 34, and 30:15, 18, 20; Deut 25:6, 7.

[6]   1 Cor 7:9.

a just cause to fear poisoning or other sort of murder, he may secure his life against a wife as well as against an enemy. Christ excepted not that case, because nature supposeth such exceptions.

Q. 14. But if utter unsuitableness make their cohabitation an insuperable temptation, or intolerable misery, may they not part by consent for their own good; seeing it is their mutual good, which is the end of marriage?

A. (1) The public good is a higher end of all men's worldly interests and actions than their own: and when the example would encourage unlawful separaters, they must not seek their own ease to the public detriment. (2) And if it be their own sinful distempers which maketh them unsuitable, God bindeth them to amend, and not to part: and if they neglect not his grace, he will help them to do what he commandeth: and it is in his way, and not their own, by the cure of their sin, and not by indulging it, that they must be healed: but as the apostle saith, in another case, if the faulty person depart, and the other cannot help it, a brother or sister is not left in bondage, but may stay till the allay of the distemper incline them to return.[7]

Q. 15. What is inward heart-fornication, or uncleanness?

A. (1) Inordinate filthy thoughts are some degree. (2) Inordinate desires are a higher degree. (3) Inordinate contrivance and consent are yet a higher. And when such thoughts and desires become the ordinary inhabitants of the soul, and pollute it when they lie down and when they rise, and shut out holy and sober thoughts, and become a filthy habit in the mind, then the degree is so great as that an unclean devil hath got great advantage, if not a kind of possession of the imagination and the soul.[8]

Q. 16. Which way are the other senses guilty of this sin?

A. (1) When an ungoverned eye is suffered to fetch in lustful thoughts and desires into the mind. (2) Much more when to such immodest or unchaste looks there is added immodest actions and dalliance, unfit to be named. (3) And when fleshly appetite and ease do bring in fuel to

---

[7] Matt 5:32, and 19:6.

[8] Matt 5:28, 29; Eph 5:4, 5; Jas 1:21; 2 Pet 2:18; 1 John 2:16; Job 31:1.

unchaste inclinations. (4) And when the ear is set open to ribald and defiling words.

Q. 17. How is the tongue guilty of uncleanness?

A. By the aforesaid filthy or wanton talk, reading alluring books, using alluring words to others; but, worst of all, by defending, extenuating, or excusing any filthy lusts.

Q. 18. What are the chief causes of this sin?

A. It is supposed that God put into nature an ordinate governable appetite to generation in mankind: but that which rendereth it inordinate, and unruly, and destructive, is, (1) Overmuch pampering the flesh by pleasing meats and drinks. (2) Idleness; not keeping under the body by due labour, nor keeping the mind in honest employment about our callings, and the great matters of our duty to God, and of our salvation, which leave no room for filth and vanity. (3) Want of a sanctified heart and tender conscience to resist the first degrees of the sin. (4) Specially wilful running into temptation.[9]

Q. 19. By what degrees do persons come to fornication?

A. (1) By the aforesaid cherishing the causes, appetite and idleness.

(2) By this means the lustful inclinations of the flesh grow as strong and troublesome in some as a violent itch, or as a thirst in a fever.[10]

(3) Then an ungoverned eye must gaze upon some tempting piece of flesh.

(4) And if they get opportunity for frequent privacy and familiarity, and use it in immodest sights and actions, they are half overcome.

(5) For then the devil, as an unclean spirit, gets possession of the imagination, and there is a strong inclination in them to think of almost nothing else but fleshly filth, and the pleasure that their sense had in such immodest brutishness. When God should have their hearts morning and night, and perhaps at church and in holy actions, this unclean spirit ruleth their thoughts.

(6) Then conscience growing senseless, they fear not to feed these pernicious flames with ribald talk, and romances, and amorous foolish plays, and conversing with such as are of their own mind.

---

[9]　Deut 6:21; Ezek 16:49.

[10]　Eph 2:3; Jud. 12:7, 8; 2 Pet 2:14, 16, 18; 1 John 2:16 Gal 5:19, 20.

(7) After this, where their fancy is infected, they study and contrive themselves into further temptation, to get that nearness, opportunity, and secrecy which may encourage them.

(8) And from thence Satan hurrieth them, usually against conscience, into actual fornication.

(9) And when they are once in, the devil and the flesh say, 'Twice may be pardoned as well as once.'

(10) And some, at last, with seared consciences, grow to excuse it as a small sin; and sometimes are forsaken to fall into utter infidelity or atheism, that no fear of judgment may molest them. But others sin on in horror and despair; of whom, of the two, there is more hope, as having less quietness in their sins to hinder their repentance.

Q: 20. What are the best remedies against all unchastity and uncleanness of mind and body?

A. (1) The principal is the great work of renewing grace, which taketh up the heart of man to God, and maketh him perceive that his everlasting concerns are those that must take up his mind and life; and this work still mortifieth the flesh, with the affections and lusts thereof.

(2) Another is to make it seriously a great part of our religion to subdue and destroy all fleshly, sinful lusts: and not to think a bare conviction or wish will do it: but that it requireth more labour than to kill weeds in your ground, or to tame unruly colts or cattle.[11]

(3) Another means is, to resolve upon a constant diligence in a lawful calling. Poor labouring men are seldom so vicious in lust as idle gentlemen are.[12]

(4) Temperance and fasting, when there is need, and avoiding fulness, and flesh-pleasing meats and drinks. Gluttons and drunkards are fitted to be boars and stallions.

(5) To keep a conscionable government of the eye, and thoughts, and call them off as soon as Satan tempteth them.

(6) Above all, to be sure to keep far enough from tempting persons. Touch them not; be not private with them. There is no safety when fire

---

[11] Rom 8:1, 5, 7, 12, 13; 2 Pet 2:10; Gal 5:13, 17, 21.

[12] Jude 23; 1 Cor 9:17; Rom 13:13, 14; Prov 5:8; Gen 34.

and gunpowder are long near, and in an infectious house. Distance is the greatest means of safety.

(7) Another means is to foresee the end, and think what will follow: specially think of death and judgment. Consider what the alluring flesh will be when the small-pox shall cover it with scabs, or when it shall have lain a few weeks stinking in a grave. This must be. But O the thoughts of the judgment of God, and the torment of a guilty conscience, should be more mortifying helps. To go to the house of mourning, and see the end of all men, and see what the dust and bones of men are when they are cast up out of the grave, and to think where the souls are and must be for ever, methinks should cure the folly of lust.

Q. 21. Is it unlawful for men and women, especially the unmarried, to set out themselves in such ornaments of apparel as may make them seem most comely and desirable?

A. (1) The common rule is to be clothed with decent, but modest apparel, such as shows the body without deceit to be what it is, which is neither loathsome nor alluring. (2) And persons must be invited to conjugal desires by truth, and not by deceit, and by the matters of real worth, such as wisdom, godliness, patience, and meekness, and not by fleshly snares; for marriages so contracted are like to turn to continued misery to both, when the body is known without the ornaments, and deceit and diseases of the soul become vexatious.

(3) But there is much difference to be made of the time, and ends.[13] A young woman that hath a suitor, and intendeth marriage, may go further in adorning herself to please him that chooseth her, and a wife to please her husband's eye, than they may do to strangers, where there is no such purpose or relation. To use a procatious garb to be thought amiable to others, where it may become a snare, but can do no good, is the act of one that hath the folly of pride, and some of the disposition of a harlot; even a pleasure and desire to have those think them amiable, desirable persons, in whom it may kindle concupiscence likelier than good.

Q. 22. But may not a crooked or deformed person hide their deformity by apparel, or other means?

---

[13] Jer 2:32; 1 Pet 3:3, 4; Gen 38:16; Prov 7:10.

A. Yes, so far as it only tends to avoid men's disdain in a common conversation; but not so as to deceive men in marriage desires, or purposes, or practice.

Q. 23. What if one's condition be such that marriage is like to impoverish them in the world, and cast them into great straits and temptations, and yet they feel a bodily necessity of it?

A. God casteth none into a necessity of sinning. Fornication must not be committed to avoid poverty. If such can by lawful means overcome their lust, they must do it; if not, they must marry, though they suffer poverty.

Q. 24. What if parents forbid their children necessary marriage?

A. Such children must use all lawful means to make marriage unnecessary to them. But if that cannot be done, they must marry whether their parents will or not. For man hath no power to forbid what God commandeth.

Q. 25. Is that marriage void which is without the consent of parents, and must such be separate as adulterers?

A. Some marriage, as aforesaid, is lawful without their consent; some is sinful, but yet not null, nor to be dissolved, which is the most usual case. Because all at age do choose for themselves, even in the matters of salvation: and though they ought to be ruled by parents, yet when they are not, their own act bindeth them. But if the incapacity of the persons make it null, that is another case.

Q. 26. How shall men be sure what degrees are prohibited, and what is incest, when Moses's law is abrogated, and the law of nature is dark and doubtful in it, and Christ saith little of it?

A. (1) Those passages in Moses's laws, which are but God's explication of a dark law of nature, do still tell us how God once expounded it, and consequently how far it doth extend, though Moses's law as such be abrogated.

(2) The laws about such restraint of marriage are laws of order; and therefore bind when order is necessary for the thing ordered, but not when it destroyeth the good of the thing ordered, which is its end. Therefore incest is unlawful out of such cases of necessity; but to Adam's sons and daughters it was a duty: and all the children of Noah's three sons must needs marry either their own brothers and sisters, or

the children of their father's brethren, which moved Lot's daughters
to do what they did.

(3) In these matters of order some laws of the land must be obeyed,
though they restrain men more than the laws of God.

Q. 27. Is marriage in every forbidden degree to be dissolved?

A. Not if it be a degree only forbidden by man's laws: or if it were
in such foresaid cases of absolute necessity, but that which God doth
absolutely forbid, must not be continued but dissolved; as the case of
Herod, and him, 1 Cor. 5, tells us.

41

Of the Eighth Commandment

Q. 1. What are the words of the eighth commandment?

A. Thou shalt not steal.

Q. 2. What is the stealing here forbidden?

A. All injurious getting or keeping that which is another's.

Q. 3. When is it injurious?

A. When it is done without right: and that is, when it is done without the owner's consent, or by a fraudulent and forcible getting his consent, and without just authority from a superior power, who may warrant it.

Q. 4. What power may allow one to take that which is another's?

A. (1) God, who is the only absolute owner of all, did allow the Israelites to take the Egyptians' and Canaanites' goods; and so may do by whom he will. (2) And a magistrate may take away the goods of a delinquent who forfeiteth them; and may take from an unwilling subject such tribute as is his due, and as much of his estate as the law alloweth him to take for the necessary defence of the commonwealth, and may force him to pay his debts: and a father may take from his child, who is but a conditional sub-proprietor, what he seeth meet.

Q. 5. But what if it be so small a matter, as will be no loss to him? Is it sinful theft to take it?

A. Yes; if there be none of his consent, nor any law to warrant you, it is theft, how small soever the thing be. But if the common sense of mankind suppose that men would consent if they knew it; or if the law of God, or the just law of man, enable you to take it, it is no theft.

And so God allowed the Israelites to pluck the ears of corn, or eat fruit as they passed through a vineyard in hunger, so be it that they carried none away. And a man may gather a leaf of an herb for a medicine in another man's ground, because humanity supposeth that the owner will not be against it.[1]

Q. 6. But what if he can spare it, and I am in great necessity, and it be his duty to relieve me, and he refuseth?

A. You are not allowed to be your own carver; the common good must be preferred before your own. And if every one shall be judge when their necessity alloweth them to take from another, the property and right of all men will be vain, and the common order and peace be overthrown. And while you may either beg, or seek to the parish or magistrate for relief, there is no place for a just plea of your necessity.

Q. 7. But should a man rather die by famine, than take from another that is bound to give, and will not?

A. If his taking will, by encouraging thieves, do the commonwealth more hurt than his life will do good, he is bound rather to die than steal. But I dare not say that it is so, where all these following conditions concur. (1) If it be so small a thing as is merely to save life (as God allowed the aforesaid taking of fruit and corn). (2) If you have first tried all other means, as begging, or seeking to the magistrate. (3) If by the secrecy, or by the effect, it be no hurt to the commonwealth, but good. As for instance, if to save life, one take an apple from a tree of him that is unwilling; or eat pease or corn in the field: if children have parents that would famish them; if a company in a ship should lose all their provision save one man's, and he have enough for them all, and would give them none, I think the law of nature alloweth them to take as much as will save their lives, against his will. If David, the Lord's anointed, and his six hundred men, want bread, they think they may take it from a churlish Nabal.[2] If an army, which is necessary to save a kingdom from a foreign enemy, should want money and food, and none would give it them, it seemeth unnatural to say, that they should all famish, and lose the kingdom, rather than take free quarter, or things absolutely

---

[1]　Deut 23:25; Matt 12:1; Luke 6:1.

[2]　Even King Ahab might not take Naboth's vineyard.

necessary, from the unwilling. The commonwealth's right in every subject's estate is greater than his own, as the common good is better than his. But these rare cases are no excuse for the unjust taking of the least that is another's without his consent.

Q. 8. But may not a child, or servant, take that meat or drink which is but meet, if the parents and masters be unwilling?

A. No, unless, as aforesaid, merely to save life. If children have hard parents, they must patiently bear it. If servants have hard masters, they may leave them, or seek remedy of the magistrate for that which they are unable to bear. But the world must not be taught to invade other men's property, and be judges of it themselves.

Q. 9. But what if he owe me a debt and will not pay me, or keep unjust possession of my goods, may I not take my own by stealth or force, if I be able?

A. Not without the magistrate, who is the preserver of common order and peace, when your taking it would break that order; and such liberty would encourage robbery. If you take it, you sin not against his right, but you sin against the greater right and peace of the commonwealth.

Q. 10. But what if I owe him as much as he oweth me, may I not stop it, and refuse to pay him?

A. Yes, if the law and common good allow it, but not else; for you must rather lose your right, than hurt the commonwealth, by breaking the law which keeps its peace.

Q. 11. What if I win it by gaming, or a wager, when he consented to run the hazard?

A. Such gaming as is used in a covetous desire of getting from another, without giving him any thing valuable for it, is sinful in the winner and the loser; and another's covetous, sinful consent to stand to the hazard, maketh it not lawful for you to take it. You forfeit it on both sides, and the magistrate may do well to take it from you both. But if a moderate wager be laid, only to be a penalty to the loser for being confident in some untruth, it is just to take his wager as a penalty, and give it to the poor. But the just law of exchanging rights by contract is, to take nothing that is another's, without giving him for it that which is worth it.

Q. 12. Is it lawful to try masteries for a prize or wager; as running of men, or horses, cockfights, fencing, wrestling, contending in arts, &c.?

A. It is not lawful to do it. (1) Out of covetousness desiring to get another man's money, though to his loss and grief. (2) Nor by cruelty, as hazarding men's lives by over-striving, in running, wrestling, fencing, &c. But if it be used as a manly recreation, and no more laid on the wager than is meet to be spent on a recreation, and may be justly spared without covetousness, or hurting another, I know not but it may be lawfully done.

Q. 13. What are the rules to avoid sinful injury, in buying and selling?

A. (1) That you give the true worth, that is, the market price for what you buy, and desire not to have it cheaper, unless it be of a rich man that abateth you the price in kindness or charity, or one that, having bought it cheaper, can afford to sell accordingly.[3] And that you neither ask nor desire more than the said true worth for what you sell, unless it be somewhat that you would not otherwise part with, which is worth more to some one man than to others, or one that in liberality will give you more.

(2) That you do as you would be done by, if you were in the same circumstances with the other, supposing your own desires just.

(3) That you work not on the ignorance or necessities of another, to get more or take less than the worth.

(4) And, therefore, that you deceive him not by hiding the fault of what you sell, nor by any false words or wiles.

(5) That if a man be overseen, you hold him not to his bargain to his loss, if you can release it without a greater loss. Yet that you stand to your own word to him if be will not discharge you. More I omit.[4]

Q. 14. Is it lawful to take usury, or gain, for money lent?

A. The great difference of men's judgments about usury, should make all the more cautelous to venture on none that is truly doubtful. I shall give my judgment in some conclusions.

(1) It is evident that usury of other things, as well as of money, was forbidden the Jews. (Deut. 23:19, 20; Lev. 25:36, 37; Exod. 22:25.) And by usury is meant any thing more than was lent taken for the use of it.

---

[3] Lev 25:14; Prov 20:14.

[4] Amos 8:6.

(2) It is manifest, the word "nesheck," signifying biting usury, that it is unmerciful hurting another that is here meant.

(3) It is manifest that it was to the poor that this manner of lending was not to be used: and that only to a brother or Israelite, who also might not be bought as a forced servant: but to a stranger it was lawful.

(4) The Israelites then used no merchandise, or buying and selling for gain. They lived on flocks, herds and vineyards, and fig-trees. So that it is only taking usury of any thing that was lent to the needy, when charity bound them to relieve them by lending, that is here meant.

(5) To exact the principal, or thing lent, was as truly forbidden, when the poor could not pay it. And so it was to deny to give him freely in his need.

(6) All this plainly showeth that this supposeth a case in which one is bound to use mercy to another in want, and that it is mere unmercifulness that is here forbidden.

(7) The law described the sin, and the prophets, when they speak against usury, do but name it; making no new law, but supposing it described in the law before.

(8) The law of Moses, as such, bound not the rest of the world, nor bindeth Christians now. (2 Cor. 3)

(9) Therefore there is no usury forbidden but what is against the law of nature, or the supernatural revelation of Christ.

(10) The law of nature and of Christ forbid all injustice and uncharitableness, and therefore all usury which is against justice or charity. Every man must in trading, lending, and giving, keep the two grand precepts; "Do as you would (justly) be done by," and "Love your neighbours as yourselves."

(11) To take more for the use than the use of the money, horse, goods, or any thing, was really worth to the user, is injustice. And to take either use or principal when it will do more hurt to him that payeth it, than it is like to do good to ourselves, or any other to whom we are more obliged, is contrary to charity: and so it is not to give where we are obliged to give.

(12) Merchandise, or trading by buying and selling for gain, is real usury. They that lay out money on goods, and sell them for more than they gave for them, do take use or increase for their money of the buyer: which was forbidden the Israelites to poor brethren. And it is all one to

make a poor man pay one shilling in the pound for the use of the money to buy cloth with, as to make him pay one shilling more than was paid for the cloth. And if a draper be bound to lend a poor man money to bay cloth, without use, he is as much bound to sell him cloth without gain.

(13) Merchandise, or trading for gain, is not unlawful, being used without injustice and uncharitableness.

(14) Every one that hath money is not bound to lend it at all: and not to lend it at all is as much against the good of some borrowers as to lend it and take but what the use of it was worth to them.

(15) No more must be taken for use than the user had real profit by it; unless it be when the rich are willing to pay more, or run the hazard, or what a man loseth by one bargain he gets by another.[5]

(16) Some usury is an act of great charity: viz., a landlord offereth to sell his tenant his land for much less than the worth: the tenant hath not money to buy it: a rich neighbour told him, 'The land is also offered to me; but if you will, I will lend you money on use to buy it, and pay me when you can.' It was wood land: the tenant borrows the money; and in two years sells the wood, which paid it all, and had the land for almost nothing. Was not this charitable usury?[6]

I knew a worthy person that, trading in iron-works, did, partly for himself and partly in charity, take to use the monies of many honest, mean people, that knew not else how to live or to use it; and from a small estate he grew to purchase at least seven thousand pounds per annum to himself and his sons. Was there any uncharitableness in this usury?[7]

(17) It is great uncharitableness in some not to give use for money, and cruelty to set it out without use: as when poor orphans are left with nothing but a little money to maintain them, and abundance of poor widows that have a little money, and no trade to use it in, and must beg if they presently spend the stock; if they lend it the rich, or those that gain by it in trading, the gainers are unmerciful if they pay not use for it, as well as unjust.

---

5   Deut 23:20.

6   Matt 25:27; Luke 19:23.

7   Prov 22:16.

(18) They that say, 'We must not lend to make men rich, but only to the needy,' do put down all common trading; and forbid most young men to marry: for that which will maintain a single man plentifully will not maintain a wife and children, and provide them necessary portions: and if he must not endeavour to grow richer than he is, how shall he maintain them, who had but enough for himself before? And how shall he be able to relieve the poor, or do any such good works, if he may not endeavour to grow richer?

Q. 15. If a merchant find that it is usual to deceive the Custom-house, or poor men think chimney money, or other legal taxes, to be an oppression, may they not, by concealment, save what they can?

A. No; the law hath given it the king; if you like not to be his subjects on the terms of the law, remove into another land; if you cannot, you must patiently suffer here. It is no more lawful to rob the king than to rob another man.

Q. 16. Is it necessary to restore all that one hath wrongfully got?

A. Yes, if he be able.[8]

Q. 17. What if he be not able?

A. If he can get it by his friends, he must; if not, he must humble himself to him that he wronged, and confess the debt, and bind himself to pay him if ever he be able.

Q. 18. But what if it be a malicious man, that will disgrace or ruin him if he know it, is he bound to confess it?

A. Humanity itself will tell a man, that repentance is the greatest honour, next to innocence; and that a repenting person, that will do it at so dear a rate, is unlike to wrong him any more: and, therefore, we may suppose that there are few so inhuman as to undo such a penitent. But if he that knoweth him have good cause to judge that the injured person will make use of his confession, (1) To the wrong of the king or the commonwealth, or the honour of Christianity, (2) Or to a greater hurt of the confessor than the confession is like to prove a good to any, he may then forbear such a confession to the person injured, and send him secretly his money by an unknown hand: or, if he cannot pay him, confess it to God and his spiritual guide.

---

[8] Exod 22:5, 6, 12; Lev 6:4; Luke 19:8.

Q. 19. What if a man can restore it, but not without the wrong or ruin of his wife and children, who knew not of his sin?

A. His wife took him with his debts, as he did her; and this is a real debt: she can have no right by him in that which he hath no right himself to; and he cannot give his children that which is none of his own.

Q. 20. What if I wronged a master but in some small matter in marketing, which is long since gone?

A. The debt remaineth: and if you have the value, you must offer satisfaction; though it is like, that for small things few will take it: but you must confess the fault and debt; and forgiveness is equal to restitution.

Q. 21. What if those that I wronged be dead?

A. You owe the value to those that they gave their estate to: or, if they be dead, to the next heirs: and if all be dead, to God, in some use of charity.

Q. 22. What if any father got it ill, and left it me?

A. He can give you no right to that which he had none to himself; sinful keeping is theft, as well as sinful getting.

Q. 23. What if the thing be so usual as well as small, as that none expect confession or restitution: as for boys to rob orchards?

A. Where you know it would not be well taken, restitution is no duty: but if you have opportunity, it is safest to confess.

Q. 24. Is it thievery to borrow and not pay?

A. Deceitful borrowers are of the worst sort of thieves, against whom one cannot so well save his purse as against others: and they would destroy all charitable lending, by destroying mutual belief and trust. Many tradesmen that after break, do steal more, and wrong more, than many highway robbers that are hanged. But it is not all breakers that are so guilty.[9]

Q. 25. What borrowing is it that is theft?

A. (1) When you have no intent to pay. (2) When you know that you are not able to pay, nor like to be able. (3) When there is a great hazard and danger of your not paying, with which you do not acquaint the lender, and so he consenteth not to run the hazard.[10]

---

[9] Rom 13:8, 9.

[10] Ps 37:21.

Q. 26. What if it would crack my credit, and ruin my trade, if I should reveal the hazard and weakness of my estate?

A. You must not rob others for fear of ruin to yourself. If you take his money without his consent, you rob him. And no man that is ignorant is said to consent: if you hide that which would hinder him from consenting if he knew it, you have not really his consent, but rob him.

Q. 27. What is the duty required in this eighth commandment?

A. To further the prosperity or estate of your neighbour as you would do your own, that is, with the same sincerity.

Q. 28. Must a man work at his trade for his neighbour as much as for himself; or as much use his estate for others?

A. I said 'with the same sincerity' not in the same manner and degree. For there are some duties of beneficence proper to ourselves as the objects, and some common to others. And as nature causeth the eye to wink for itself, and the gust to taste for itself immediately, and yet also consequently for every member's good, and principally for the whole man; so every man must get, possess, and use, what he can immediately for himself. But as a member of the body which hath a due I regard to the good of every member, and is more for the whole than for himself.[11]

Q. 29. Who be the greatest breakers of this commandment?

A. (1) They that care for nobody but themselves, and think they may do with their own as they list, as if they were absolute proprietors, whereas they are but the stewards of God: and it is the pleasure of the flesh which is the use they think they may put all their estates to.

(2) Those that see their brother have need, and shut up the bowels of their compassion from him;[12] that is, relieve him not when it is not for want of ability, but of compassion and will; or that drop out some inconsiderable pittance to the poor, like the crumbs or bones to the dogs; the leavings of the flesh, while they please their appetites and fancies with the rest, and live as he (Luke 16) who was clothed in purple and silk, and fared sumptuously or deliciously daily, while the poor at the door had but the scraps. That make so great a difference between themselves and others as to prefer their own superfluities and pleasures

---

[11] 1 Cor 12:21; Eph 4:28.

[12] Deut 15:8, 11; Eph 4:28; Jas 2:16; 1 John 3:17; Matt 25; Prov 31:20; Ps 72:13; Ezek 16:49.

before the necessities of others, even when multitudes live in distressing poverty.

(3) Those that live idly, because they are[13] rich or slothful, and think they are bound to labour for none but themselves; whereas God bindeth all that are able to live in some profitable labour for others, and to give to them that need. So also they that by prodigality, drunkenness, gaming, luxury, or other excess, disable themselves to relieve the poor.

(4) Those that out of a covetous, worldly mind heap up riches for themselves and their children,[14] to leave a name and great estate behind them; (that their children may as hardly be saved as themselves;) as if all that they can gather were their children's due, while others better than they are utterly neglected.

(5) Those that give with grudging, or make too great a matter of their gifts, and set too high a price upon them, and must have it even extorted from them.

(6) Those that neglect to pay due wages to them that labour for them, and would bring down the price below its worth, so that poor labourers cannot live upon it: and that strive in all their bargainings to have every thing as cheap as they can get it, without respect to the true worth or the necessities of others.[15]

(7) Those that help not to maintain their own families and kindred as far as they are able.

Q. 30. Who are the greatest robbers, or breakers of both parts of this command, negative and preceptive?

A. (1) Emperors, kings, and other chief rulers, who oppress the people, and impoverish them, while they are bound by office to be God's ministers for their good.[16]

(2) Soldiers who, by unjust wars, destroy the countries, or, in just war, unjustly rob the people. O, the woeful ruins that such have made! So that famine hath followed the poverty and desolation, to the death of thousands.

---

[13] Prov 31; 2 Thess 3.

[14] Nabal.

[15] 1 Tim 5:8; Jas 4, 5.

[16] Exod 3:9, 10; Ps 12:5, 6, and 73:8; Prov 28:16; Eccl. 4:1, 2; 1 Sam 12:3, 4.

(3) Unrighteous judges, who for bribes or partiality, or culpable ignorance, do fine righteous men, or give away the estates of the just, and do wrong men by the pretence of law, right, and justice, and deprive the just of their remedy.

(4) Perfidious patrons, who simoniacally sell, or sacrilegiously alienate, the devoted maintenance of the church.

(5) Much more those rulers and prelates who factiously, maliciously, or otherwise culpably, silence and cast out faithful ministers, sacrilegiously alienating them from the work of Christ, and the church's service, to which they were consecrated and devoted, and casting them out of their public, ministerial maintenance.[17]

(6) All persecutors who unjustly fine men, and deprive them of their estates, for not sinning against God by omission or commission, especially when they ruin multitudes.

(7) Cruel, oppressing landlords, who set their poor tenants such hard bargains as they cannot live on.[18]

(8) Cruel lawyers, and other officers, who take such fees as undo the clients; so that men that have not money to answer their covetous expectations, must lose their right.

(9) Unmerciful physicians, who consider not the scarcity of money with the poor, but by chargeable fees, and apothecaries' bills, put men to die for want of money.[19]

(10) Unmerciful usurers and creditors, that will not forgive a debt to the poor, who have it not to pay.

(11) People that rob the ministers of their tithes.

(12) Cheaters, who by gaming, false plays, and tricks of craft, or false writings, concealments, or by quirks in law that are contrary to equity, do beguile men of their right.[20] And especially the poor, who cannot contend with them; yea, and some their own kindred.

---

[17] 2 Cor 7:2.

[18] Isa 5:7; Jer 6:6.

[19] Isa 3:12; 16:4, and 19:20.

[20] Lev 19:13; 1 Cor 6:7, 8; 1 Thess 4:6.

42

Of the Ninth Commandment

Q. 1. What are the words of the ninth commandment?

A. Thou shalt not bear false witness against thy neighbour.

Q. 2. What is it which is herein forbidden?

A. All falsehood injurious to the innocency, right, or reputation of another; especially in witness-bearing, accusations, or judgments, contrary to public justice. The act forbidden is falsehood; the object against which it is done is our neighbour's good or right of any sort; whether his good name, or estate, or life, especially as it perverteth the hearer's judgment and love, or public justice.[1]

Q. 3. Is all lying here forbidden, or only injurious lying?

A. All lying is injurious, and forbidden.[2]

Q. 4. What injury doth a jesting lie do to any one? or a lie which only saveth the speaker from some hurt, without hurting any other? Yea, some lies seem to be profitable and necessary. As if a parent, or physician, tell a lie to a child or patient, to get them to take a medicine to save their lives; or a subject tell a lie to a traitor, or enemy, to save the life of the king; tell me, I pray you, why God forbiddeth all such lies?

A. (1) You must consider, that God is the Author of order; and order is to the world its useful disposition to its operations and ends. Just as it

---

[1] Lev 19:11; Prov 15:4.

[2] Col 3:9; Rev 21:17, and 22:15.

is to a clock, or watch, or a coach, or ship, or any such engine; disorder the parts, and it is good for nothing. A kingdom, army, church, or any society, is essentiated by order, without which it is destroyed. And the world of mankind being made up of individual persons, the ordering of particular men is the chief thing to the order of the human world. As we die, when disorder of parts or humours maketh the body incapable of the soul's operations, so a man's soul is vitiated and dead to its chief ends, when its order is overthrown. All godliness and morality is nothing but the right order of the dispositions and acts of man, in our subordination to the governing will of God, which is our law. It is not another substance that grace maketh in us, but another order. And all sin is nothing but the contrary disorder; and that man's words be the true and just expression of his mind is a great part of the order of his words, without which it were better man were speechless.

And, (2) You must consider, that God hath made man a sociable creature, and each one a part of the world, which is one kingdom of God, the universal King. And that each part is more for the whole than for itself, because the common welfare of the whole is better than of any part, as being a higher end of government, and more illustriously showing the glory of God.

And, (3) You must consider, that because God only knoweth the heart, there can be no society and conversation but by words, and other signs. And that without mutual trust there can be no society of love, concord, or mutual help. But utter distrust is a virtual war. There can be no prince and subjects, no husband and wife, no pastor and flocks, without some trust. And trustiness is truth-telling. So far as a man is taken for a liar, he is not believed or trusted.[3]

(4) You must consider, that if God should leave it to man's discretion in what cases to lie, and in what not, and did not absolutely forbid it, selfishness, interest, and folly, would scarce leave any credibility or trustiness in mankind; for how can I know whether your judgment now bid you not lie, for some reason that I know not?

(5) So that you see that leave to lie when we think it harmless would be but to pluck up a flood-gate of all deceit, untrustiness, and utter

---

[3] Prov 6:17; 12:19, 28; 13:5, and 17:7; 1 Tim 1:10.

confusion, which would shame, and confound, and ruin societies and the world. And then it is easy to know that it is better that any man's commodity or life miscarry (which yet was scarce ever done merely for want of a lie), than that the world should be thus disordered and confounded. As men sick of the plague must be shut up rather than go about to infect the city; and some houses must be blown up rather than the fire not be stopped. And as soldiers burn suburbs to save a city, &c., so no man's private good must be pretended for the corruption and misery of the world.[4]

(6) And remember that lying is the devil's character and work, and so the work and character of his servants. And truth is the effect of God's perfection, and his veracity so necessary to mankind, that without it we could have no full assurance of the future blessedness which he hath promised. If God could lie, our hopes were all shaken; for we should be still uncertain whether his word be true. And God's laws and his image must signify his perfection.[5]

Q. 5. Wherein doth the truth of words consist?

A. In a threefold respect: (1) In a suitable significancy of the matter. (2) In an agreeable significancy of the mind of the speaker. (3) And both these, as suited to the information of the hearer.

Q. 6. What is false speaking?

A. (1) That which is so disagreeable to the matter as to represent it falsely. (2) That which is so disagreeable to the speaker's mind as to represent it falsely to another. (3) That which speaketh the matter and mind aptly as to themselves and other hearers, but so as the present hearer, who we know takes the words in another sense, will by our design be deceived by them.[6]

Q. 7. Is all false speaking lying, or what is a lie?

A. Lying properly, signifieth a culpable speaking of falsehood; and it hath divers degrees of culpability. When falsehood is spoken without the speaker's fault, it is not morally to be called a lie. Though improperly the Hebrews called any thing a lie which would deceive those that

---

[4] Rom 3:7.

[5] 1 Kgs 22:22; John 8:44; Titus 1:2; Heb 6:18.

[6] Rom 3:4.

trust in it; and so all men and creatures, though blameless, are liars to such as overtrust them.[7]

Q. 8. Which are the divers degrees of lying, or culpable false speaking?

A. (1) One is privative; when men falsely represent things by diminutive expressions. Things may be falsely represented by defective as well as by excessive speeches. He that speaks of God, and heaven, and holiness, faintly as good, saith a grammatical truth; but if he speak not of them as best, or excellent, it is, morally, a false expression through defect. He that saith coldly, 'To murder, to be perjured, to silence Christ's ministers unjustly is not well,' as Eli said of his sons' wickedness; or only saith, 'I cannot justify it,' or 'It is hard to justify it,' saith a grammatical truth; but a moral falsehood, by the extenuating words, as if he would persuade the hearer to think it some small or doubtful matter, and so to be impenitent.

(2) He that speaketh falsely through rashness, heedlessness, neglect of just information, or any ignorance which is culpable, is guilty of some degree of lying; but he that knowingly speaketh falsely, is a liar in a higher degree.

(3) He that by culpable forgetfulness speaks falsely, is to be blamed; but he that remembereth and studieth it, much more.

(4) He that lieth in a small matter, which seemeth not to hurt, but perhaps to profit, the hearer, is to be blamed; but he that lieth in great matters, and to the great hurt of others, much more.

(5) He that speaketh either contrary to his mind, or contrary to the matter culpably, lieth; but he that speaketh both contrary to his mind and the matter, lieth worse.

(6) He that by equivocation useth unapt and unsuitable expressions, to deceive him that will misunderstand them, is to be blamed; but he that will stand openly, bold-faced, in a lie, much more.

(7) It is sin to speak untruths of our own, which we might avoid; but it is much worse to father them on God, or the holy Scripture.[8]

(8) It is sin, by falsehood, to deceive one; but much more to deceive multitudes, even whole assemblies, or countries.

---

[7] Prov 12:17; Ps 52:4; 116:11, and 120:7; Eph5:6.

[8] 1 Cor 15:15; 1 John 5:10.

(9) It is sin in a private man to lie to another about small things; but much more heinous for a ruler, or a preacher, to deceive multitudes, even in matters of salvation.

(10) It is a sin rashly to drop a falsehood; but much greater to write books, or dispute for it, and justify it.

(11) It is a sin to lie from a good intent; but much more out of envy, malice, or malignity.

(12) It is a sin to lie in private talk; but much more to lie to a magistrate or judge who hath power to examine us.

(13) It is a sin to assert an untruth as aforesaid; but much greater to swear it, or offer it to God in our profession or vows.

Q. 9. Is all deceiving of another a sin?

A. No; there is great difference, (1) Between deceiving one that I am bound to inform, and one that I am not bound to inform. (2) And between deceiving one to his benefit or harmlessly, and to his hurt and injury. (3) And between deceiving him by just means, and by unjust, forbidden means.

(I) I am under no obligation to inform a robber, or an usurping persecutor, as such; but to others I may be obliged to open the truth.

(II) I may deceive a patient, or child, to profit him, when I may not do it to hurt him.

(III) I may deceive such as I am not bound to inform, by my silence, or my looks, or gestures, which I suppose he will misunderstand, when I may not deceive him by a lie.

Q. 10. Is it not all one to deceive one way or another?

A. No; (1) I am not bound to open my mind to all men. What right hath a thief to know my goods or my heart; or a persecutor to know where I hide myself?

(2) But I have before largely showed you that lying is so great an evil against common trust and society in the world, as is not to be used for personal commodity or safety.

(3) And other signs, looks, and gestures being not appointed for the natural and common indications of the mind, are more left to human liberty and prudence, to use for lawful ends. As Christ (Luke 24) made by his motion, as if he would have gone further; and even by words about Cæsar's tribute, and other cases, concealed his mind, and oft denied the pharisees a resolution of questions which they put to him.

Stratagems in a lawful war are lawful, when, by actual shows and seemings, an enemy is deceived.

Q. 11. But the Scriptures mention many instances of equivocation and flat lying, in the Egyptian midwives, in Rahab, in David, and many others, without blame, and some of them with great commendation and reward. (Heb. 11)

A. (1) It is God's law that tells us what is sin and duty, when the history oft tells us but what was done, and not how far it was well or ill done.

(2) It is not the lie that is commended in the midwives and Rahab, but their faith and charity.

(3) That which God pardoneth, as he did polygamy and rash divorce, to godly men that are upright in the main, and especially such as knew it not to be sin, is not thereby justified; nor will it be so easily pardoned to us, who live in the clearer gospel light.

Q. 12. But when the Scripture saith that all men are liars, and sad experience seemeth to confirm it, what credit do we owe to men, and what certainty is there of any history?

A. History, by writing or verbal tradition, is of so great use to the world, that Satan maketh it a chief part of his work, as he is the deceiver and enemy of mankind, to corrupt it: and false history is a most heinous sin, and dangerous snare, by which the great deceiver keeps up his kingdom in the world. Heathenism, Mahometanism, popery, heresy, and malignity, and persecution, are all maintained by false tradition and history. Therefore we must not be too hasty or confident in believing man; and yet denying just belief will be our sin and great loss.

Q. 13. How then shall we know what and whom to believe?

A. (1) We must believe no men that speak against God or his word: for we are sure that God cannot lie; and the Scripture is his infallibly sealed word.

(2) We must believe none that speak against the light of nature and common notices of all mankind; for that were to renounce humanity: and the law of nature is God's first law. But it is not the sentiments of nature, as depraved, which is this law.

(3) We must believe no men against the common senses of makind, exercised on their duly qualified objects. Faith contradicteth not common sense, though it go above it. We are men before we are

Christians, and sense and reason are presupposed to faith. The doctrine which saith there is no bread nor wine, after consecration, in the sacrament, doth give the lie to the eyes, taste, and feeling, and intellectual perception of all sound men, and therefore is not to be believed; for if sense be not to be trusted, we know not that there is a church, or a man, or a Bible, or any thing in the world, and so nothing can be believed. Whether all sound senses may be deceived or not, God hath given us no surer way of certainty.

(4) Nothing is to be believed against the certain interest of all mankind, and tending to their destruction. That which would damn souls, or deny their immortality and future hope, or ruin the christian world or nations, is not to be believed to be duty or lawful; for truth is for good, and faith is for felicity, and no man is bound to such destructive things.[9]

(5) Nothing is to be believed as absolutely certain, which depends on the mere honesty of the speakers; for all men are liable to mistake, or lie.

(6) The more ignorant, malicious, unconscionable, factious, and siding any man is, the less credible he is; and the wiser and nearer to the action any man is, and the more conscionable, peaceable, and impartial he is, the more credible he is. An enemy speaking well of a man, is far more credible than a friend: multitudes, as capable and honest, are more credible than one.

(7) As that certainty which is called moral, as depending on men's free will, is never absolute, but hath many degrees, as the witness is more or less credible; so there is a certainty by men's report, tradition, or history, which is physical, and wholly infallible, as that there is such a place as Rome, Paris, &c., and that the statutes of the land were made by such kings and parliaments to whom they are ascribed; and that there have been such kings, &c. For proof of which know, (1) That besides the free acts, the will hath some acts as necessary as it is to the fire to burn, viz., to love ourselves and felicity, and more such. (2) That when all men of contrary interest, friends and foes, agree in a matter that hath sensible evidence, it is the effect of such a necessitating cause.

---

[9] 1 John 4:1, 2.

(3) And there is no cause in nature that can make them so agree in a lie. Therefore it is a natural certainty. Look back to the sixth chapter.

Q. 13. Why is false witness in judgment so great a sin.

A. Because it containeth in all these odious crimes conjunct: (1) A deliberate lie. (2) The wrongful hurting of another contrary to the two great principles of converse, justice and love. (3) It depriveth the world of the benefit of government and judicatures. (4) It turneth them into the plague and ruin of the innocent. (5) It blasphemeth or dishonoureth God, by whose authority rulers judge, as if he set up officers to destroy us by false witness, or knew it not, or would not revenge injustice. (6) It overthroweth human converse and safety, when witnesses may destroy whom they please, if they can but craftily agree.[10]

Q. 14. Is there no way to prevent this danger to mankind?

A. God can do it. If he give wise and righteous rulers to the world they may do much towards it; but wicked rulers use false witness as the devil doth, for to destroy the just, as Jezebel did.

Q. 15. How should rulers avoid it?

A. (1) By causing teachers to open the danger of it to the people. (2) Some old canons made invalid the witness of all notorious wicked men: how can he be trusted in an oath, that maketh no conscience of drunkenness, fornication, lying, or other sin?

Q. 16. How, then, are so few destroyed by false witnesses?[11]*

A. It is the wonderful providence of God, declaring himself the Governor of the world; that when there are so many thousand wicked men who all have a mortal hatred to the godly, and will daily swear and lie for nothing; and any two of these might take away our lives at pleasure, there are yet so few this way cut off. But God hath not left himself without witness in the world, and hath revenged false witness on many, and made conscience a terrible accuser for this crime.

Q. 17. What is the positive duty of the ninth commandment?

A. (1) To do justice to all men in our places.

---

[10] Matt 26:62, and 27:13; Mark 14:55, 56; Num 35:30; Acts 6:15; Deut 19:16–18; Prov 6:19; 12:17; 21,28,and 25:18; Ps 35:11.

[11] * Prov 19:5, 9.

(2) To defend the innocent to the utmost of our just power. If a lawyer will not do it for the love of justice and man, without a fee when he cannot have it, he breaketh this commandment.

(3) To reprove backbiters, and tell them of their sin.

(4) To give no scandal, but to live so blamelessly that slanderers may not be believed.

(5) On all just occasions especially to defend the reputation of the gospel, godliness, and good men, the cause and laws of God, and not silently for self-saving, to let Satan and his agents make them odious by lies; to the seduction of the people's souls.[12]

---

[12] Prov 25:23; Ps 15:3, 5.

43

Of the Tenth Commandment

Q. 1. What are the words of the tenth commandment?

A. Thou shalt not covet thy neighbour's house; thou shalt not covet thy neighbour's wife, nor his man-servant, nor his maid-servant, nor his ox, nor his ass, nor any thing that is thy neighbour's.

Q. 2. What is forbidden here, and what commanded?

A. (1) In some, the thing forbidden is selfishness, and the thing commanded is to love our neighbour as ourselves.

Q. 3. Is not this implied in the five foregoing commandments?

A. Yes; and so is our love to God in all the nine last. But because there are many more particular instances of sin and duty that can be distinctly named and remembered, God thought it meet to make two general, fundamental commandments, which should contain them all, which Christ called the first and second commandment; "Thou shalt love the Lord thy God with all thy heart," &c. And "Thou shalt love thy neighbour as thyself." The first is the summary and root of all the duties of the other nine, and especially of the second, third, and fourth. The other is the summary of the second table duties; and it is placed last, as being instead of all unnamed instances. As the captain leads the soldiers, and the lieutenant brings up the rear.[1]

Q. 4. What mean you by the sin of selfishness?

---

[1] Matt 19:10; Luke 10:27; Rom 13:9; Lev 16:24; Mark 8:34.

A. I mean that inordinate self-esteem, self-love, and self-seeking, with the want of a due, proportionate love to others, which engageth men against the good of others, and inclineth them to draw from others to themselves: it is not au inordinate love of ourselves, but a diseased self-love.[2]

Q. 5. When is self-love ordinate, and when is it sinful?

A. That which is ordinate, (1) Valueth not a man's self blindly above his worth. (2) It employeth a man in a due care of his own holiness, duty, and salvation. (3) It regardeth ourselves but as little members of the common great body, and therefore inclineth us to love others as ourselves, without much partial disproportion, according to the divers degrees of their amiableness, and to love public good, the church and world, and, much more, God above ourselves. (4) It maketh us studious to do good to others, and rejoice in it as our own, rather than to draw from them to ourselves.[3]

Sinful selfishness, (1) Doth esteem, and love, and see self-interest above its proper worth: it is over-deeply affected with all our concerns. (2) It hath a low, disproportionate love and regard of all others' good. (3) And when it groweth to full malignity, it maketh men envy the prosperity of others, and covet that which is theirs, and desire and rejoice in their disgrace and hurt, when they stand against men's selfish wills, and to endeavour to draw from others to ourselves: selfishness is to the soul like an inflammation or imposthume to the body; which draweth the blood and spirits to itself from their due and common course, till they corrupt the inflamed part.

Q. 6. What mean you by loving others as ourselves?

A. Loving them as members of the same body or society (the world or the church as they are) impartially with a love proportionable to their worth, and such a careful, practical, forgiving, patient love, as we love ourselves.[4]

Q. 7. But God hath made us individual persons, with so peculiar a self love, that no man can possibly love another as himself?

---

[2] Jer 14:6; Matt 16:22, 23; Luke 14:26, 29, 32, 33.

[3] Phil 2:4, 21; 1 Cor 12, and 10:24.

[4] Col 3:12, 13; 1 Cor 13; Eph 4:1, 2.

A. (1) You must distinguish between sensitive natural love, and rational love. (2) And between corrupt and sanctified nature.

(1) Natural sensitive love is stronger to one's self (that is, more sensible of self-interest) than to all the world. I feel not another's pain or pleasure, in itself: I hunger and thirst for myself: a mother hath that natural sensitive love to her own natural child (like that of brutes) which she hath not for any other.[5]

(2) Rational love valueth, and loveth, and preferreth every thing according to the degree of its amiableness, that is, goodness.

Rational love destroyeth not sensitive; but it moderateth and ruleth it, and commandeth the will and practice to prefer, and desire, and seek, and delight in higher things (as reason ruleth appetite, and the rider die horse); and so deny and forsake all carnal or private interests, that stand against a greater good.

Common reason tells a man, that it is an unreasonable thing in him that would not die to save a kingdom; much more that when he is to love both himself and the Kingdom inseparably, yet cannot love a kingdom, yea, or more excellent persons, above himself. But yet it is sanctification that must effectually overcome inordinate self-love, and clearly illuminate this reason, and make a man obey it.[6]

To conquer this selfishness is the sum of all mortification, and the greatest victory in this world: and therefore it is here perfectly done by none: but it is done most where there is the greatest love to God, and to the church and public good, and to our neighbours.

Q. 8. What is the sinfulness and the hurt of selfishness?

A. (1) It is a fundamental error and blindness in the judgment: we are so many poor worms and little things; and if an ant or worm had reason, should it think its life, or ease, or other interest, more valuable than a man's, or than all the country's?

(2) It is a fundamental pravity and disorder of man's will: it is made to love good as good, and therefore to love most the greatest good.

(3) Yea, it blindly casteth down, and trampleth on, all good in the world which is above self-interest. For this prevailing selfishness taketh

---

5 Prov 15:10.

6 1 Cor 10:33; Titus 1:8; Jas 3:15, 17; Col 1:24.

a man's self for his ultimate end, and all things else but as means to his own interest: God and heaven, and all societies and all virtue, seem no further good to him than they are for his own good and welfare. And selfishness so over-cometh reason in some, as to make them dispute for this fundamental error as a truth, that there is nothing to be accounted good by me, but that which is good to me as my interest or welfare: and so that which is good to others is not, therefore, good to me.[7]

(4) And thus it blasphemously deposeth God in the mind of the sinner; making him no further good to us than as he is a means to our good; and so he is set quite below ourselves: as if he had not made us for himself, and to love him as God, for his own goodness.

(5) I told you before (of the first commandment) how this, maketh every man his own idol, to be loved above God.

(6) Yea, that the selfish would be the idols of the world, and have all men conformed to their judgment, wills, and words.

(7) A selfish man is an enemy to the public peace of all societies, and of all true unity and concord: for whereas holy persons, as such have all one centre, law, and end, even God and his will, the selfish have as many ends, and centres, and laws as they are persons. So that while every one would have his own interest, will, and lust, to be the common rule and centre, it is by the wonderful, overruling power of God that any order is kept up in the world; and because when they cannot be all kings, they agree to make that use of kings which they think will serve their interest best.

(8) A selfish man so far can be no true friend; for he loveth his friend but as a dog doth his master, for his own ends.

(9) A selfish person is so far untrusty, and so false in converse and all relations; for he chooseth, and changeth, and useth all, as he thinks his own interest requireth. If he be a tradesman, believe him no further than his interest binds him; if he be a minister, he will be for that doctrine and practice which is for his carnal interest; if he be a ruler, wo to his inferiors! And therefore it is the highest point in policy, next conscience and common obedience to God, to contrive, if possible, so

---

[7] Prov 3:5; 20:6; 23:4; 25:27; 26:5, 12, 16; 27:2, and 28:11.

to twist the interest of princes and people, that both may feel that they are inseparable, and that they must live, and thrive, or die, together.[8]

(10) In a word, inordinate selfishness is the grand pravity of nature, and the disease and confusion of all the world: whatever villanies, tyrannies, rebellions, heresies, persecutions, or wickedness you read of in all history, or hear of now on earth, all is but the effects of this adhering by inordinate self-love to self-interest. And if Paul say of one branch of its effects, "The love of money is the root of all evil," we may well say it of this radical, comprehensive sin.

Q. 9. Alas! who is it that is not selfish? How common is this sin! Are there then any saints on earth; or any hope of a remedy?

A. It is so common and so strong, as that, (1) All Christians should most fear it, and watch, and pray, and strive against it. (2) And all preachers should more open the evil of it than they do, and live themselves as against it and above it.

(1) How much do most over-value their own dark judgments and weak reasonings, in comparison of others![9]

(2) How commonly do men measure the wisdom or folly, goodness or badness, of other men, as they are for or against their selfish interest, opinions, side, or way!

(3) How impatient are men if self-will, reputation, or interest, be crossed!

(4) How will they stretch conscience in words, deeds, or bargaining for gain!

(5) How soon will they fall out with friends or kindred, if money or reputation come to a controversy between them!

(6) How little feeling pity have they for another in sickness, poverty, prison, or grief, if they be but well themselves!

(7) How ordinarily doth interest of body, reputation, wealth, corrupt and change men's judgment in religion: so that selfishness and fleshly interest chooseth not only other conditions and actions of life, but also the religion of most men, yea, of too many teachers of self-denial.[10]

---

[8] Phil 2:4, 21.

[9] 1 Kgs 22:8; 2 Chron. 18:7.

[10] 1 John 2:15.

(8) And if godly people find this and lament it, how weakly do they resist it, and how little do they overcome it.

(9) And though every truly godly man prefer the interest of his soul above that of his body, how few get above a religion of caring and fearing for themselves; to study more the church's good, and, more than that, to live in the delightful love of God, as the infinite good.

(10) And of those that love the church of God; how many narrow it to their sect or party, and how few have an universal impartial love to aft true Christians, as such.[11]

Q. 10. Where then are the saints, if this be so?

A. All this sin is predominant in ungodly men; (saving that common grace so far overcometh it in some few, that they can venture and lose their estates and lives for their special friends, and for their country;) but in all true Christians it is but in a subdued degree.[12] They hate it more than they love it: they all love God and his church with a far higher estimation than themselves, though with less passion. They would forsake estate and life, rather than forsake Christ and a holy life.[13] They were not true Christians if they had not learned to bear the cross, and suffer. They seek and hope for that life of perfect love and unity, where selfishness shall never more divide us.

Q. 11. What is it that maketh the love of others so great a duty?

A. (1) It is but to love God, his interest and image in others. No man hath seen God; but rational souls, and especially holy ones, are his image, in which we must see and love him. And there is no higher duty than to love God.

(2) Love maketh us meet and useful members in all societies, especially in the church of God. It maketh all to love the common good above their own.

(3) It maketh all men use their utmost power for the good of all that need them.

(4) It overcometh temptations to hurtfulness and division; it teacheth men patiently to bear and forbear; it is the greatest keeper of peace and

---

[11] Col 1:4, 8.

[12] 2 Tim 3:2.

[13] Luke 14:26, 27, 33; 1 Cor 13.

concord. As one soul uniteth all parts of the body, one spirit of love uniteth all true believers. It is the cement of individuals; the vital, healing balsam which doth more than art to cure our wounds.[14]

If all magistrates loved the people as themselves, how would they use them? If bishops and teachers loved others as themselves, and were as loth to hurt them as to be hurt, and to reproach them as be reproached, and to deliver them from poverty, prison, or danger, as to be safe themselves, what do you think would be the consequent?

How few would study to make others odious, or to ruin them? How few would backbite them, or censoriously condemn them, if they loved them as themselves? If all this city and kingdom loved each other as themselves, what a foretaste would it be of heaven on earth! how delightfully should we all live together! every man would have the good of all others to rejoice in as his own, and be as ready to relieve another as the right hand will the left. We can too easily forgive ourselves our faults and errors, and so should bear with others.[15]

Love is our safety: who is afraid of any one who he thinks loveth him as himself? Who is afraid that he should persecute, imprison, or destroy himself, unless by ignorance or distraction? Love is the delight of life, when it is mutual, and is not disappointed: what abundance of fears, and cares, and passions, and lawsuits, would it end? It is the fulfilling of the preceptive part of the law; and as to the penal part, there is no use for if Where love prevaileth. To such, saith Paul, there is no law; they are not without it, but above it, so far as it worketh by fear.[16]

(5) Love is the preparation and foretaste of glory. Fear, care, and sorrow, are distantly preparing works; but it is joyful love, which is the immediate preparation and foretaste. There is no war, no persecution, no hatred, wrath, or strife in heaven; but perfect love, which is the uniting grace, will there more nearly unite all saints, than we that are in a dividing world and body can now conceive of, or perfectly believe.

---

[14] 1 Cor 12; Eph 4:1–3, 16; Rom 12:9, 10.

[15] 2 Cor 2:4, 8, and 8:7, 8, 24.

[16] Rom 13:10; Gal 5:6, 13, 22; Phil 1:15, 17, and 2:1–3; 1 Thess 4:4; 1 Tim 6:11; Heb 13:1, 2; 1 John 4:7, 18; Eph 4:16.

Q. 12. Is there any hope that love should reign on earth?[17]

A. There is hope that all the sound believers should increase in love, and get more victory over selfishness. For they have all that spirit of love, and obey Christ's last and great command, and are taught of God to love one another; yea, they dwell in love, and so in God, and God in them; and it will grow up to perfection.

But I know of no hope that the malignant aped of Cain should cease the bating of them that are the holy seed, save as grace converteth any of them to God. Of any common or universal reign of love, I see no prognostics of it in rulers, in teachers, or any others in the world; prophecies are dark; but my greatest hope is fetched from the three first petitions of the Lord's prayer, which are not to be put up in vain.

Q. 13. What should we do toward the increase of love?

A. (1) Live so blamelessly, that none may find just matter of hatred in you.[18]

(2) Love others, whether they love you or not. Love is the most powerful cause of love.

(3) Do hurt to none, but by necessary justice or defence; and do as much good as you can to all.

(4) Praise all that is good in men, and mention not the evil without necessity.

(5) Do all that you can to make men holy, and win them to the love of God; and then they will love each other by his Spirit, and for his sake.

(6) Do all that you can to draw men from sinful, worldly love; for that love of the world which is enmity to God, is also enmity to the love of one another. Further than you can draw men to centre in Christ, and in holy love, there is no hope of true love to others.

(7) Patiently suffer wrongs, rather than provoke men to hate you, by unnecessarily seeking your right or revenge.

Q. 14. Is all desire of another man's unlawful?

---

[17] Jas 2:8.

[18] 1 Pet 2:17, and 3:8.

A. All that is to his hurt, loss, and wrong. You may desire another man's daughter to wife, by his consent; or his house, horse, or goods, when he is willing to sell them; but not else.[19]

Q. 15. But what if in gaming, betting, or trading, I desire to get from him, though to his loss?

A. It is a covetous, selfish, sinful desire: you must desire? to get nothing from him to his loss and hurt.

Q. 16. But what if he consent to run the hazard, as in a horse race, a game, a wager, &c.? It is no wrong to a consenter.

A. The very desire of hurtful drawing from him to yourself is selfish sin: if he consent to the hazard, it is also his covetous desire to gain from you, and his sin is no excuse for yours; and you may be sure it was not the loss that he consented to; but if he do it as a gift, it is another case.[20]

Q. 17. What be the worst sorts of covetousness?

A. (1) When the son wisheth his father's death for his estate.

(2) When men that are old, and near the grave, still covet what they are never like to need or use.

(3) When men that have abundance, are never satisfied, but desire more.

(4) When they will get it by lying, extortion, or other wicked means, even by perjury and blood, as Jezebel and Ahab got Naboth's vineyard.

(5) When princes, not content with their just dominions, invade other men's, and plague the world with unjust wars, blood, and miseries, to enlarge them.[21]

Q. 18. How differ charity and justice?

A. Charity loveth all, because there is somewhat in them lovely; and doth them good without respect to their right, because we love them. Justice respecteth men as in the same governed society (under God or man) and so giveth every man his due.

Q. 19. Is it love or justice that saith, "Whatever you would that men should do to you, do ye also to them?"

---

[19] Ps 10:3; 1 Cor 5:10, 11, and 6:10; Eph 5:5; Luke 12:15.

[20] Acts 20:23; 1 Tim 6:10.

[21] Josh. 7:21; Mich.2:2; Prov 21:26, and 28:16; Hab. 2:9; Exod 18:21.

A. It is both. Justice saith, 'Do right to all, and wrong to none, as you would have them do to you.' Charity saith, 'Love, and pity, and relieve all in your power, as you would have them love, pity, and relieve you.'

Q. 20. Hath this law no exceptions?

A. It supposeth that your own will, for yourselves, be just and good; if you would have another make you drunk, or draw you to any sinful or unclean pleasure, you may not therefore do so by them. But do others such right and good as you may lawfully desire they should do to you.

Q. 21. What are those foundations on which this law is built?

A. (1) That as God hath made us individual persons, so he is the free distributor of his allowance to every person, and therefore we must he content with his allowance, and not covet more.

(2) That God hath made us for holiness, and endless happiness in heaven: and therefore we must not so love this world as to covet fulness, and desire more of it than God alloweth us.[22]

(3) That God hath made every man a member of the human world, and every Christian a member of the church, and no one to be self-sufficient, or independent, as a world to himself. And therefore, all men must love themselves but as members of the body, and love the body, or public good, above themselves, and love other members, as their place and the common interest doth require.[23]

(4) That we are not our own, but his that did create us and redeem us: and therefore must love ourselves and others, as his, and according to his will and interest; and not as the selfish, narrow interest tempteth us.

(5) That the faithful are made spiritual by the sanctifying Spirit, and therefore savour the things of the Spirit, and refer all outward things thereto; and therefore must not so over-value provision for the flesh, as to covet and draw from others for his pleasure.[24]

So that, (1) As the first greatest command engageth us wholly to God, as our Creator, Redeemer, and Sanctifier, against that selfishness, which is the idol enemy to God, including the privation of our love to him, and against the trinity of his enemies; the flesh, which would be

---

[22] Heb 13:5; 1 Tim 6:8; Phil 4:11; 1 John 2:15; Ps 119:36; Esek. 33:31.

[23] 1 Cor12; 6:20. and 7:23.

[24] Rom 8:6–8, and 13:13; Luke 12:21; Matt 7:22.

first pleased; the world, which it would be pleased by; and the devil, who deceiveth and tempteth men by such baits of pleasure; even so this tenth (which is the second summary command) engageth us to love God in our brethren, and to love them according to his interest in them, as members of the same society, with an impartial love, against that selfishness, which is the enemy of impartial love, and common good; and against the lust of the flesh, which would be first pleased; and the world, which is the provision which it coveteth; and the devil, who would, by such worldly baits, and fleshly pleasure, deceive mankind into ungodliness, sensuality, malignity, mutual enmity, contention, oppression, persecution, perfidiousness, and all iniquity; and finally into endless misery, in separatiou from the God of love, and the heavenly, perfected, united society of love.[25]

And this is the true meaning of the tenth commandment.

---

[25] Eph 5:3; Col 3:5.

PART V

44

Of the Sacred Ministry, and Church, and Worship

Q. 1. Though you have opened the doctrine of the catholic church and the communion of saints before, in expounding the Creed, because the sacraments cannot be understood without the ministry and church, will you first tell us what the ministerial office is?

A. The sacred ministry is an office instituted by Christ, in subordination to his prophetical office to teach; and to his priestly office, to intercede in worship; and to his kingly office, to be key-bearers of his church, to try and judge of men's title to its communion: and this for the converting of the infidel world, the gathering them into the christian communion, and the helping, guiding, and edifying them therein.[1]

Q. 2. Are they ministers in office to any but the church?

A. Yes: their first work is upon the world, to make them Christians, and gather them into the church by teaching and baptising them.[2]

Q. 3. Is not that the common work of laymen, that are no officers?

A. Laymen must do their best in their capacity and station; but (1) Officers do it as separated to this work, as their calling. (2) And accordingly do it by a special commission and authority from Christ. (3) And are tried, chosen, and dedicated thereto, as specially qualified.

---

[1] Matt 16:19; 22:3, 4; 24:45, and 28:19, 20; Acts 2:42; Rom 1:1, 2; 1 Cor 4:1, 2.

[2] Acts 14:23, and 20:28; Titus 1:5; 1 Tim 3.

Q. 4. What must Christ's ministers say and do for the World's conversion?

A. Luke 16, and Matt. 22, tell you: they must tell men of the marriage-feast, the blessed provision of grace and glory by Christ, and, by evidence and urgency, compel them to come in. More particularly:

(1) They must speak to sinners as from God, and in his name, with a "Thus saith the Lord." They must manifest their commission, or at least that the message which they bring, is his; that men may know with whom they have to do; and that he that despiseth, despiseth not men, but God.[3]

(2) They must make known to sinners their sinful, dangerous, and miserable state, to convince them of the necessity of a Saviour. As if they should say, 'He that hath no sin, that is no child of Adam, that shall not die and come to judgment, that needs no Saviour, pardon, and deliverance, let him neglect our invitation: but sin and misery are all men's necessity.'

(3) They are to tell men what God hath done for them by Christ; what a Saviour he hath given us; what Christ hath done and suffered for us.[4]

(4) They are to tell men what grace and glory is purchased for them, and offered to them, and what they may have in Christ, and by him.

(5) They are to tell men how Willing God is of men's recovery, so that he beseecheth them to be reconciled to him, and ministers are sent to entreat them to accept his grace; who refuseth none that refuse not him.

(6) They are to acquaint men with God's conditions, terms, and expectations: not that they give him any satisfying or purchasing price of their own, but that they accept his free gift according to its proper nature and use, and come to Christ that they may have life; but that they come in time, and come sincerely and resolvedly, and believe, and penitently return to God, for which he is ready to assist them by his grace.[5]

(7) They must acquaint men with the methods of the tempter, and the hinderances of their faith and repentance, and what opposition

---

[3] Acts 26:17, 18; Luke 10:16, and 24:47; 1 Thess 4:8; Matt 9:13.

[4] John 3:16; Heb 10:14; Rom 3:1, 10; Titus 2:14.

[5] 2 Cor 5:19, 20; Luke 14:17.

they must expect from the flesh, the world, and the devil, and how they must overcome them.

(8) They must acquaint men what great assistances and encouragements they shall have from Christ: how good a master; how perfect a Saviour and Comforter, how sure a word, how sweet a work, how good and honourable company, and how many mercies here, and how sure and glorious a reward for ever; and that all this is put in the balance for their choice, against a deceitful, transitory shadow.[6]

(9) They must answer the carnal objections of deceived sinners, and show them clearly that all is folly that is said against Christ and their conversion.

(10) They must make men know how God will take it, if they unthankfully neglect or refuse his grace, and that this will leave them without remedy, and greatly add to their sin and misery, and that there is no more sacrifice for sin, but a fearful looking for of judgment, from that God who to such is a consuming fire; and that it will be easier for Sodom in the day of judgment than for such.[7]

Q. 5. In what manner must Christ's ministers preach all this?

A. (1) With the greatest gravity and holy reverence; because it is the message of God.

(2) With the greatest plainness; because men are dull of understanding.

(3) With the greatest proof and convincing evidence, to conquer prejudice, darkness, and unbelief.

(4) With powerful winning motives, and urgent importunity, because of men's disaffection and averseness. And O what powerful motives have we at hand, from self-love, from God, from Christ, from necessity, from heaven and hell![8]

(5) With life and fervency, because of the unspeakable importance of the matter, and the deadness and hardness of men's hearts.

---

[6] 1 Thess 3:5; Eph 6:11; 2 Cor 2:11, and 4:16, 18; Heb 11, and 12:28,29.

[7] 2 Tim 2:26; Titus 2:8; Heb 2:8, and 10:22, 23.

[8] Titus 2:6–8; Heb 5:10, 11; 1 Cor 1:17, 18; Matt 7:29; Acts 2:37.

(6) With fervency, in season and out of season, because of men's aptness to lose what they have heard and received, and their need still to be carried on.

(7) With constancy to the end, that grace may be preserved and increased by degrees.

(8) With seemly and decent expressions, because of captious, cavilling hearers, and the holiness of the work.

(9) With concord with all the church of Christ, as preaching the same faith and hope.

(10) By the example of holy practice, doing what we persuade them to do, and excelling them in love, and holiness, and patience, and victory over the flesh and world, and winning them, not by force, but by light and love.[9]

Q. 6. What is it that all this is to bring men to?

A. (1) To make men understand and believe what God is to them; what Christ is; what grace and glory are; as is aforesaid in the christian faith.

(2) To win men's hearts to the love of these, from the love of sinful, fleshly pleasure, and to fix their wills in a resolved choice.

(3) To engage them in the obedient practice of what they love and choose, and help them to overcome all temptations to the contrary.[10]

Q. 7. Why will God have all this and the rest which is for the church, to be an office, work of chosen, separated, consecrated persons?

A. (1) It is certain that all men are not fit for it; alas! too few. The mysteries of godliness are deep and great. The chains of sinners are strong, and God useth to work according to the suitableness of means. Great abilities are requisite to all this: and God would not have his cause and work dishonoured by his ministers' unfitness. Alas! unfit men have been the church's great calamity and reproach![11]

(2) God would have his work effectually done; and, therefore, by men that are wholly devoted to it. Were they never so able, if they have avocations, and do it by the halves, dividing their labours between it

---

[9] 1 Cor14; 2 Tim 2:15; 1 Pet 3:16; Acts 20:25, 29, 31,32.

[10] Acts 20:21.

[11] 1 Tim 3:16, and 4:15; 2 Tim 2:2, 15; Titus 1:6, 9.

and the world, this will not answer the necessity and the end: even a Paul must do it publicly, and from house to house, night and day, with tears. (Acts 20:20, 28.) It must be done in season and out of season. (2 Tim. 4:1, 2.) Timothy must meditate on these things, and give himself wholly to them. (1 Tim. 4:15.) Paul was separated to the gospel of God. (Rom. 1) And ministers are stewards of his mysteries, to give the children their meat in season.

(3) It is much for the comfort of the faithful to know that it is by God's own ordained officer that his message of invitation, and his sealed covenant, pardon, and gift of Christ and grace, are delivered to them.[12]

(4) The very being of an ordered church requireth a guiding official part. It is no ruled society without a ruler: no school without a teacher. Men must know to whom to go for instruction: the law was to be sought from the mouth of the priest, as the messenger of the Lord of Hosts. (Mal. 2:7.) Read Acts 14:23; Tit. 1:5: Eph. 4:14–16; 1 Thes. 5:12, 13; Luke 12:42, 43.

(5) The safety and preservation of the truth requireth the ministerial office. As the laws of England would never be preserved without lawyers and judges, by the common people; so the Scriptures, and the faith, sacraments, and worship, would never have been brought down to us as they are, without a stated ministry, whose interest, office, and work it is continually to use them. (See 1 Tim. 5:20; Eph. 4:14; Rom. 16:16, 17; 1 Tim. 3:15: Heb. 13:7, 9, 17.) None have leisure to do this great work as it must be done, but those that by office are wholly separated thereto. Will you leave it to magistrates, or to the people, who, if they were able, have other work to do? Deny the office, and you destroy the church and work.

Q. 8. How are men called and separated to the sacred ministry?

A. There are many things concur thereto. The first ministers were called immediately by Christ himself, and extraordinarily qualified: but ever since all these things must concur.

(1) A common obligation on all men to do their best in their places to propagate the gospel and church, and to save men's souls, is presupposed, as a preparatory antecedent.

---

[12] 2 Cor 5:19.

(2) There must be necessary qualifying abilities: (1) Natural wit and capacity. (2) Acquired improvement, and so much knowledge as must be exercised in the office. (3) If apt to teach and able signified no more than to read what is prescribed by others, a child, fool, or an infidel, were apt and able, Ability for competent utterance and exercise. (4) And to his acceptance with God and his own salvation, saving faith and holiness is necessary. If you would know the necessary degrees of ability, it is so much without which the necessary acts of the office cannot be done. "The things that thou hast heard of me among many witnesses, the same commit thou to faithful men, who shall be able to teach others also." (2 Tim. 2:2.)

(3) The approving judgment of other senior ministers is ordinarily necessary; for men are not to be the only judges themselves where the public interest is concerned. And the investing ordination of such is the orderly solemnizing of their entrance, and delivery of Christ's commission; and is that to the general office of the ministry which baptism is to Christianity, and solemn matrimony to marriage, or coronation to a king. This is not done by the election of the people; it is not their work to choose ministers to the general office, or men to call the world.[13]

(4) To make a man the pastor of a particular church or flock, the consent both of the man and of the flock is necessary; and to the well-being also, the consent of the neighbour pastors; and to peace and liberty, the prince's. This is an ordination or relation, which may be often renewed and changed; but the ordination to the general office is to be but once: to license a physician, and to choose him for my physician, are divers things: and so it is here.

Q. 9. What laws or canons have pastors power to make for the church?

A. (1) None to the universal church, for that hath no ruler, or lawmaker, or judge, but Christ; man being utterly incapable of it.

(2) None which shall cross the laws of Christ, in nature or Scriptures.

(3) None which are of the same kind and use with Christ's own universal laws, and no more needful to one place or age than to all: for this

---

[13] 2 Tim 2:2; Titus 1:5; Acts 14:23; 9, and 13:2.

will accuse Christ, as if he had been defective in his own legislation, when more must be added of the same kind.[14]

(4) Taking the word "laws" strictly, pastors, as such, have no legislative power. But, taking it laxly for mandates, or directions given by just power, such as a parent or tutor hath, they may make such laws as these: (1) Such as only enjoin the obeying of Christ's own laws. (2) And such as only determine of such mere accidents of doctrine, worship, and discipline, as Christ hath commanded in general, and virtually, and left the particular sort to human determination of governors (as time, place, utensils, &c). (3) Such as are not extended beyond the churches of which they are pastors, to others of whom they are no rulers. (4) Such as, being indifferent, are not made more necessary than their nature and use requireth; nor used to the church's destruction or hurt, but to its edification. (5) Such as, being mutable in the reason or cause of them, are not fixed. And continued when the reason of them ceaseth.[15]

Christ maketh us ministers that we may not think we are lords of his heritage: our work is to expound and apply his laws, and persuade men to obey them, and not to make laws of our own of the same kind, as if we were his equals, and lords of his church. It is true he hath bid us determine of circumstances to the church's edification, and the pastor is judge for the present time and place, what chapter he shall read, what text he shall preach on, and in what method; what psalm shall be sung, and in what tune, and such like: but who made him lord of other churches, to impose the like on them? or, how can he prove that the very same circumstances are necessary to all, when a day may alter the case with himself, which depends on mutable causes? If all the world or land be commanded on such a day to read the same psalm and chapter, and occurrents make any subject far more suitable, who hath power to deprive the present pastor of his choice, and to suppose ministers unable to know what subject to read or peach on, unless it be they that make such men ministers, that they may so rule them?
Q. 10. Why must there be stated worshipping congregations?

---

[14] Isa 33:22; Jas 4:12; 1 Tim 4:6; 1 Cor 3:5, and 4:1.

[15] Matt 20:27, 28; 2 Cor 1:24, and 3:6; 1 Pet 5:1-9, and 4:9-11.

A. (1) For the honour of God and our Redeemer, who is best honoured in united, solemn assemblies, magnifying him with one mind, and heart, and mouth.[16]

(2) For the preservation of religion, which is so best exercised, honoured, and kept up.

(3) For the benefit and joy of Christians, who, in such concordant societies, receive encouragement, strength, and comfort.

(4) For the due order and honour of the particular churches and the whole.

Q. 11. Is every worshipping congregation a church?

A. The name is not much worthy of a debate: there are divers sorts of christian assemblies, which may be called churches. (1) There are occasional, accidental assemblies that are not stated. (2) There are stated assemblies, like chapels, which have only curates, and are but parts of the lowest political, governing churches. (3) Christians statedly associated under such pastors as have the power of the church keys for personal communion in holy doctrine, worship, and conversation, are the lowest sort of political governed churches. (4) Synods, consisting of the pastors and delegates; these may be called churches in a lax sense. (5) And so may a christian nation under one king. (6) And all the christian world is one catholic church as headed by Jesus Christ. (7) And the Roman sect is a spurious church, as it is headed by a human, incapable sovereign, claiming the power of legislation and judgment over all the churches on earth.

Q. 12. But how shall I know which is the true church, when so many claim the title; and the papists say it is only theirs?

A. I have fully answered such doubts on the article of the "Holy Catholic Church, and Communion of Saints," in the Creed. Either you speak of the whole church, or of a particular church, which is but a part. If of the whole church, it is a foolish question, How shall I know which is the true church? when there is but one. If of a particular church, every true christian society (pastors and flocks) is a true church, that is, a true society, as a part of the whole.

---

[16] 1 Cor 14; Heb 10:21, 23; Acts 14:23.

Q. 13. But when there are divers contending churches, how shall I know which of them I should join with?

A. (1) If they are all true churches, having the same God, and Christ, and faith, and hope, and love, you must separate from none of them, as churches, though you may separate from their sins; but must communicate with them in all lawful exercises, as occasion requireth. (2) But your fixed relation to a particular pastor and church peculiarly, must be chosen, as your own case and benefit, all things considered, doth require. When you can have free choice, the nearest and ablest, and holiest pastor and society should be chosen: when violence interposeth, a ruler's will may do much to turn the scales for a tolerable pastor and society, if it make it most for the common good, and your edification.

Q. 14. May men add any thing to the prescribed worship of God?

A. Worship is a doubtful word; if you will call mere mutable accidents and circumstances by the name of worship, man may add to them, such as is putting off the hat, the metre and tune of psalms, and such like. But men may do nothing which implieth a defect in the law of Christ, and therefore may make no new articles of faith, or religion, or any thing necessary to salvation, or any sacraments or ordinances of worship of the same kind with Christ's, much less contrary thereto.

Q. 15. May we hold communion with a faulty church and worship?

A. Or else we must have communion with none on earth: all our personal worship is faulty; we join with them for christian faith and worship. If the minister say or do any thing contrary, it is his sin, and our presence maketh it not ours. Else we must separate from all the world. But we may not by false professions, subscribing, swearing, or practice, commit any sin ourselves for the communion of any church on earth.[17]

---

[17] Luke 4:16, and 6:6; Matt 8:4.

45

Of Baptism

Q. 1. What is baptism?

A. It is a sacred action, or sacrament, instituted by Christ, for the solemnizing of the covenant of Christianity between God and man, and the solemn investing us in the state of Christianity, obliging us to Christ, and for his delivering to us our relation and right to him as our Head, and to the gifts of his covenant.[1]

Q. 2. Why did Christ institute such a ceremony as washing in so great and weighty a work as our christening?

A. (1) A soul in flesh is apt to use sense, and needs some help of it. (2) Idolaters had filled the world with images and outward ceremonies, and the Jews had been long used to abundance of typical rites; and Christ being to deliver the world from these, and teach them to worship in spirit and truth, would not run into the extreme of avoiding all sensible signs and helps, but hath made his sacraments few and fitted to their use, to be instead of images, and men's vain inventions, and the Jewish burdens, as meet and sufficient helps of that kind to his church, that men might not presume to set up any such things of their own, on pretence of need, or usefulness.

Q. 3. What doth this great sacrament contain?

---

[1] Matt 28:10; Acts 2:38, 41; 8:12, 13, 16, 37, 38; 19:5, and 22:16; Rom 6:3, 4; 1 Cor 12:13; Gal 3:27; Eph 4:5; Col 1:12; 1 Pet 3:21.

A. (1) The parties covenanting and acting. (2) The covenant as on both parts, with the benefits given of God, and the duty professed and promised by man. (3) The outward signs of all.

Q. 4. Who are the parties covenanting and acting?

A. God and man; that is, (1) Principally God the Father, Son, and Holy Ghost; and, ministerially under him, the baptising ministers; (2) The party baptised; and if he be an infant, the parent or owner on his behalf.

Q. 5. In what relation is God a covenanter with man?

A. (1) As our Creator and Governor, offended by sin, and reconciled by Christ, whom his love gave to be our Saviour. (2) As Christ is our Redeemer and Saviour. (3) As the Holy Ghost is our Regenerator and Comforter; sent by the Father and the Son.

Q. 6. In what relation stands the person to be baptised?

A. As a sinner, miserable by guilt and pravity, and loss of his blessed relation to God, but redeemed by Christ, and called by him, and coming to receive him and his saving grace.

Q. 7. What is it that God doth as a covenanter with the baptised?

A. You must well understand that two covenanting acts of God are presupposed to baptism, as done before. (I) The first is God's covenant with Jesus Christ, as our Redeemer, by consent, in which God requireth of him the work of man's redemption as on his part, by perfect holiness, righteousness, satisfactory suffering, and the rest: and promiseth him, as a reward, to be Lord of all, and the saving and glorifying of the church, with his own perpetual glory.[2]

(II) A promise and conditional covenant, or law of grace, made to lost mankind by the Father and the Son, that whoever truly believeth, that is, becometh a true Christian, shall be saved.[3]

Now baptism is the bringing of this conditional promise, upon man's consent to be an actual mutual covenant.

Q. 8. And what is it that God there doth as an actual covenanter?

A. First he doth by his minister stipulate, that is, demand of the party baptised whether he truly consent to his part. And next on that

---

[2]   John 17:1–3; 3:35; 5:22, 27, and 6:39.

[3]   John 3:16; 2 Cor 5:19, 20; 1 John 5:11, 12.

supposition, he delivereth him the covenant gifts, which at present are to be bestowed.[4]

Q. 9. What be those?

A. (1) The relation of a pardoned, reconciled sinner and adopted child of God, or that God will be his God in love through Christ.

(2) A right and relation to Christ as his actual Saviour, Head, Teacher, Intercessor, and King.

(3) A right and relation to the Holy Ghost, to be to him the illuminating, sanctifying, quickening Spirit of light and love, and holy life; and deliverance from the devil, the world, and flesh, and from the wrath of God.[5]

Q. 10. What is it that God requireth of man, and he professeth?

A. That he truly believe in this God the Father, Son, and Holy Ghost, and presently and resolvedly consenteth to be his in these relations, taking him as his God and Father, his Saviour, and his Sanctifier, repenting of his sins, and renouncing the Contrary government of the devil, world, and flesh.[6]

Q. 11. What are the outward signs of all this?

A. (1) The water. (2) And the actions of both parties. (1) The action of the minister on God's part is to wash the body of the baptised with the water, which, in hot countries, was by dipping them overhead, and taking them up: to signify, (1) That they are washed from the guilt of sin by the blood of Christ. (2) And are as dead and buried to sin and the world and flesh, and risen to a new and holy life and heavenly hope. (3) And that by this act we are solemnly bound by God to be Christians.

(II) The action of the baptised is, to be a willing receiver of this washing, to signify his believing and thankful receiving these free gifts of Christ, and his solemn self-engagement to be henceforth a Christian.

Q. 12. Are infants capable of doing all this?

A. No: they are personally capable of receiving both the sign and the grace, even right to Christ and life, but not themselves, of actual believing and covenanting with Christ.

---

[4] 1 Pet 3:21, 22.

[5] Gal 3:27; 1 Cor12, 13.

[6] Matt 28:19, 20; 1 John 5:7, 11, 12.

Q. 13. Why then are they baptised who cannot covenant?

A. That you may understand this rightly, you must know, (1) That as children are made sinners and miserable by their parents without any act of their own; so they are delivered out of it by the free grace of Christ, upon a condition performed by their parents; else they that are visibly born in sin and misery should have no visible or certain way of remedy: nature maketh them as it were parts of the parents, or so near as causeth their sin and misery: and this nearness supposed, God, by his free grace, hath put it in the power of the parents to accept for them the blessings of the covenant; and to enter them into the covenant of God, the parents' will being instead of their own, who yet have none to choose for themselves.[7]

(2) That baptism is the only way which God hath appointed for the entering of any one into the christian covenant and church.

(3) That the same sacrament hath not all the same ends and uses to all, but varieth in some things, as their capacities differ. Christ was baptised, and yet not for the remission of sin: and the use of circumcision partly differed to the old and to the infants.

(4) It is the will of God that infants be members of the christian church, of which baptism is the entrance. For, (1) There is no proof that ever God had a church on earth in any age, of which infants were not members.

(2) The covenant with Abraham, the father of the faithful, was made also with his infant seed, and sealed to them by circumcision. And the females who were not circumcised, were yet in the church and covenant: and when the males were uncircumcised forty years in the wilderness, they were yet members of the Jewish church: and (Deut. 19) the parents entered their little ones into the renewed covenant: and Christ came not to cast all infants out of the church who were in before.

(3) Christ himself saith, that he would have gathered Jerusalem as a hen gathereth her chickens, and they would not: so that he would have taken in the whole nation, infants, and all that were in before.[8]

---

[7] 1 Cor 7:14; Isa 65:23; Ps 37:26; Acts 2:39.

[8] Matt 23:37.

(4) And in Rom. 11 it is said, that they were broken off by unbelief: therefore, if their parents had not been unbelievers, the children had not been broken off.

(5) And Christ himself was Head of the church in his infancy, and entered by the sacrament then in force, though, as man, he was not capable of the work which he did at age: therefore infants may be members.[9]

(6) And he rebuked his disciples that kept such from him, because of such is the kingdom of God: he would have them come as into his kingdom.

(7) And plainly the apostle saith to a believing parent, that the unbeliever is sanctified to the believing, (for the begetting of a holy seed,) else were your children unclean, but now they are holy; mere legitimation is never called holiness, nor are heathens' children bastards.[10]

(8) And most plainly, Christ, when he instituteth baptism, saith, 'Go, disciple me all nations, baptising them.' Which fully showeth that he would have ministers endeavour to disciple and baptise nations, of all which infants are a part.[11]

(9) And accordingly many prophecies foretell, that nations shall come in to Christ; and Christians are called "A holy nation." And it is said, "The kingdoms of the world are become the kingdoms of the Lord and of his Christ."

Q. 14. But though infants be church members, is it not better that their baptism be delayed till they know what they do?

A. Christ knows what is best: and he hath told us of no other door of entrance into the visible church regularly, but by baptism. And if he had intended so great a change to the believing Jews as to unchurch all their infants, he would have told it. And the apostles would have had more ado to quiet them in this, than they had for casting off circumcision: but we read of no such thing, but the constant baptising of whole households.

---

[9] Matt 19:13, 14, and 18:8.

[10] 1 Cor 7:14.

[11] Matt 28:19, 20; Rev 9:15.

Q. 15. But infant baptism seems to let in all the corruption of the churches, while infants receive they know not what, and are all taken after for Christians, how had soever, or without knowing what Christianity is: whereas, if they stayed till they understood it, it would engage them to be resolved Christians indeed?

A. This is not along of infant baptism, but of unfaithful parents and ministers. For, (1) If the parents were told their duty, and also what a blessing it is to have their children in Christ's church and covenant, it would awaken them better to do their part, and comfort them in their children's state of grace.

(2) And if infants were not betime engaged, the usage would tempt multitudes to do as some did of old, even sin on as long as they durst, that baptism might wash it away at last.

(3) And doubtless, with unfaithful ministers, baptism at age also would be made but a ceremony, and slubbered over as confirmation is now, and as customary going to the church and sacrament is.

(4) But that which should be done is, that at age every baptised person, before he is admitted among adult communicants, should be as diligently catechised, and as solemnly own and renew his baptismal vow and covenant, as if it were now to be first done. The full nature of baptism is best to be understood by the case of the adult, who were capable of more than infants are. And no adult person must be baptised without serious, deliberate understanding, profession of faith, repentance, and holy obedience to Christ. Infants cannot do this, though they must not do that again which they did and could do, viz., receive baptism; yet they must do that which they did not nor could do.

I confess to you, of the two evils, I think the church is more corrupted for want of such a solemn, serious renewing of the baptismal covenant at age, and by turning confirmation into a ceremony, than by those anabaptists, who call people to be seriously re-baptised, as the Afric council did those that had been baptised by heretics.

Q. 16. Do you think that anabaptists should be tolerated, or that all should not be forced to bring their children to baptism?

A. (1) Infant baptism is no such easy controversy or article of faith, as that no one should be tolerated that receiveth it not.

(2) The ancient church, which we most reverence, left all men to their liberty to be baptised only when they pleased, and compelled none

for themselves or their children. Tertullian was for the delay till they understood. Gregory Nazianzen was for staying some years. Augustine, and others of the Fathers, were baptised at age.

(3) Baptism giveth so great a gift, even Christ, and pardon, and adoption, and right to life eternal, on condition of thankful acceptance and believing consent, that undoubtedly the unwilling have no right at all to it. The ancient church baptised none till they desired and sought it for themselves or children. Yea, they must be willing of it on self-denial terms, forsaking the flesh, the world, and the devil, and taking God instead of all. So that to force any to be baptised by mulcts and penalties, and baptise those so forced, is to deceive souls, defile Christ's church, and profane the sacred ordinance of God.

Q. 17. I have oft wondered what harm twice baptising doth, that it should be accounted a heresy and intolerable?

A. It is a fault, because it is contrary to Christ's appointed order: baptism is the sacrament of our new birth, and we are born but once. To be baptised again implieth an untruth, that we were not baptised before: but I suppose none do it bat through ignorance. And Cyprian, and the bishops of many countries in many councils, were so ignorant as to be guilty of re-baptising all that heretics baptised. The great fault of the anabaptists is their schism, that they cannot be contented when they are re-baptised to live in love and communion with others, but grow so fond of their own opinion as to gather into separated churches, and avoid communion with all that are not of their mind, and spend their time in contentious endeavours to draw men to them.

Q. 18. What the better are infants for being baptised?

A. The children of the faithful are stated by it in a right to the foresaid benefits of the covenant, the pardon of their original sin, the love of God, the intercession of Christ, and the help of the Holy Ghost, when they come to age, and title to the kingdom of heaven, if they die before they forfeit it.

Q. 19. But how can we judge all such in a state of salvation, when we see many at age prove wicked, and enemies?

A. This is a point of so great difficulty, that I may but humbly propose my opinion to trial. (1) There is a degree of grace or goodness, which doth only give a man a power to believe or obey God, but not give a rooted, habitual determination to his will. Such the fallen angels had, and Adam before his fall, who was thereby in a state of life, till he fell from it by wilful sin: and so it may be with the baptised infants of believers. But when the special sanctifying gift of the Holy Ghost is given them, and they are habitually rooted in the love of God, as the seed sown in good ground, they fall not totally away. (2) As parents and children are covenanters for their several duties, if parents will perfidiously neglect their promised duty for the holy education of their children, or children rebelliously sin against that power and measure of grace which they received, they may perish by apostasy, as the angels did, or need, as Adam, a renewing by repentance. All Christ's grace is not confirming: as the best may lose much, and fall into foul sin, and grow worse than they once were, so common grace, and I think this middle infant grace which children have, as related to their parents, may be lost.

Q. 20. But is it not safer to hold that baptism puts none but the elect, who never lose it, into a title to salvation?

A. (1) Then it would be little comfort to parents, when their children die, who know not whether one of ten thousand be elect. (2) And it would be little satisfaction to the minister to baptise them, who knoweth not the elect from others. (3) It is plain that it is not another, but the same covenant of grace which is made with infants and adult; and that the covenant giveth pardon of sin, and right to life, to all that have the requisite qualification: and as that qualification in the adult is faith and repentance, so in infants it is nothing but to be the children of the faithful dedicated to God. God never instituted any baptism which is not for remission of sin. If I thought infants had no visible right to remission in which baptism should invest them, I durst not baptise them. I think their holiness containeth a certain title to salvation.

Q. 21. But is it not enough to know that they are of the church visible?

A. All at age that are of the visible church are in a state of salvation, except hypocrites. Therefore all infants that are of the visible church, are also of the mystical church, except such as had not the requisite qualification, and that is such as were not the children of the faithful.

All the world are in the kingdom of the devil, who are not in the kingdom of God; and if there be no visible way of salvation for them, what reason have we to hope that they are saved?

Q. 22. Some say we must leave their case to God as unknown to us, and that he will save such of them as he electeth?

A. True faith and hope is grounded on God's promise. What reason have we to believe and hope that any are saved whom God never promised to save? This would teach wicked men to presume that God will save them too, though he do not promise it: and this giveth no more comfort to a Christian than to an infidel. How know we, but by his promise, whether God elect one of ten thousand, or any at all: but God hath promised a special blessing to the seed of the faithful, above all others.

Q. 23. You make the mercy so very great, as maketh the denial of it seem a heinous sin in the anabaptists?

A. There are three sorts of them greatly differing. (1) Some say that no infants have original sin, and so need no baptism nor pardon: or, if it be sin, it is done away by Christ's mere death, and all infants in the world are saved.

(2) Others say that infants have original sin, but have no visible remedy; nor are any in covenant with Christ, nor members of his church, because no pardon is promised but to believers.

(3) Others hold that infants have original sin, and that the promise is to the faithful and their seed, and that parents ought thankfully to acknowledge this mercy, and devote them to Christ as infant members of his church; but that baptism is not for infant members, but only as the Lord's supper for the adult. This last sort are they whom I speak of as such whom I would not separate from, if they separate not from us; but the other two sorts are dangerously erroneous. When God hath made so many plain promises to the seed of his servants, and, in all ages before Christ, hath taken infants for church members, and never made a covenant but to the faithful and their seed, to say that Christ, the Saviour of the world, came to cast all infants out of the visible church, into the visible kingdom of Satan, and give them no greater mercy instead of it, seemeth to me very great ingratitude, and making Christ too like to Satan, as coming to do much of his destroying work.

Q. 24. But every where salvation is promised only to believers.

A. The promise is to them and their seed, keeping covenant. The same text that saith, "He that believeth shall be saved," saith, "He that believeth not shall be damned." Which showeth that it is only the adult that it speaketh of; or else all infants must be damned for unbelief. It shuts them no more out of baptism than out of heaven.

Q. 25. But the Scripture speaks of no infants baptised.

A. (1) No infants are to be baptised but the infants of the faithful; therefore the parents were to be made believers first. (2) The Scripture speaks of baptising divers households. (3) No Scripture mentioneth that ever any child of a believer was baptised at age. 4. The Scripture commandeth it, and that is enough: "Disciple nations, baptizing them." (Matt. 28:19).[12]

Q. 26. How can infants be disciples that learn not?

A. (1) Did Christ mistake when he sent them to disciple nations, of which infants are a part? (2) Cannot infants be disciples of Christ, if Christ, an infant, can be the Master and King of his church? Christ was our Teacher, Priest, and King, in his infancy, by right, relation, and destination, and undertaking, and obligation to what he was after to do; and so may infants be his subjects and disciples. May not an infant be a king that cannot rule? And are not infants the king's subjects, though they cannot obey May not they be knights and lords, and have right to inheritances? (3) Yea, are not infants called God's servants? (Levit. 25:42;) yea, and Christ's disciples? (Acts 15:10.) Peter saith, those that would have imposed circumcision would put a yoke on the neck of the disciples: but it was infants on whom they would have put it.

Q. 27. We are all by nature children of wrath, and none can enter into heaven that is not regenerate, and born of the Spirit?

A. But we are all the children of God, we and our seed, by the grace of Christ; and infants are capable of being regenerate by the Spirit. Or else they would not be called holy. (1 Cor. 7:14.)

Q. 28. The apostle only giveth a reason why a believing husband may lawfully live with an unbelieving wife.

A. True; but what is the reason which he giveth? The doubt was not whether it be fornication: that was past doubt; but the faithful must, in all their relations, be a peculiar, holy people, and the doubt was, whether their conjugal society became not such as infidels, common and unholy; and Paul saith, no. To the pure all things are sanctified. The unbeliever

---

[12] Acts 16:15, 20, and 18:8.

is not holy in herself, but sanctified to the husband for conjugal society; else, saith he, "Your children were unclean," not bastards, but unholy, as those without are; "but now are they holy," as the Israelites' adult and infants were a holy people, separated from the world to God, in the covenant of peculiarity, and not common and unclean.

Q. 29. Is it the infants of ell professed Christians and hypocrites, or only the infants of sincere Christians, who have the promise of pardon and salvation delivered and sealed by baptism?

A. As the church is to receive all the adult who make a credible profession, so are they to receive all their infants, for God only knoweth the heart. But it is with the heart that man believeth to righteousness, (Rom. 10) And as adult hypocrites are not pardoned by God, who knoweth the heart, so neither is there any promise of pardon to their seed. No text of Scripture giveth any pardon but to sincere believers and their seed. And the child is in the covenant as the child of a believer devoted to God. And that faith which qualifieth not the parent for pardon, cannot qualify the child for it. I know no more promise of pardon and life to an hypocrite's than to a heathen's child.

Q. 30. But what if the godfather, or grandfather, be a true Christian, or the ancestors and the parents both infidels, may not the child be baptised and pardoned?

A. The further you go from the parent the darker is the case. We are all the offspring of righteous Noah, and yet that maketh not the infants of heathens baptisable or pardoned. But the case of Abraham's covenant maketh it probable, that whoever is the true owner of the child by nature, purchase, or adoption, may devote it acceptably to God in baptism: because the infant having no choosing power, the will of his owner goeth for his own, in accepting the mercies of the covenant, and obliging him to such conditions as are for his good; which, if he like them not, he may renounce when he comes to age. But if the grandfather or godfather be no owner of the child, I know no proof that their causing him to be baptised helps him to pardon and salvation. If we dream that baptism giveth pardon to all infidels, and heathens' children, whose owners were not in the covenant themselves, we make a gospel, which, as far as I can find, Christ never made.

Q. 31. May not any man take an infant out of the street, and give him food and raiment, much more offer him to baptism, which is an act of greater charity?

A. The first God alloweth: but pardon and salvation is none of ours to give, but God's; and we can ministerially deliver the investing signs to none that have no title to which God hath promised the gift. If, as some think, bare redemption hath given a right to all the world, then all infidels and heathens shall be saved, if baptised. If they say it is to all infants in the world, then, whether they have godfathers or no, they may be baptised. And if all that are baptised are saved, it is irrational to think that want of baptism without their fault shall hinder their salvation. But though God offer to all men pardon and life for themselves and their infants, yet no Scripture giveth it to either without acceptance and consent of the adult. We must not make a gospel of our own.

Q. 32. Some say, that so much faith will serve for a title to baptism, as taketh Christ for a teacher, and maketh us disciples, that we may after attain to saving holiness; but that it is not special, saving faith that must needs be then professed.

A. This is to make a new baptism and Christianity to vie with that which alone Christ made. No adult person is a Christian, in Scripture sense, who believeth not in Christ as Christ. Which is as Saviour, as Prophet, Priest, and King. The essentials of Christ's office and gifts, as offered, are essential to that accepting faith which makes us Christians. A disciple and a Christian were words of the same importance. (Acts 11)[13] Christ made no baptism but for the remission of sin, and giving men a relation right to Father, Son, and Holy Ghost: baptism saveth by the answer of a good conscience to God. "Arise and wash away thy sins," was the word to Saul. We are sacramentally buried and risen with Christ, as dead to sin, and made new creatures, when we are baptised. (Rom. 6) Therefore it is called "The laver of regeneration." (Tit. 3:5.) All the church of Christ, from the apostles, taught that baptism put away the guilt of sin, to all that were truly qualified for that sacrament. And they required the profession of a saving faith and repentance; and all the form of baptism used in England, and the whole christian world,

---

[13] Mark 16:16; Rom 10:10, 14.

so happily agreeth in expressing this, that whoever will bring in the opinion, That the profession of a faith short of that which hath the promise of pardon and life, entitleth to baptism, must make a new baptismal form.

Q. 33. But many divines say, that baptism is not administered to infants on the title of a present faith, nor to give present pardon; but on a promise that they shall believe at age, and so have the benefits of baptism at age.

A. None dare say so of the adult. If they say, 'We repent not, nor believe now, but we promise to do it hereafter,' no wise man will baptise them. It is present believing, and not a mere promise to believe, that is their title. An infant's title is the parent's faith and dedication. By this doctrine infants of Christians are not in the same covenant or baptism as their parents, nor are they any more pardoned than heathens.[14]

Q. 34. What use are we to make of our baptism ever after?

A. It is of great and manifold use. (1) We must live under the humble sense of that miserable state of sin, from which Christianity doth deliver us.[15]

(2) We must live in the thankful sense of that grace of God in Christ which did deliver us, and in the exercise of our belief of that truth and love which was then sealed to us.

(3) We must live in the faithful remembrance of that covenant which we sealed, and that obedience which we promised, and in that war against the devil, the world, and the flesh, in which we then engaged ourselves.

(4) It is the knowledge of the baptismal covenant which tells us what Christianity is, and who we must take and love as Christians, while sects and dividers, by narrow, false measure, do limit their christian love and communion, and hate or cast off the disciples of Christ.

(5) Accordingly it is the baptismal covenant that must tell us what true faith is; viz., such a belief as causeth us truly to consent to that covenant; and what true conversion is: viz., such a change as containeth a true consent to that covenant. And so it tells us how to judge of our

---

[14] Acts 2:39.

[15] Rom 3, and 6:1–3; Rev 1:5, and 7:14; 1 Cor 6:10–12; Heb 10:22.

sincerity of grace; viz., when we unfeignedly consent to that covenant; and tells us what sin is mortal, that is, inconsistent with true grace and title to salvation; viz., all sin which is not consistent with an unfeigned consent to the covenant of grace.[16]

(6) It tells what the catholic church is; viz., visibly all that profess consent to the baptismal covenant, and forsake it not; and mystically all that sincerely do consent to it.

And, (7) So it tells us how to exercise church discipline, that we cast not out those as none of Christ's members, for their infirmities, who are not proved by sufficient witness to have done that which cannot stand with the sincere keeping of that covenant.

And thus baptism, not as a mere outward washing, but as including the grace which it signifieth, and the covenant and vow which it sealeth, is the very kernel of the christian religion, and the symbol, or livery, of the church and members of Christ.

Q. 35. Are all damned that die unbaptised?

A. Baptism is the solemn devoting men in covenant to Christ. All that hear the Gospel are condemned that consent not to this covenant. But the heart consent for ourselves and children is our title condition before God, who damns not men for want of an outward ceremony, which, by ignorance or necessity, is omitted. Believers' children are holy, because they and theirs are devoted to God before baptism. Baptism is to Christianity what public matrimony is to marriage, ordination to the ministry, enlisting to a soldier, and crowning to a king.

---

[16] John 13:8; Eph 5:26; Tit 3:5; Acts 22:16.

46

Of the Sacrament of Christ's Sacrificed Body and Blood

Q. 1. What is the sacrament called the Lord's supper, or eucharist?

A. It is a sacred action in which, by bread and wine consecrated, broken, and poured out, given and taken, and eaten and drunk, the sacrifice of Christ's body and blood for our redemption is commemorated, and the covenant of Christianity mutually and solemnly renewed and sealed, in which Christ, with the benefits of his covenant, is given to the faithful, and they give up themselves to Christ, as members of his church, with which they profess communion.[1]

Q. 2. Here are so many things contained, that we must desire you to open them severally: and first, what actions are here performed?

A. (1) Consecration. (2) Commemoration. (3) Covenanting and communication.

Q. 3. What is the consecration?

A. It is the separating and sanctifying the bread and wine, to this holy use; by which it ceaseth to be mere common bread and wine, and is made sacramentally, that is, by signification and representation, the sacrificed body and blood of Christ.

Q. 4. How is this done, and what action consecrateth them?

---

[1] Matt 26:26–28; Luke 22:19; 1 Cor 10:16, 17, and 11:23–26, 28

A. As other holy things are consecrated, as ministers, utensils, church maintenance, oblations, the water in baptism, &c., which is by an authorised devoting it to its proper holy use.

Q. 5. But some say it is done only by saying these words, "This is my body;" or by blessing it.

A. It is done by all that goeth to a dedication or separation from its holy use; and this is, (1) By declaring that God commandeth and accepteth it, (which is best done by reading his institution,) and that we then accordingly devote it. (2) By praying for his acceptance and blessing. (3) By pronouncing ministerially that it is now, sacramentally, Christ's body and blood.

Q. 6. Is the bread and wine the true body and blood of Christ?

A. Yes, relatively, significantly, representatively, and sacramentally: that is, it is consecrated bread and wine, on these accounts so called.

Q. 7. But why do you call it that which it is not really, when Christ saith, "This is my body," and not, 'This signifieth it?'

A. The name is fitly taken from the form; and a sacramental form is a relative form. If you see a shilling of the king's coin, and the question be, whether this be a shilling, or the king's coin, or silver? You will answer, it is all three; the matter of it is silver; the general relation is money or coin; the special relative form is, it is a shilling. And this is the fittest name, when the value is demanded. So the question is, whether this be bread and wine, or a sacrament, or Christ's sacrificed body and blood. It is all these, and the answer must be according to the meaning of the question.

It is usual to say of pictures, this is the king, and this is such an one, and this is my father, &c. Certainly the two parts of the sacrament must be understood alike. And of one, Christ saith, "This cup is the New Testament in my blood which is shed for you." (Luke 22:20; 1 Cor. 11:25.) Where none can deny, that by "cup," is meant the wine, and by "is the New Testament," is meant, is the exhibition and sealing of the New Testament, and not the very Testament itself.

And it is known that Christ's common teaching was by parables and similitudes, where he saith, (Matt. 21:28,) "A certain man had two sons," &c., (v. 33,) "A certain householder planted a vineyard," &c. And so frequently, (Matt. 13:21–23, 37–39.) "He that soweth is the Son of Man; the field is the world; the good seed are the children of the kingdom; the tares are the children of the wicked one; the enemy is the devil; the reapers are the angels;" that is, they are signified. This is ordinary in the gospel, (John 15:1,) "I am the Vine, and my Father is the Husbandman." (John 10:7, 9, 14.) "I am the Door; I am the good Shepherd." As David, (Psalm 22:6,) "I am a worm, and no man." (Matt. 15:13, 14.) "Ye are the salt of the earth, the lights of the world;" that is, ye are like these things.

Yea, the Old Testament useth "is," for "signifieth," most frequently, and hath no other word so fit to express it by.

Q. 8. Why then do the papists lay so much stress on the word "is;" yea, why do they say, that there is no bread and wine after the consecration, but only Christ's body and blood, under the show of them?

A. The sacrament is exceedingly venerable, being the very eating and drinking Christ's own sacrificed body and blood, in similitude or representation. And it was meet that all Christians should discern the Lord's body and blood in similitude, from common bread and wine. And in time, the use of the name, when the church was drowned in ignorance, was taken (about one thousand years after Christ) for the thing signified without the sign; as if they had said, 'This is the king;' therefore it is not a picture, nor is it cloth, or colours. And it being proper to the priests to consecrate it, they found how it exalted them to be judged able to make their Maker, and to give or deny Christ to men by their authority; and so they set up transubstantiation, and by a general council made it heresy to hold that there is any bread or wine left after consecration.

Q. 9. Wherein lieth the evil of that opinion?

A. The evils are more and greater than I must here stay to recite. In short, (1) They feign that to be Christ's body and blood, which was in his hand, or on the table when he spake the words, as if he had then two bodies.

(2) They feign his body to be broken, and his blood shed before he was crucified.

(3) They feign him to have flesh and blood in heaven, which two general councils have condemned; his body being a spiritual body now.

(4) They feign either himself to have eaten his own flesh and drunk his own blood, or at least his disciples to have done it while he was alive.

(5) They feign him to have been the breaker of his own flesh, and shedder of his own blood, and make him to do that which was done only by the Jews.

(6) They contradict the express words of the Scripture, which three times together call it bread, after the consecration in 1 Cor. 11.[2] When yet they say, it is not bread.

(7) They condemn the belief of the soundest senses of all men in the world, as if it were heresy. All our eyes, touch, taste, &c., tell us that there is bread and wine, and they say there is none.

(8) Hereby they deny all certainty of faith, and all other certainty; for if a man may not be certain of what he seeth, feeleth, and tasteth, he can be certain of no sensible thing: for we have no faculties but sense to perceive things sensible as such: nor any way to transmit them to the intellect but by sense. And we can no otherwise know that there is a bible, a church, a council, a pope, a man, or any thing in the world, and therefore much less can believe any of them. So that all human and divine faith are thus destroyed; yea, man is set below a beast that hath the benefit of sense.

(9) Hereby they feign God to be the grand deceiver of the world; for things sensible are his works, and so is sense; and he makes us know no supernatural revelation but by the intromission of some sense, and if God may deceive all men by the way of sense, we can never be sure but he may do it otherwise.

(10) They set up men, who confess their own senses are not to be credited, to be more credible than all our senses, and to be the lords of the understandings of all princes and people in despite of sense, and he that is to be believed before our senses is an absolute lord.

(11) They deny it to be a sacrament, for if there be no sign, there is no sacrament.

(12) They feign every ignorant, drunken priest, every time he consecrateth, to work greater miracles than ever Christ wrought, and so to make miracles common, and at the wills of thousands of wicked men. I must not here stay to handle all this, but in a small book called 'Full and Easy Satisfaction, which is the True Religion,' I have showed

---

[2] So 1 Cor 10:15, and 11:25–28; Acts 20:7, 11, and 2:42, 46.

thirty-one miracles with twenty aggravations, which all priests are feigned to work at every sacrament.

Q. 10. What is it that is called the mass, which the papists say that all the fathers and churches used in every age, and we renounce?

A. In the first ages, the churches were gathered among heathens, and men were long instructed and catechised hearers before they were baptised Christians; and the first part of the day was spent in public, in such common teaching and prayer as belonged to all, and then the deacon cried, Missa est; that is, dismissed the unbaptised hearers, and the rest that were Christians spent the rest of the time in such duties as are proper to themselves, especially the Lord's Supper and the praises of God. Hereupon all the worship following the dismission of the unchristened and suspended, came to be called barbarously the mass or dismission. And this worship hath been quite changed from what it was in the beginuing, and the papists, by keeping the name 'mass' or dismission, make the ignorant believe, that the worship itself is the same as of old.

Q. 11. What be the changes that have been made?

A. More than I may now stay to number. Justin Martyr and Tertullian describe it in their time to be just such as the Scripture mentioneth, and we now commonly perform, that is, in reading the Scripture, opening and applying it, praying as the minister was able, praising God, baptising and administering the Lord's Supper. After this, ministers grew less able and trusty, and they decreed that they should pray and officiate in set forms; yet so that every bishop might choose his own, and every presbyter must show it to the bishops and have their approbation; the Creed, Lord's Prayer, and Commandments, and the words of baptism, and delivery of the Lord's Supper, were always used in forms before. After this, they grew to use the same forms called a liturgy in whole provinces; some ceremonies were so ancient, that we cannot find their original, that is, the anointing of the baptised, the giving them milk and honey to taste; dipping them thrice; clothing them in a white garment after; to worship with their faces toward the east, and not to kneel in prayer or adoration any Lord's day in the year, nor any weekday between Easter and Whitsuntide, and especially to observe those two yearly festivals, and Good Friday's fast.

And quickly after the encouraging of persecuted Christians to suffer, drew them to keep a yearly day at the place where a martyr was killed or buried, to honour their memories, and give God thanks for them. After this, they built altars over them, and they built their churches where their graves or some of their bones were laid, and in honour of their memory, called the churches by their names. Next, they brought their names daily into the church liturgies, and next they added to the names of such bishops of those particular churches as had left an honourable memorial behind them. And the Lord's supper was celebrated much like as it is in our English liturgy (save these names). And thus far the changes were then accounted laudable, and were not indeed such as should discourage any Christians from communion, nor do we read of any that were against them. Besides which they overvalued the use of crossing.

But quickly (though by degrees) a flood of ceremonies came in, and popes and prelates added at their pleasure, till God's public worship was made quite another thing.

(I) God who is a Spirit, and will be worshipped in spirit and truth, is by mass priests and papists worshipped by such a mass of ceremonies, as makes it like a stage play, and representeth God so like the heathen idols, delighted in mummeries and toyish actions, as is greatly to the dishonour of religion and God.[3]

(II) They have brought in the worshipping of God, in a language which the people understand not, and praying for they know not what.

(III) They have locked up the very Scriptures from the people, and forbid all to use it in their known tongue translated, but those that get a special license for it.

(IV) They abolish all substantial signs in the Sacrament, as is aforesaid, and say, there is no bread or wine, and so make it no Sacrament.

(V) They give the laity the bread only, without the cup.

(VI) They call the consecrated bread by the name of their Lord God, and taking it to be no bread, but Christ's body, worship it with divine worship, which seemeth to me flat idolatry.

(VII) They reserve it as their God, long after the Sacrament, to adore and to work pretended miracles by.

---

[3] John 4:20, 22-24, and 5:39; Acts 17:11, 23, 25; Phil 3:3; 1 Cor 14:2-27; Luke 11:52; 2 Tim 3:15.

(VIII) They solemnly celebrate a Sacrament before the congregation, where none communicate but the priests, and the people look on.

(IX) They say these masses by number, to deliver souls out of the flames of purgatory.

(X) They have many prayers for the dead as in purgatory, for their ease and deliverance.

(XI) They pray to the dead saints to intercede for them, and help them, and to the virgin Mary, for that which is proper to Christ.

(XII) They worship God by images, and adore the images as the representations of saints and angels; yea, and of God: and some profess that the cross, and the images of the Father, Son, and Holy Ghost, are to be worshipped with honour participatively divine.[4]

These, with abundance more, and many false doctrines on which they depend, are brought into God's public worship, and called the mass, and are added by degrees to that sounder worship, which was called the mass at first.

Q. 12. You have spoken much about the consecration in the Sacrament; what is it which you call the commemoration?

A. It containeth the signal representation of the sacrificing of Christ, as the Lamb of God, to take away the sins of the world. Where the signs are, (1) The materials, the bread and wine. (2) The minister's breaking the bread and pouring out the wine. (3) The presenting them to God, as the commemoration of that sacrifice in which we trust; and declaring to the people, that this is done to this commemoration?

The things signified, are, (1) Christ's flesh and blood, when he was on earth. (2) The crucifying of Christ, the piercing of his flesh, and shedding his blood. (3) Christ's offering this to God as a sacrifice for man's sin. And this commemoration is a great part of the Sacrament.

Q. 13. What think you of the name sacrifice, altar, and priest, here?

A. The ancient churches used them all, without exception from any Christian that ever I read of. (I) As the bread is justly called Christ's body, as signifying it, so the action described was of old called a sacrifice, as representing and commemorating it. And it is no more improper than

---

[4] Col 2:18.

calling our bodies, and our alms, and our prayers sacrifices. (Rom. 12:1; Eph. 5:2; Phil. 2:17, and 4:18; Heb. 13:15, 16; 1 Pet. 2:5.[5])

(II) And the naming of the table an altar as related to this representative sacrifice is no more improper than that other. "We have an altar whereof they have no right to eat," (Heb. 13:10,) seems plainly to mean the sacramental communion. And the Scripture (Rev. 6:9; 8:3, 5, and 16:7) oft useth that word.

(III) And the word 'priest,' being used of all Christians that offer praise to God, (1 Pet. 2:5, 9; Rev. 1:6; 5:10, and 20:6,) it may sure as well be used of those whose office is to be sub-intercessors between the people and God, and their mouth to God, in subordination to Christ's priesthood: causeless scruples harden the papists. We are not offended that the Lord's day is called the Sabbath, though the Scripture doth never so call it; and a Sabbath in Scripture sense was a day of ceremonial rest: and the ancient church called it the christian Sabbath, but by such allusion as it (more commonly) used the word sacrifice and altar.

Q. 14. But we shall too much countenance the papists' sacrifice by using the same names.

A. We can sufficiently disclaim their turning a commemoration of Christ's sacrifice into the feigned real sacrificing of his flesh and blood, without renouncing the names. Else we must, for men's abuse, renounce the name of a Sabbath too, and a temple, &c., if not also of a church and bishop.

Q. 15. You have spoken of the sacramental consecration, and commemoration; what is it which you call the covenanting part and communication?

A. It containeth the signs, and the things signified, as communicated. The signs are, (1) The actual delivering of the consecrated bread and wine (first broken and poured out) to the communicants, with the naming what it is that is given them. (2) Bidding them take, eat, and drink. (3) Telling them the benefits and blessings given thereby: and all this by a minister of Christ, authorized thus to act in his name, as covenanting, promising, and giving what is offered.[6]

---

[5]   Luke 22:19; 1 Cor 11:24, 26, 27.

[6]   Matt 26:26; John 6:53, 54, 57, 58.

And on the receiver's part the signs are, (1) Freely taking what is offered (the bread and wine). (2) Eating and drinking. (3) Vocal praise and thanksgiving to God, and professed consent to the covenant.

Q. 16. What are the things signified and given?

A. (I) (1) On God's part, the renewed giving of a sacrificed Saviour to the penitent believes.

(2) The will and command of Christ, that as sacrificers feasted on the sacrifice, so the soul by faith should thankfully and joyfully feast on Christ by hearty acceptance of the free gift.[7]

(3) The actual applicatory gift of the benefits of Christ's sacrifice; which are, (1) Our confirmed relation to Christ as our Head and Saviour, and to God as our Father reconciled by him, and to the Holy Ghost as our Sanctifier, and to the church as his kingdom or body. (2) The pardon of our sins by his blood. (3) Our right confirmed to everlasting life. (4) The strengthening of our faith, hope, love, joy, patience, and all grace.[8]

(4) Christ's promise and covenant for all this sealed to us.

(II) On the receiver's part is signified, (1) That in the sense of his own sin, misery, and need, he humbly and thankfully received his part in Christ as sacrificed. (2) That he endeavoureth by faith to feast on him. (3) And that he thankfully receiveth the blessings purchased, to wit, his relation to Christ as his Head, to God, as his Father, and to the Holy Ghost, as his Sanctifier, and Comforter, with the pardon of sin, the sealed promise, and right to heaven, and all the helps of his faith and other graces. (4) That he resolvedly reneweth the dedication of himself to God the Father, Son, and Holy Ghost, as thus related to these ends; covenanting fidelity in these relations, and renouncing the contraries. (5) Doing all this as in communion with all the church of Christ, as being united to them in the same Head, the same faith, and hope, and love. (6) Thankfully praising God and our Redeemer for this grace.

Q. 17. Should not one prepare for the Lord's supper by fasting and humiliation before? Or how should we prepare?

A. We must always live in habitual preparation, and special fasts are not ordinarily necessary thereto: the primitive church did communicate

---

[7]   Zec. 9:11; Heb 10:29, and 13:20.

[8]   1 Cor 10:16; 2 Cor 13:14; Luke 22:20; Heb 9:15–18.

not only every Lord's day, but on other days when they met to worship God; and therefore used not every week to spend a day in fasting for preparation. But as Christians must use fasting on just occasions, so must they do before this Sacrament in case that any heinous sin, or heavy judgment or danger call for it; and preparing considerations and, prayers are necessary.

Q. 18. May one communicate who is uncertain of the sincerity of his faith?

A. By faith you mean either objective or active faith.

(1) One that is so far uncertain that the gospel is true, and that there is a life to come, as that he dare not say, I have no wavering or doubt of it, may yet be a true believer and may communicate, if his persuasion be but so prevalent, as to resolve him to consent to the covenant of grace, and take God for his God, and Christ for his Saviour, and the Holy Ghost for his Sanctifier, God's law for his rule, his promise for his security, and heaven for his happiness, and here to place his hope and trust, forsaking all that stands against it. A weak and doubting faith may bring a man to martyrdom and to heaven, if it bring him to trust Christ with soul and body in the way of obedience to him.[9]

(2) If by faith you mean the act of believing and consenting, God hath made the sincerity of our faith necessary to our salvation, but not the certainty that it is sincere. Every man must do his best to discern the trust, consent, and choice of his own heart: and he that truly believeth, and yet is not sure of it, if he can say, 'As far as I am able to know my own heart by trial, I seriously think that I resolvedly consent to the covenant of grace, and prefer Christ, holiness, and heaven, before all this world, and trust to Christ and his promises for my felicity;' ought to come to the table of the Lord, notwithstanding his uncertainty.[10]

Q. 19. Whence is it that so many Christians are more terrified than comforted by the Lord's supper?

A. (1) Some of them, by an excess of reverence to this above all other ordinances of God, which, by degrees, brought in the papist's transubstantiation and adoration: and by a dread lest, by unworthy receiving,

---

[9] Acts 8:37; Mark 9:24; Matt 6:30; 8:26; 14:31, and 16:8; Luke 17:5.

[10] John 20:25; Matt 28:17; Acts 13:39.

they should eat and drink their own damnation; and so coming thither with a deeper sense of the danger than of the benefit, and mistaking their imperfections for this unworthy receiving. (2) And some come with too high expectations that God must suddenly give them joy, or all the grace that is signified by the sacrament, while they have not the holy skill to fetch in comfort by the exercise of their faith: and when they miss of what they expected, they are cast down. (3) And too many, by wilful sin or negligence, deal falsely with God, and break their covenant, and renew their wounds of conscience, and deprive themselves of the comforts of the love of God, and the grace of Christ, and the communion of the Holy Spirit.[11]

Q. 20. Is not the Lord's supper a converting ordinance, which therefore should be used by the unbelievers, or ungodly?

A. Many things may accidentally, by God's grace, convert a man, which are not to be chosen and used to that end. Plagues, sickness, death approaching, may convert men; falling into a heinous sin hath affrighted some to leave their sin. But these are not means to be chosen for such ends, and the fear and care of preparing for a sacrament hath converted some, when it was not the receiving that did it. It is so evident as not to need long proof that God never appointed the Lord's supper to be chosen and used by infidels, or impenitent, ungodly persons, as a means to convert them. (1) Because it is presupposed that they be baptised who communicate: and I have proved that baptism to the adult presupposed the profession of faith and repentance, and that it delivereth pardon and title to salvation.

(2) Because faith, and repentance, and covenant-consent renewed, are also to be professed by all before they communicate.

(3) Because it was ever an ordinance proper to the church, which consisteth of professors of faith and holiness.

(4) And the communicants are said to be one bread and one body, and to eat Christ's flesh, and drink his blood, and Christ to dwell in them by faith, and to have eternal life hereby.

And as for them that say it is not saving faith, but some commoner, preparatory sort, which is necessarily to be professed in baptism and

---

[11] 1 Cor 11:20, 30, 31.

the Lord's supper, I have at large confuted them in a treatise of Right to Sacraments, and the reasons before and now named confute it. I add, that their opinion is destructive to true christian love; for by them no one should be taken for a child of God, and in a state of salvation, for being baptised, and communicants, and so not loved as such. And how poor a charity is it to love all visible church members, but as the children of the devil must be loved!

Q. 21. Must we love all as true Christians who are baptised, and communicate, and profess Christianity?

A. Yes, with these three exceptions; (1) That it is not as a certain truth, that we must judge them as sincere, but as probable. (2) That there be divers degrees of probability as there be of profession. Some, we are almost sure, are sincere; and some we have more fear than hope of: and we must measure our love and trust accordingly. (3) If men by word or life apostatise, or plainly contradict and destroy their profession of Christianity, thereby they nullify our obligation to take them for Christians: but till men render their profession incredible by contrary profession or practice, we are, by the rules of christian and human charity, to take all professed, baptised, communicating Christians to be sincere, but only in various degrees of probability.[12]

Q. 22. How must the Lord's supper be improved after the receiving?

A. By a serious remembering with joy and thankfulness, how great mercies we have received of God; and, with cheerful obedience, what a covenant we have made, and what duty we have most solemnly promised; and in how near a relation and bond we are tied to the whole church of Christ, and to all our fellow Christians: and frequently to plead these great receivings and great obligations, to quicken our faith, and hope, and joy, and to overcome all temptations to the world and flesh, to unbelief, disobedience, and despair.[13]

Q. 23. Some say that no man should be kept from the sacrament, or excommunicated, because it is the food of their souls, &c.

---

[12] Acts 9:26; 2:38, 41, 42, 44–46, and 4:32, 34; Mark 16:16; 1 Cor 10:16, 17, and 12:8, 11, 13; 2 Cor 11:2; Gal 3:28; Eph 4:3, 5; John 4:1, and 13:35; Rom 6:3, 5; Matt 10:42; Luke 14:26, 33.

[13] 1 Cor 12:16, 20–22.

A. (1) If none be kept from baptism, heathens and infidels, and professed deriders of Christianity might be baptised to make a mock of baptism. We must make men Christ's disciples before we baptise them. (Matt. 28:19.) And then baptism would be no baptism, nor the ministry no ministry, the specifying end and use being changed. (2) Then the church would be no church, but lie common with the world. (3) And then Christ would be no King, and Head, and Husband of his church, that is, no Christ.[14] (4) If all may not be baptised, all may not communicate: for baptism entereth them into a state of communion, else the unbaptised, and all infidels, might communicate. (5) Some baptised persons turn atheists, sadducees, or infidels, after; and these are worse than common infidels that never were baptised. The church is no church if it be common to these. (6) Some that continue a nominal Christianity, openly hate and persecute the practice of it, and live in common adultery, perjury, murder; and the church is holy, and a peculiar people, a holy nation, a royal priesthood:[15] and repentance and obedience are necessary to the church as well as faith. If, therefore, these notorious, flagitious, impenitent persons, must be members in communion with the church, it will be a swine sty, and not a church; a shame to Christ, and not an honour. If his church be like the rest of the world, Christ will not be honoured as the Saviour of it, nor the Spirit as its Sanctifier. It is the unity of the spirit that all Christians must keep in the bond of peace.[16] But these have none of his Spirit, and therefore are none of Christ's.

The sacraments are symbols of the church as differenced from the world; and Christ will have them be a visibly distinct society. (7) Communicants come to receive the greatest gift in the world, pardon, justification, adoption, right to heaven. The gospel giveth these to none but penitent believers. To say that Christ giveth them to flagitious, impenitent rebels, whose lives say, "We will not have him reign over us," is to make a new gospel, contrary to Christ's gospel, which

---

[14] Matt 28:19; Mark 16:16; 1 Cor 11:27–30; Eph 1:22, 23.

[15] Titus 2:14; 1 Pet 2:9.

[16] Eph 4:3, 16; Rom 8:9.

Paul curseth, were it done by an angel. (Gal. 1:7, 8.) They are not yet capable of these precious gifts.

(8) The objectors take no notice of 1 Cor. 5:2; 2 Thess. 3; Rom. 16:16, 17; Tit. 3:10; Rev. 2 and 3; where the churches are reproved for suffering defilers; nor Heb. 13:7, 17, 24; Luke 12:42, 43; 1 Thess. 5:12, 13, which describe the office of church guides; nor 1 Tim. 3 and 4, &c., where the governing of the church, and avoiding communion of the impenitent, are described.

(9) In a word, Christ's office, works, and law, the nature of the church and sacrament, the office of the ministry, the frequent precepts of the apostles, and the constant practice of the church in its greatest purity, down from the apostles' days, do all speak so plainly for keeping and casting out infidels and impenitent, wicked men, and for keeping the church as a society of visible saints, separated from the world, that I can take him for no better than a swine or an infidel, who would have the church keys cast away, and the church turned common to swine and infidels.

Q. 24. But it will make ministers lords and tyrants to have such power?

A. (1) Somebody must be trusted with the power, if the work must be done. The church must be differenced from the world. Therefore some must try and judge who are fit to be baptized, and to have its communion; and who are fitter than these whom Christ, by office, hath thereto appointed. Would you hare magistrates, or the people, do it? Then they must be prepared for it by long study and skill, and wholly attend it, for it will take up all their time.[17]

Q. 25. Must ministers examine people before they communicate?

A. They must catechise and examine the adult before they baptise them, and, consequently, those who were baptised in infancy, before they number them with adult communicants; or else atheists and infidels will make up much of the church, who will come in for worldly interest. This examination should go before confirmation, or the public owning of their baptism; but there is no necessity of any more examination before every sacrament, except in case of scandal, or when persons need and crave such help.

---

[17] 1 Cor 4:1, 2; Matt 24:45, 46, 47; 1 Thess 5:12.

Q. 26. Who be they that must be excommunicated, or refused?

A. Those who are proved to be impenitent in gross, scandalous sins, after sufficient admonition and patience. And to reject such, is so far from tyranny, that it is necessary church justice, without which a pastor is but a slave, or executioner of the sinful will of others; like a tutor, philosopher, or schoolmaster, who is not the master of his own school, but must leave it common to all that will come in, though they scorn him, and refuse his conduct. But no man must play the pastor over other men's flocks, nor take the guidance of a greater flock that he can know and manage, much less be the only key-bearer over many score or hundred churches; and, least of all, take upon him to govern and judge of kings and kingdoms, and all the world, as the Roman deceiving tyrant doth.

47

Of Preparation for Death and Judgment

Q. 1. How must we prepare for a safe and comfortable death?

A. I have said so much of this in my family book, that to avoid repetition I must refer you thither, only in brief: (1) Preparation for death is the whole work of life, for which many hundred years are not too long, if God should so long spare and try us. And all that I have hitherto said to you, for faith, love, and obedience, upon the Creed, Lord's prayer, and commandments, is to teach you how to prepare for death. And though sound conversion at last may tend to pardon and salvation, to them that have lived a careless, wicked life, yet the best, the surest, the wisest preparation, is that which is made by the whole course of a holy, obedient, heavenly life.[1]

Q. 2. What life is it that is the best preparation?

A. (I) When we have so well considered of the certain vanity of this world, and all its pleasures, and of the truth of God's promises of the heavenly glory, as that by faith we have there placed our chiefest hopes, and there expect our chief felicity, and make it our chief business in this world to seek it, preferring no worldly thing before it, but resolved,

---

[1] Phil 2:12; Heb 5:9, and 12:28; Titus 2:11, 12; Luke 19:9, and 14:26, 33; Rom 10:10, 11; 2 Pet 3:11, 12; 1 Pet 1:9.

for the hopes of it to forsake them all when God requireth it: this is the first part of our preparation for death.[2]

(II) When we believe that this mercy is given by Christ, the Mediator between God and man, and trust in his merits and intercession with the Father, and take him for our teacher also, and our ruler, resolving to obey his word and Spirit. This is the second part of our preparation for death.[3]

(III) When the Holy Spirit hath shed abroad God's love upon our hearts, and turned their nature into a habit of love to God and holiness, and given us a victory over that love of the world, and fleshly prosperity, and pleasure, which ruleth in the hearts of carnal men, though yet our love show itself but in such mortification, and endeavour, and grief for what we want, we are prepared for a safe death.[4]

But if the foretastes of heavenly glory, and sense of the love of God, do make our thoughts of heaven sweeter to us than our thoughts of our earthly hopes, and cause us, out of love to God and our glorified Redeemer and his church, and out of love to a life of perfect knowledge, love, and joy, to long to depart and be with Christ, then we are prepared not only for a safe but a joyful death.[5]

Q. 3. O! But this is a great and difficult work.

A. It is not too hard for the Spirit of Christ, and a soul renewed by it. It is our great folly and naughtiness that maketh it hard: why else should it be hard for a man that loveth himself, and knoweth how quickly a grave, and rotting in the dark, must end all his pleasures in this world, to be earnestly desirous of a better after it? And why should it be hard for one that believeth that man's soul is immortal, and that God hath sent one from heaven, who is greater than angels, to purchase it for us, and promise it to us, and give us the first-fruits by his Holy Spirit; to rejoice that he dieth not as an unpardoned sinner, nor as a beast, but

---

[2] Matt 6:33.

[3] 2 Cor 4:16, 18; John 3:16.

[4] 2 Cor 5:17; Heb 12:14; Rom 8:9, 13.

[5] 2 Cor 5:1, 3, 8; Phil 1:21, 23.

shall live in perfect life, and light, and love, and joy, and praise, for ever? What should rejoice a believing, considerate man like this?[6]

Q. 4. O! But we are still apt to doubt of things unseen?

A. (1) You can believe men for things unseen, and be certain by it; for instance, that there is such a place as Rome, Paris, Venice, that there have been such kings of England as Henry VIII., King James, &c. You know not, but by believing others, whether ever you were baptised, nor who was your father or mother. (2) You see not your own soul, nor any one's that you talk with; and yet you feel and see such things as may assure any sober man that he hath a soul. God is not seen by us, yet nothing is more certain than that there is a God.

(3) We see plants, flowers, fruits, and all vital acts, produced by an unseen power; we see vast, lucid, glorious regions above us, and we see and feel the effects of invisible powers: therefore, to doubt of things because they are unseen, is to doubt of all the vital, noblest part of the world, and to believe nothing but gross and lowest things, and to lay by reason, and become brutes. But of this I have said more near the beginning.

Q. 5. What should we do to get the soul so familiar above as to desire to be with Christ?

A. (I) We must not live in a foolish forgetfulness of death, nor flatter our souls into delays and dulness, by the expectations of long life on earth; the grave must be studied till we have groundedly got above the fears of it.

(II) We must not rest quiet in such a human belief of the, gospel and the life to come, as hath no better grounds than the common opinion of the country where we live, as the Turks believe Mahomet, and his Alcoran; for this leaveth the soul in such doubts and uncertainty as cannot reach to solid joy, nor victory over the world and flesh. But the true evidence of the gospel, and our hopes, must be well digested, which I have opened to you in the beginning, of which I give you a breviate in two sentences.

(1) The history of the gospel of Christ's life, miracles, death, resurrection, ascension, sending down the Spirit, the apostles' miracles, and

---

[6] 1 Pet 1:6, 8; 1 Thess 5:16; Phil 2:16–18, and 4:4; Heb 3:6.

preaching, and writing, and sufferings, is a true history: else there is none sure in the world, for none of such antiquity hath greater evidence.

(2) And if the history aforesaid be true, the doctrine must needs be true; for it is part of the history, and owned and sealed certainly by God.[7]

(III) We must not be content to be once satisfied of the truth of the life to come, but we must mentally live upon it and for it, and know how great business our souls have every day with our glorified Lord, and the glorified society of angels, and the perfected spirits of the just, and with the blessed God of love and glory: we must daily fetch thence the motives of our desires, hopes, and duties, the incentives of our love and joy. The confutation of all temptations from the flesh and the world, and our supporting patience in all our sufferings and fears. Read oft John 17:22–24, and 20:17. Heb. 12:22–24; Matt. 6:19-21, 33; Col. 3:4, 5; 2 Thess. 1:10, 11; Heb. 11; 2 Cor. 4:16, 17, and 5:1-3, 5, 7, 8; Phil. 1:21, 23, and 3:18, 19, 20. They that thus live by faith on God and glory will be prepared for a joyful death.

(IV) We must take heed that no worldly hope or pleasure vitiate our affections, and turn them down from their true delight.[8]

(V) We must live wholly upon Christ, his merit, sufficiency, love, and mediation; his cross and his kingdom must be the sum of our learning, study, and content.[9]

(VI) We must take heed of grieving the Spirit of consolation, and wounding our consciences by wilful sin of omission or commission.

(VII) We must faithfully improve all our time and talents to do God all the service, and others all the good, that we can in the world, that we may be ready to give an account of our stewardship.

(VIII) We must be armed against temptations to unbelief and despair.

(IX) We must, while we are in the body, in our daily thoughts fetch as much help from sensible similitudes as we can, to have a suitable imagination of the heavenly glory. And one of the most familiar is, that which Christ calleth the coming of the kingdom of God, which was his

---

[7] Phil 3:18–20; Col 3:1–3; Heb 12:22-24.

[8] Eph 3:17, 18.

[9] Eph 4:10.

transfiguration with Moses and Elias in glorious appearance in the holy mount, (Matt. 17:1,) which made Peter say, "It is good to be here."[10] Christ purposely so appeared to them to give them a sensible apprehension of the glory which he hath promised. And Moses, that was buried, appeared there in a glorified body.

And we must not think only of God, but of the heavenly society, and even our old acquaintance, that our minds may find the more suitableness and familiarity in their objects and contemplations.

(X) We must do our best to keep up that natural vivacity and cheerfulness, which may be sanctified for spiritual employment; for when the body is diseased with melancholy, heaviness, or pains, and the mind diseased with griefs, cares, and fears, it will be hard to think joyfully of God, or heaven, or any thing.

(XI) We must exercise ourselves in those duties which are nearest akin to the work in heaven. Specially labouring to excite hope, love, and joy, by faith, and praising God, especially in psalms in our families and the sacred assemblies, and using the most heavenly books and company.

(XII) We must not look when all is done to have very clear conceptions of the quality and acts of separated souls, or the world of spirits, but must be satisfied with an implicit trust in our Father and our glorified Lord, in the things which are yet above our reach: and, giving up soul and body to him, we should joyfully trust them with him as his own, and believe that while we know as much as may bring us well to heaven, it is best for us that the rest is known by Christ, in whose hand and will we are surer and better than in our own.

As for the special preparations in sickness, I refer you to the family book.

Q. 6. What shall one do that is tempted to doubt, or to think hardly of God, because he hath made heaven for so few?

A. (1) Those few may be assured that he will never forsake them whom he hath so chosen out of all the world, and made his jewels and his treasure.

(2) It is improbable rashness to say, heaven it but for few: all this earth is no more to the glorious world above us (even so far as we see)

---

[10] Matt 17:4.

than one inch is to all the earth, and what if God forsake one inch or molehill. (Heb. 12:23, 24.)

Again I say, I take hell to be at the gallows, and this earth to be as Newgate gaol, where some prisoners are that shall die, and some shall live; and the superior world to be like the city and kingdom. Who will say that the king it unmerciful, because malefactors have a prison and a gallows, if all else in the kingdom live in peace?

And though this world seems almost forsaken at the prison-way to hell, yet, while the elect are saved, and the superior, lucid, glorious world is many thousand, and thousand, and thousand times greater than all this earth, I doubt not but experience will quickly tell us, that the glory of God's love is so unmeasurably manifested in heaven, as that the blindness, wickedness, confusions, and miseries of this earth and hell shall be no eclipse or dishonour to it for ever.

Finitur, Jan. 10, 1681/2